200 Fast & Easy
Artisan Breads
No-Knead, One Bowl

200 Fast & Easy
Artisan Breads
No-Knead, One Bowl

Judith Fertig

For complete cataloguing information, see page 306.

Disclaimer
The recipes in this book have been carefully tested by our kitchen and our tasters. To the best of our
knowledge, they are safe and nutritious for ordinary use and users. For those people with food or other
allergies, or who have special food requirements or health issues, please read the suggested contents of
each recipe carefully and determine whether or not they may create a problem for you. All recipes are used
at the risk of the consumer.

We cannot be responsible for any hazards, loss or damage that may occur as a result of any recipe use.

For those with special needs, allergies, requirements or health problems, in the event of any doubt,
please contact your medical adviser prior to the use of any recipe.

Design and Production: Daniella Zanchetta/PageWave Graphics Inc.
Editor: Sue Sumeraj
Recipe Editor and Tester: Jennifer MacKenzie
Proofreader: Sheila Wawanash
Indexer: Gillian Watts
Photography: Colin Erricson
Food Styling: Kathryn Robertson
Prop Styling: Charlene Erricson

Cover image: Baby Boule (page 25) and Batard (page 27)

We acknowledge the financial support of the Government of Canada through the Book Publishing Industry
Development Program (BPIDP) for our publishing activities.

Published by Robert Rose Inc.
120 Eglinton Avenue East, Suite 800, Toronto, Ontario, Canada M4P 1E2
Tel: (416) 322-6552 Fax: (416) 322-6936

Printed and bound in Canada

2 3 4 5 6 7 8 9 CPL 17 16 15 14 13 12 11 10 09

For my family

Contents

Acknowledgments

Many thanks to all the people who helped taste and test and nudge this book into being: Karen Adler, Dee Barwick, Mary Ann Duckers, Lisa Ekus, Sarah Fertig, Nick Fertig, Julie Fox, Jack Merkle, Jean Merkle, Kathy Moore, Roxanne Wyss, everyone at Robert Rose — especially Bob Dees, Sue Sumeraj and Jennifer MacKenzie — and Daniella Zanchetta of PageWave Graphics.

Introduction

ALTHOUGH ARTISAN BREAD baking is a time-honored tradition, with classic forms and methods, there has been a recent surge of revision. Baking experts such as Jim Lahey, Peter Reinhart, Jeff Hertzberg, Zoë François, Dorie Greenspan, Nancy Silverton, Maggie Glezer, Nancy Baggett and the late Julia Child; food scientists such as Shirley Corriher; and innovative bread bloggers have taken a fresh look at old recipes and come up with new, easier ways to achieve the same or similar results.

As a cookbook author, culinary instructor and avocational baker, I've built on their combined expertise and gone a step further in streamlining artisan bread baking into an achievable — and rewarding — activity for busy people. I've questioned, challenged and tested my way to the best methods for baking artisan-quality breads in an easier, faster manner.

I've also used a sequential, step-by-step approach known as "benchmarking." With each dough, with each recipe, you learn and master new techniques.

The result is *200 Fast & Easy Artisan Breads*, which shows how you can achieve incredible results in just minutes a day.

What's so easy about easy artisan breads?

- You use basic equipment: a large mixing bowl, a Danish dough whisk or wooden spoon, measuring cups, a cutting board or cookie sheet, an instant-read thermometer, a serrated knife, a rolling pin, a broiler pan and a baking stone.

- You make enough dough for several loaves, store the dough in the refrigerator, then bake when you're ready. Many of the doughs keep in the refrigerator for over a week.

- You skip traditional bread-making steps. No need to proof (active dry) yeast over water to make sure it works; you use instant or bread machine yeast and simply stir it into the flour. No need to knead, as you use a moist dough that does the work of activating the gluten for you. No need to bake the bread the same day — you can if you want to, but you can also wait several days, up to a week or more.

- You master easy methods for shaping the dough into round loaves (boules), baguettes, batards, rolls, filled rolls, flatbreads, pizzas, bagels, pastries and more.

- You know when your bread is done in one easy step — by using an instant-read thermometer. No tapping, thumping, guessing, hoping.
- You learn similarly easy, streamlined ways to make complements to bread, such as artisan butter (in the food processor in 5 minutes) and caramelized onions (in the slow cooker).

The "fast" part of the *200 Fast & Easy Artisan Breads* title means that your hands-on activity (not including rising, resting or baking time) with these breads is only minutes a day. You can make the dough one day, form and bake in the days afterwards.

If you can bake a batch of brownies from a box mix, you are ready to start *200 Fast & Easy Artisan Breads*. So let's get started!

Part 1
Let's Get Started

One-bowl, no-knead artisan bread. Is it as easy as it sounds? Let's get some hands-on experience.

If you follow the steps in making the dough, forming the loaves and baking the bread, you can't go wrong. Each easy step takes you closer to great artisan bread — and helps you avoid common pitfalls experienced by novice bread bakers. If you just scoop the flour out of the bag and dump it in the bowl, you could end up with a heavy, lackluster loaf, but by measuring the flour correctly, you'll end up with just the right amount. If you add hot water, it can kill the yeast and your bread won't rise, but by taking the temperature of the water, you'll know it is lukewarm. If you only thump or tap to test for doneness, you could end up with bread that is still gummy inside, but by taking the temperature of your loaf, you'll know it's done.

So relax. Just follow the steps and you're on your way to your first boules and baguettes.

Equipment You'll Need

EACH PIECE of kitchen equipment listed below is simple but necessary to artisan bread, from the start of making the dough to the process of baking it. To make the first master recipe, Easy Artisan Dough, you'll need basic kitchenware, including a wooden spoon or a Danish dough whisk. If you've never seen a dough whisk before, you'll be amazed at how often you'll use it once you get one. The dough whisk has a long wooden handle, and the whisk end looks like a freeform mitten made with thick stainless steel wire. The dough whisk does a great job with all of the doughs in this book, but is especially effective with heavier whole-grain doughs.

You'll also need something with which to slide artisan bread onto the baking stone in the oven. A simple three-sided cookie sheet will do, but as you get going, you might want to purchase a wooden baker's peel, sort of a flat shovel for getting breads and pizzas in the oven. A flexible cutting board is indispensable for scooping up and sliding baguettes or batards from the floured surface to the baker's peel or baking stone. The baking stone helps replicate the even heating of a brick oven. The broiler pan of water underneath it adds steam for better baking results.

Essential Equipment

- Measuring cups and spoons (liquid and dry)
- Instant-read thermometer
- 16-cup (4 L) mixing bowl
- Wooden spoon or Danish dough whisk
- Serrated knife
- Dough scraper
- Three-sided cookie sheet or baker's peel
- Flexible cutting board
- Baking stone
- Broiler pan

Ingredients You'll Need

THE BASIC INGREDIENTS for artisan bread are also simple, but each one is crucial to success.

Yeast

To bake bread the Easy Artisan way, you'll need instant or bread machine yeast, which is packaged in jars, in individual packets or in larger vacuum-sealed bags. Active dry or quick-rise yeasts need to be proofed in water first, and we're eliminating that step. The smaller granules of instant or bread machine yeast can simply be stirred into the flour and other dry ingredients. Because of the way instant or bread machine yeast is formulated, you'll use a little bit more of it than you're used to with active dry yeast bread recipes. Once you've opened your instant or bread machine yeast jar or vacuum-sealed bag, store it in the refrigerator so it stays fresh longer.

Two More Things To Know About Yeast

1. **Temperature affects it.** Both manufactured and wild yeasts in the air slow down their activity in a cold refrigerator and go into hibernation in the freezer. (That's why you can buy frozen yeast bread dough, then come home and bake it off.) Warmer temperatures help yeast release carbon dioxide to be trapped within the muscular layers of gluten, helping bread to rise. According to food scientist Shirley Corriher in *BakeWise*, manufactured yeast is most active between 86°F (30°C) and 95°F (35°C), while wild yeasts prefer lower temperatures. Yeast cells die between 138°F (59°C) and 140°F (60°C). For the artisan baker, this means that judging the temperature of liquids you stir into the dry ingredients is very important — use your instant-read thermometer so you don't inadvertently kill the yeast with hot liquids. Knowing how yeast works helps you understand the mechanics of baking better: how the bread rises in the hot oven until the dough itself reaches between 138°F (59°C) and 140°F (60°C), and then the excess moisture bakes out, the crust forms and the bread is done at 190°F (90°C).

2. **Leaving yeast to do its work slowly results in bread with better, more developed flavor.** So room temperature resting and rising, or even an overnight stay in the refrigerator, results in tastier bread.

Flour

Artisan bread made with a no-knead method requires flour with good protein content, because protein equals gluten. Gluten helps form the muscular structure of bread, thereby helping it rise. It can be activated either by kneading, which we're not going to do, or by adding extra liquid, which we are. The more gluten, the better rise we'll get in the bread. Unbleached all-purpose flour and bread flour have the protein and gluten content we're looking for. With some recipes, you can use either/or, while others specify bread flour to do really heavy lifting. If you want to use unbleached organic flours, all the better. Why unbleached flour? Because with less processing, unbleached flours retain more of their protein.

Baking with Canadian Flour

Canadian flour has a higher protein content than some U.S. flours and therefore absorbs more water. If you are using Canadian unbleached bread flour, start by adding about ½ cup (125 mL) less than called for, and add just enough of the remaining ½ cup (125 mL) to make a thick, paste-like dough. To get the best texture from your bread, you want to avoid a dough that is too dry. You don't need to adjust the amount of Canadian unbleached all-purpose flour.

Salt

We'll start off using table salt, but as we go along and get to purer artisan baking, we'll want the good stuff: fine kosher or sea salt. You can certainly use fine kosher or sea salt for all the recipes, if you wish.

Water

We'll start off by using tap water, but as we go along, we'll use filtered or bottled spring water, as it has fewer chemicals and a purer, cleaner taste (if you like, use filtered or bottled water for every recipe). Use your instant-read thermometer to measure the temperature of the water in the first few recipes; eventually, you'll be able to tell by touch how warm the water needs to be. Hot water, 138°F (59°C) and above, will kill the yeast.

Ten Basic Steps to Artisan Bread

NOW THAT WE HAVE the equipment and ingredients, what will we do with them?

1. *Measure.* How you measure the flour makes an enormous difference in the final product. If you just stick a measuring cup in a bag or container of flour and scoop, the flour packs into the measuring cup more. One cup (250 mL) of scooped flour will weigh around $5\frac{1}{4}$ ounces (about 157 g). If you spoon flour from the bag or container into the measuring cup, leveling it off with a knife or your finger, the flour gently settles in. One cup (250 mL) of spooned flour will weigh around $4\frac{1}{2}$ ounces (about 140 g). Multiply that by the number of cups you need in a recipe, and you'll see that the measuring method makes a big difference. More flour means denser, heavier baked goods. And that's not what we want. So we'll spoon and measure.

2. *Mix.* Because we're working with instant or bread machine yeast, we'll stir the dry ingredients together first — usually the yeast, flour and salt — then stir in the liquid. We'll stir the dough together until just moistened, then beat 40 strokes, just as you would with brownie batter made from a mix. The dough should be lumpy, but it will get smoother and bigger as it rests and rises.

3. *Rise.* Now we'll let the yeast, flour and water do their work. The yeast will give off carbon dioxide bubbles, and the water will join with the gluten in the flour to form fibrous bands. The result is dough that rises. Cover the bowl with plastic wrap — it's easy to get the wrap to stick if you moisten the rim of the bowl with a little water, then attach the wrap. If you like, spray the underside of the plastic wrap, where the dough might touch, with olive oil before covering the bowl, so the dough won't stick as it rises. Let the dough rise at room temperature (72°F/22°C) for 2 hours or until it has risen nearly to the top of the bowl, or about doubled in bulk, and has a sponge-like appearance. If your kitchen is warmer, this may take less time. If your kitchen is cooler, it may take a little longer. The dough will even rise in the refrigerator.

4. _Use right away or refrigerate._ Use the dough to bake that day or place the bowl of dough, covered with plastic wrap, in the refrigerator for up to 9 days before baking. Each master dough recipe has a different "use by" date; some sweetened, naturally leavened or enriched doughs will only last several days in the refrigerator. Just read the recipe to make sure. If you like, use a permanent marker to write the date you made the dough on the top of the plastic wrap.

5. _Form._ To form loaves, rolls, flatbreads and more, you'll remove half or one-quarter of the dough with a serrated knife and a dough scraper — or you might use all of it. The serrated knife helps mark the line on top and through the dough; the dough scraper helps remove the dough from the bowl. Each recipe will give you a guideline as to how big the portion should be: the size of a softball for a quarter of the dough, or the size of a small volleyball for half the dough. It doesn't matter if your dough portion isn't exact; the bread will be happy and delicious anyway, and you'll be using an instant-read thermometer to tell when it is done, so don't worry. After you've taken some of the dough out of the bowl, the remaining dough will deflate somewhat, but it will rise again.

You'll transfer your portion of dough to a floured surface and dust it very lightly with flour. You'll also want to flour your hands, because no-knead doughs are fibrous and stickier than doughs you knead. Work the dough as little as possible and sprinkle on flour as necessary. You want enough flour that you'll be able to work the dough, with the help of your dough scraper, without it sticking to your hands, but not so much flour that you'll get a heavy loaf. When the dough is soft but not sticky, you've added enough flour.

Next, you'll form the dough into a geometric shape, depending on the type of bread you're making: circle, oval, rectangle, cylinder and so on. This dough won't form precise shapes, so don't worry about getting it just right. The main thing is to form the loaf so that the surface has a soft, non-sticky skin, without any cracks or seams. Pinch any seams together to prevent "blow-outs" as the loaf bakes. Lightly flour any sticky places on the dough. The dough should feel soft and smooth all over, like a baby's skin, but not at all sticky.

6. *Rest.* Sprinkle cornmeal on a three-sided cookie sheet or baker's peel and place the dough on the cornmeal. Cover with a tea towel and let rest at room temperature for 40 minutes.

7. *Prepare oven for artisan baking.* About 30 minutes before baking, place a broiler pan on the lower shelf and a baking stone on the middle shelf of the oven. Preheat the oven to 450°F (230°C). Most of the artisan breads in this book need the high temperature to do their final rise in the hot oven.

8. *Slash with serrated knife.* When it's ready to bake, the dough won't have risen much, but it will finish rising dramatically in the oven. For many (but not all) of the breads, you'll use a serrated knife to make evenly spaced diagonal slashes, about $1/2$ to 1 inch (1 to 2.5 cm) deep, across the loaf, exposing the moist dough under the surface. The slashes help the bread bake more evenly and add an attractive pattern where the exposed moist dough "blows out."

9. *Slide formed dough onto baking stone and add water to broiler pan.* First, make sure the dough isn't sticking to the cookie sheet by scooping under it in several places with the dough scraper. The cornmeal will act as little ball bearings to help move the dough from the cookie sheet to the hot baking stone. If you like, practice this beforehand. Using a quick forward-and-back jerk of your arms, slide the dough from the cornmeal-dusted cookie sheet back onto the floured surface, so you feel more confident. You'll see that it's a lot easier than it seems. When you're ready, use an oven mitt to carefully pull the middle rack of the oven out several inches. Hold the cookie sheet level with the rack, so that the dough will slide onto the center of the hot baking stone. With a quick forward jerk of your arms, slide the formed dough from the cookie sheet to the stone. If your baguette, for example, doesn't land straight on the baking stone, use a long-handled metal pancake turner to push it into shape (but even an irregular baguette will be delicious). Push the middle rack back in place. Pull the lower rack out, pour hot water into the broiler pan and push the lower rack back in place. Close the oven door immediately so the steam will envelop the oven. When we get to the intermediate and advanced recipes, you'll be spraying the dough with water before and during baking to help create a blistered crust. And as we go along, you'll be able to slide two loaves onto the baking stone.

10. *Bake.* Keep the oven light on in the beginning so you can see how the bread bakes. At first, the formed dough won't appear to do anything. A couple of minutes in, it will start to rise dramatically and the slashed seams will burst open (but hopefully not any "hidden" seams you didn't pinch closed; even if this happens, though, your irregular bread will be delicious). You don't have to wonder if your bread is done, because you'll test it with an instant-read thermometer inserted in the center of the loaf. When the thermometer registers at least 190°F (90°C), your bread is done. As you bake more, you'll know by how fast the needle goes around or the temperature jumps that your bread is done. No thumping, tapping, worrying. You'll know. Wearing oven mitts, remove the loaves by hand to cool on a wire rack.

> **Every bowl of master dough will make at least two to four different breadstuffs, from boules and baguettes to batards, breadsticks, flatbreads, pizzas, rolls, bagels, coffee cakes, pastries and more.**

What Easy Artisan Dough Is Like

IF YOU'VE BAKED kneaded breads before, this dough will seem looser to you — and it is! The extra moisture in the dough takes the place of kneading in activating the gluten in the flour. Gluten helps to form those muscular bands that are the structure of bread, trapping the carbon dioxide released by the yeast. When you work with the dough, use as little flour as possible and use the dough scraper as much as possible to scrape up the dough from the floured surface, turn it and even cut it. Use a pastry brush to brush away excess flour. The dough will feel more like a baby's skin than the tight doughs you usually get with a kneading method.

The looser dough also means that these breads are looser in shape. You won't get tight spirals, intricate braids, close knots or other exact forms. Braided Challah (page 202), for example, will have a rustic, feathery appearance instead of the neat and tidy loaf you see in the grocery store.

Each master dough recipe will tell you what type of color, crust and crumb to expect from the finished product. Along the way, you'll learn how to achieve all the various types.

The 3 C's of Artisan Bread

Color: In artisan bread, color comes from the interplay of flour and heat. Depending on the type of flour you use, your dough may be creamy white, pale yellow, beige, reddish brown, flecked brown or dark brown. Flavorings such as puréed squash, beer and saffron, as well as herbs, fruits, seeds and spices that you stir or fold into the dough, also contribute to color and appearance.

Crumb: The texture of the bread's interior. Each master dough recipe will produce a slightly different type of crumb, from the moist and soft custard crumb of Easy Artisan Dough to the rich and buttery crumb of Easy Artisan Brioche Dough to the muscular, honeycombed crumb of Naturally Leavened Artisan Dough.

Crust: The top exterior of the bread. Artisan bread crusts also vary with each master dough: a crisp crust with Easy Artisan Dough; a shiny, buttery crust with Easy Artisan Brioche Dough; a crisp and shiny crust with Easy Artisan Bagel Dough; and a crisp, blistered crust with Naturally Leavened Artisan Dough.

Basic Artisan Breads

Master Recipe #1
Easy Artisan Dough

This first master recipe introduces you to the basics of the Easy Artisan bread method. As you begin to make bread, all of this will get even easier. You won't have to check the temperature of the water, as you'll know what lukewarm feels like. You'll get quite good at forming the various types of loaves and sliding them onto the hot baking stone. You'll be able to tell, by how fast the temperature rises on the instant-read thermometer, when your bread reaches 190°F (90°C) and is done. Your artisan loaves will have a crisp, darkened crust, a tender, moist crumb and a mellow, toasty flavor — all with this easy method. The dough will also make delicious rolls, pizza or flatbread.

Makes enough dough for bread, rolls, pizza or flatbread to serve 12 to 16

Equipment:
- Instant-read thermometer
- 16-cup (4 L) mixing bowl
- Wooden spoon or Danish dough whisk

Tips
Combining 1½ cups (375 mL) hot with 1½ cups (375 mL) cold tap water will result in lukewarm water of approximately 100°F (38°C).

Before storing the dough in the refrigerator, use a permanent marker to write the date on the plastic wrap, so you'll know when you made your dough — and when to use it up 9 days later.

6½ cups	unbleached all-purpose or bread flour	1.625 L
1½ tbsp	instant or bread machine yeast	22 mL
1½ tbsp	fine table or kosher salt	22 mL
3 cups	lukewarm water (about 100°F/38°C)	750 mL

1. **Measure.** Spoon the flour into a measuring cup, level with a knife or your finger, then dump the flour into the mixing bowl.

2. **Mix.** Add the yeast and salt to the flour. Stir together with a wooden spoon or Danish dough whisk. Pour in the water and stir together until just moistened. Beat 40 strokes, scraping the bottom and the sides of the bowl, until the dough forms a lumpy, sticky mass.

3. **Rise.** Cover the bowl with plastic wrap and let rise at room temperature (72°F/22°C) in a draft-free place for 2 hours or until the dough has risen nearly to the top of the bowl and has a sponge-like appearance.

4. **Use right away or refrigerate.** Use that day or place the dough, covered with plastic wrap, in the refrigerator for up to 9 days before baking.

Baking with Canadian Flour
Canadian flour has a higher protein content than some U.S. flours and therefore absorbs more water. If you are using Canadian bread flour, start by adding about ½ cup (125 mL) less than called for, and add just enough of the remaining ½ cup (125 mL) to make a thick, paste-like dough. You don't need to adjust the amount of all-purpose flour.

Baby Boule

Equipment:
- Three-sided cookie sheet, flexible cutting board or baker's peel
- Broiler pan
- Baking stone

Start with this classic shape to get the feel of the dough. This recipe makes a small boule, which will rise dramatically in the oven, producing a crusty loaf with a moist and tender crumb, which four people can greedily consume. Delicious! And so easy!

Tip

When you are proficient at sliding the dough onto the baking stone, you can bake two boules at one time, if it's big enough to allow enough space between them. Place the boules on the prepared cookie sheet so that they are parallel to each other and about 4 inches (10 cm) apart. Then hold the cookie sheet level with the rack so that the boules will slide onto the hot baking stone. With a quick forward jerk of your arms, slide the boules from the cookie sheet to each side of the stone.

¼	recipe prepared Easy Artisan Dough (page 24), about the size of a softball	¼
	Unbleached all-purpose or bread flour	
¼ cup	cornmeal	50 mL
2 cups	hot water	500 mL

1. *Form.* Place dough on a floured surface and dust very lightly with flour. Flour your hands. Working the dough as little as possible and adding flour as necessary, form the dough into a 6-inch (15 cm) round. Smooth the dough with your hands to form a soft, non-sticky skin. Pinch any seams together. Lightly flour any sticky places on the dough. The dough should feel soft and smooth all over, like a baby's skin, but not at all sticky.

2. *Rest.* Sprinkle the cornmeal on the cookie sheet and place the dough round on the cornmeal. Cover with a tea towel and let rest at room temperature for 40 minutes.

3. *Prepare oven for artisan baking.* About 30 minutes before baking, place the broiler pan on the lower shelf and the baking stone on the middle shelf of the oven. Preheat to 450°F (230°C).

4. *Slash boule with serrated knife.* Using a serrated knife, make three evenly spaced slashes, about ½ inch (1 cm) deep, across the boule, exposing the moist dough under the surface.

5. *Slide boule onto baking stone and add water to broiler pan.* Using an oven mitt, carefully pull the middle rack of the oven out several inches. Hold the cookie sheet level with the rack so that the dough round will slide onto the center of the hot stone. With a quick forward jerk of your arms, slide the dough round from the cookie sheet to the stone. Push the middle rack back in place. Pull the lower rack out, pour the hot water into the broiler pan and push the lower rack back in place. Close the oven door immediately so the steam will envelop the oven.

6. *Bake.* Bake for 27 to 30 minutes or until the crust is a medium dark brown and an instant-read thermometer inserted in the center of the loaf registers at least 190°F (90°C). Wearing oven mitts, remove the loaf by hand to cool on a wire rack.

Baguette

Makes 1 baguette, to serve 4

Equipment:
- Three-sided cookie sheet, flexible cutting board or baker's peel
- Broiler pan
- Baking stone

A crusty baguette — warm from the oven — can be a regular feature of your weeknight repertoire when you have the dough ready-made in the refrigerator. Form the baguette and let the dough relax while you prepare the rest of dinner, then pop the baguette in the oven to bake.

Tip

When you are proficient at sliding the dough onto the baking stone, you can bake two baguettes at one time. Place the baguettes on the prepared cookie sheet so that they are parallel to each other and about 6 inches (15 cm) apart. Then hold the cookie sheet level with the rack so that the first baguette will slide sideways onto the hot baking stone. With a quick forward jerk of your arms, slide the first baguette from the cookie sheet to the back of the stone. With another jerk, slide the second baguette onto the front of the stone.

$^1/_4$	recipe prepared Easy Artisan Dough (page 24), about the size of a softball	$^1/_4$
	Unbleached all-purpose or bread flour	
$^1/_4$ cup	cornmeal	50 mL
2 cups	hot water	500 mL

1. **Form.** Place dough on a floured surface and dust very lightly with flour. Flour your hands. Working the dough as little as possible and adding flour as necessary, form the dough into a 14-inch (35 cm) cylinder. Smooth the dough with your hands to form a soft, non-sticky skin. Pinch any seams together. Pinch each end into a point. Lightly flour any sticky places on the dough. The dough should feel soft and smooth all over, like a baby's skin, but not at all sticky.

2. **Rest.** Sprinkle the cornmeal on the cookie sheet and place the dough cylinder on the cornmeal. Cover with a tea towel and let rest at room temperature for 40 minutes.

3. **Prepare oven for artisan baking.** About 30 minutes before baking, place the broiler pan on the lower shelf and the baking stone on the middle shelf of the oven. Preheat to 450°F (230°C).

4. **Slash baguette with serrated knife.** Using a serrated knife, make three evenly spaced diagonal slashes, about $^1/_2$ inch (1 cm) deep, across the baguette, exposing the moist dough under the surface.

5. **Slide baguette onto baking stone and add water to broiler pan.** Using an oven mitt, carefully pull the middle rack of the oven out several inches. Hold the cookie sheet level with the rack so that the baguette will slide sideways onto the center of the hot stone. With a quick forward jerk of your arms, slide the baguette from the board to the stone. Push the middle rack back in place. Pull the lower rack out, pour the hot water into the broiler pan and push the lower rack back in place. Close the oven door immediately so the steam will envelop the oven.

6. **Bake.** Bake for 25 minutes or until the crust is a medium dark brown and an instant-read thermometer inserted in the center of the loaf registers at least 190°F (90°C). Wearing oven mitts, remove the loaf by hand to cool on a wire rack.

Batard

Equipment:
- Three-sided cookie sheet
- Flexible cutting board, floured, or two metal spatulas
- Broiler pan
- Baking stone

Use half of the dough to form a larger loaf, to be baked without a loaf pan. This bread has a dark crust, a mellow flavor and a soft crumb.

½	recipe prepared Easy Artisan Dough (page 24), about the size of a volleyball	½
	Unbleached all-purpose or bread flour	
½ cup	cornmeal	125 mL
2 cups	hot water	500 mL

1. *Form.* Place dough on a floured surface and dust very lightly with flour. Flour your hands. Working the dough as little as possible and adding flour as necessary, form the dough into a 14-inch (35 cm) cylinder. Pinch the ends and any seams closed. Lightly flour any sticky places on the dough. The dough should feel soft and smooth all over, like a baby's skin, but not at all sticky.

2. *Rest.* Sprinkle the cornmeal on the cookie sheet. Using the cutting board or two metal spatulas, transfer the loaf to the prepared cookie sheet. Cover with a tea towel and let rest at room temperature for 40 minutes.

3. *Prepare oven for artisan baking.* About 30 minutes before baking, place the broiler pan on the lower shelf and the baking stone on the middle shelf of the oven. Preheat to 450°F (230°C).

4. *Slash batard with serrated knife.* Using a serrated knife, make five cross-hatch slashes, about ½ inch (1 cm) deep, diagonally across the top of the loaf, exposing the moist dough under the surface.

5. *Slide batard onto baking stone and add water to broiler pan.* Using an oven mitt, carefully pull the middle rack of the oven out several inches. Hold the cookie sheet level with the rack so that the loaf will slide sideways onto the hot stone. With a quick forward jerk of your arms, slide the loaf from the cookie sheet to the stone. If necessary, use a metal spatula to reposition the loaf. Push the middle rack back in place. Pull the lower rack out, pour the hot water into the broiler pan and push the lower rack back in place. Close the oven door immediately so the steam will envelop the oven.

6. *Bake.* Bake for 25 to 27 minutes or until the crust is dark brown and an instant-read thermometer inserted in the center of the loaf registers at least 190°F (90°C). Wearing oven mitts, remove the loaf by hand to cool on a wire rack.

Rolls

Makes 4 rolls

Equipment:
- Three-sided cookie sheet, flexible cutting board or baker's peel
- Broiler pan
- Baking stone

You can also make crusty artisan rolls with the master dough. They will look small before baking, but will at least double in size in the hot oven. They do not get as dark as the boule, baguette or loaf. These rolls are big enough to use for sandwiches — for burgers, grilled chicken or the filling of your choice.

¼	recipe prepared Easy Artisan Dough (page 24), about the size of a softball	¼
	Unbleached all-purpose or bread flour	
¼ cup	cornmeal	50 mL
2 cups	hot water	500 mL

1. *Form.* Place dough on a floured surface and dust very lightly with flour. Flour your hands. Working the dough as little as possible and adding flour as necessary, form the dough into an 8-inch (20 cm) cylinder. With a dough scraper, slice the cylinder into 2-inch (5 cm) pieces. Pinch the cut ends together. Lightly flour any sticky places on the dough. The dough should feel soft and smooth all over, like a baby's skin, but not at all sticky.

2. *Rest.* Sprinkle the cornmeal on the cookie sheet. Arrange the rolls in two horizontal lines, 4 inches (10 cm) apart, on the prepared cookie sheet. Cover with a tea towel and let rest at room temperature for 40 minutes.

3. *Prepare oven for artisan baking.* About 30 minutes before baking, place the broiler pan on the lower shelf and the baking stone on the middle shelf of the oven. Preheat to 450°F (230°C).

4. *Slash rolls with serrated knife.* Using a serrated knife, make two cross-hatch slashes, about ½ inch (1 cm) deep, in the top center of each roll, exposing the moist dough under the surface.

5. *Slide rolls onto baking stone and add water to broiler pan.* Using an oven mitt, carefully pull the middle rack of the oven out several inches. Hold the cookie sheet level with the rack so that the rolls will slide sideways onto the hot stone. With a quick forward jerk of your arms, slide the rolls from the cookie sheet to the stone. If a roll lands too close to another, use a metal spatula to reposition it. Push the middle rack back in place. Pull the lower rack out, pour the hot water into the broiler pan and push the lower rack back in place. Close the oven door immediately so the steam will envelop the oven.

6. *Bake.* Bake for 15 to 17 minutes or until the crust is lightly browned and an instant-read thermometer inserted in the center of a roll registers at least 190°F (90°C). Wearing oven mitts, remove rolls by hand to cool on a wire rack.

Pizza Blanca

This crisp-crusted, artisan-style pizza features simple toppings — olive oil, garlic and cheese — but can be customized with the toppings of your choice (see tip, below).

Tip

This type of thin-crust pizza is not meant for heavy sauce, cheese and meat toppings. Instead, use toppings that add bold flavor without bulk, such as thinly sliced onion, prosciutto or crisp-cooked pancetta, grated aged cheeses, chèvre, feta or blue cheese crumbles, olives, pesto, roasted red pepper, cooked Italian sausage crumbles, thinly sliced mushrooms, fresh herbs, fresh tomatoes, oil-packed sun-dried tomatoes, thin asparagus stalks or arugula.

¼	recipe prepared Easy Artisan Dough (page 24), about the size of a softball	¼
	Unbleached all-purpose or bread flour	
2 tbsp	olive oil	25 mL
1	clove garlic, minced	1
½ cup	grated Asiago, Parmesan or Romano cheese	125 mL
2 cups	hot water	500 mL

1. *Form.* Place dough on a floured surface and dust very lightly with flour. Flour your hands and the rolling pin. Working the dough as little as possible and adding flour as necessary, roll out the dough into a 12-inch (30 cm) circle. Lightly flour any sticky places on the dough as you roll. The dough should feel gently taut and smooth all over, like a baby's skin, but not at all sticky.

2. *Rest.* Drape the dough over the rolling pin and transfer to the prepared pan. Pat into place. Cover with a tea towel and let rest at room temperature for 40 minutes.

3. *Prepare oven for artisan baking.* About 30 minutes before baking, place the broiler pan on the lower shelf and the baking stone on the middle shelf of the oven. Preheat to 450°F (230°C).

4. *Add pizza toppings.* In a small, bowl, combine olive oil and garlic. Brush onto the dough and sprinkle with cheese.

5. *Place pizza pan on baking stone and add water to broiler pan.* Place the pizza pan on the hot stone. Pull the lower rack out, pour the hot water into the broiler pan, and push the lower rack back in place. Close the oven door immediately so the steam will envelop the oven.

6. *Bake.* Bake for 15 minutes or until the edges of the crust and the cheese have both browned.

Part 2
Now You're Baking

Once you know how to make Easy Artisan Dough, form the basic bread shapes and bake with the artisan method, it's time to add a little more to your repertoire.

True to the easy artisan method, we'll take easy artisan steps. With each master dough recipe, you'll learn a little more method, technique and science, and by the end of the book, you'll feel confident making naturally leavened breads, Danish pastries, flaky croissants and homemade bagels.

In this part, we'll start by adding a few more basic bread shapes, like Baby Baguettes (page 36), a large boat-shaped batard and pizza. You'll learn how to roll out the dough, spread on a filling and roll it up to form swirled loaves and rolls. Then we'll go on to include whole grains in a variety of ways: as dry packaged flour, freshly ground flour, cooked cereal and even ground granola, in breads such as Great Plains Granola Bread (page 84). After that, it's how to incorporate a filling into the dough or coat it with seeds for even more variety, as in Peshawari Naan (page 114). Then we're on to flavoring the dough itself, with buttermilk, beer, spices, purées, herbs and more, as in Mini Hamburger Buns (page 136).

By the time we're on to slow-rise breads such as Slow-Rise Ciabatta (page 164), which require a yeast starter and an overnight rest, you'll be quite the accomplished artisan baker. You'll be ready for something sweet — maybe Classic Cinnamon Rolls (page 194), or coffee cake, or light and airy braided challah — made with a sweetened, egg-enriched dough. Not to mention all the glazes and fillings that go with these goodies. Once you've got that type of dough mastered, you'll be ready for Butternut Brioche Dough (page 212) and Cider-Glazed Savarin (page 213), the epitome of a sweetened, egg-enriched dough and the glory of French bakers.

More Basic Artisan Breads

Master Recipe #1
Easy Artisan Dough

Let's put this dough through its paces — in more varied forms. With a bowl of this dough in your refrigerator, warm and crusty breads are about an hour away.

Makes enough dough for bread, rolls, pizza or flatbread to serve 12 to 16

Equipment:
- Instant-read thermometer
- 16-cup (4 L) mixing bowl
- Wooden spoon or Danish dough whisk

Tips

Combining 1½ cups (375 mL) hot with 1½ cups (375 mL) cold tap water will result in lukewarm water of approximately 100°F (38°C).

Baking with Canadian Flour

Canadian flour has a higher protein content than some U.S. flours and therefore absorbs more water. If you are using bread flour, start by adding about ½ cup (125 mL) less than called for, and add just enough of the remaining ½ cup (125 mL) to make a thick, paste-like dough. You don't need to adjust the amount of all-purpose flour.

6½ cups	unbleached all-purpose or bread flour	1.625 L
1½ tbsp	instant or bread machine yeast	22 mL
1½ tbsp	fine table or kosher salt	22 mL
3 cups	lukewarm water (about 100°F/38°C)	750 mL

1. *Measure.* Spoon the flour into a measuring cup, level with a knife or your finger, then dump the flour into the mixing bowl.

2. *Mix.* Add the yeast and salt to the flour. Stir together with a wooden spoon or Danish dough whisk. Pour in the water and stir together until just moistened. Beat 40 strokes, scraping the bottom and the sides of the bowl, until the dough forms a lumpy, sticky mass.

3. *Rise.* Cover the bowl with plastic wrap and let rise at room temperature (72°F/22°C) in a draft-free place for 2 hours or until the dough has risen nearly to the top of the bowl and has a sponge-like appearance.

4. *Use right away or refrigerate.* Use that day or place the dough, covered with plastic wrap, in the refrigerator for up to 9 days before baking.

Easy Artisan Breads in Minutes a Day	
Day 1	Stir the dough together and let rise. Bake, or cover and chill.
Days 2–9	Remove part of the dough, form and bake.

Boule

Makes 1 large round loaf, or boule, to serve 8

Equipment:
- Three-sided cookie sheet, flexible cutting board or baker's peel
- Broiler pan
- Baking stone

Once you've made the Baby Boule in Part 1, it's easy to go a step further and make it twice as big. This time, you'll remove half the dough from the bowl and form it into a round loaf.

Tip

Add texture and variety to your artisan bread by using 3 cups (750 mL) whole-grain flour (white whole wheat, semolina or whole wheat) plus 3½ cups (875 mL) unbleached all-purpose or unbleached bread flour to equal the 6½ cups (1.625 L) in the master recipe.

½	recipe prepared Easy Artisan Dough (page 34), about the size of a volleyball	½
	Unbleached all-purpose or bread flour	
½ cup	cornmeal	125 mL
2 cups	hot water	500 mL

1. *Form.* Place dough portion on a floured surface and dust very lightly with flour. Flour your hands. Working the dough as little as possible and adding flour as necessary, form the dough into a 12-inch (30 cm) round. Smooth the dough with your hands to form a soft, non-sticky skin. Pinch any seams together. Lightly flour any sticky places on the dough. The dough should feel soft and smooth all over, like a baby's skin, but not at all sticky.

2. *Rest.* Sprinkle the cornmeal on the cookie sheet and place the dough round on the cornmeal. Cover with a tea towel and let rest at room temperature for 40 minutes.

3. *Prepare oven for artisan baking.* About 30 minutes before baking, place the broiler pan on the lower shelf and the baking stone on the middle shelf of the oven. Preheat to 450°F (230°C).

4. *Slash boule with serrated knife.* Using a serrated knife, make three evenly spaced slashes, about ½ inch (1 cm) deep, across the boule, exposing the moist dough under the surface.

5. *Slide boule onto baking stone and add water to broiler pan.* Using an oven mitt, carefully pull the middle rack of the oven out several inches. Hold the cookie sheet level with the rack so that the dough round will slide onto the center of the hot stone. With a quick forward jerk of your arms, slide the dough round from the cookie sheet to the stone. Push the middle rack back in place. Pull the lower rack out, pour the hot water into the broiler pan and push the lower rack back in place. Close the oven door immediately so the steam will envelop the oven.

6. *Bake.* Bake for 27 to 30 minutes or until the crust is a medium dark brown and an instant-read thermometer inserted in the center of the loaf registers at least 190°F (90°C). Wearing oven mitts, remove the loaf by hand to cool on a wire rack.

Baby Baguettes

Makes 4 baby baguettes

Equipment:
- Three-sided cookie sheet, flexible cutting board or baker's peel
- Broiler pan
- Baking stone

If you can form a larger baguette, you can make smaller ones. This recipe makes four baby baguettes for individual servings. Form the baguettes and let the dough rest while you prepare dinner, then pop the baguettes in the oven to bake.

$\frac{1}{4}$	recipe prepared Easy Artisan Dough (page 34), about the size of a softball	$\frac{1}{4}$
	Unbleached all-purpose or bread flour	
$\frac{1}{4}$ cup	cornmeal	50 mL
2 cups	hot water	500 mL

1. *Form.* Place dough on a floured surface and dust very lightly with flour. Flour your hands. Working the dough as little as possible and adding flour as necessary, form the dough into a 12-inch (30 cm) cylinder. With a dough scraper, cut the dough into four 3-inch (7.5 cm) segments. Shape each segment into a baguette. Smooth the dough with your hands to form a soft, non-sticky skin. Pinch any seams together. Pinch each end into a point. Lightly flour any sticky places on the dough. The dough should feel soft and smooth all over, like a baby's skin, but not at all sticky.

2. *Rest.* Sprinkle the cornmeal on the cookie sheet and place the baguettes in two rows on the cornmeal. Cover with a tea towel and let rest at room temperature for 40 minutes.

3. *Prepare oven for artisan baking.* About 30 minutes before baking, place the broiler pan on the lower shelf and the baking stone on the middle shelf of the oven. Preheat to 450°F (230°C).

4. *Slash baguettes with serrated knife.* Using a serrated knife, make three evenly spaced diagonal slashes, about $\frac{1}{2}$ inch (1 cm) deep, across each baguette, exposing the moist dough under the surface.

If you have a leftover baguette, let it cool, place in a large plastic freezer bag (or cut the baguette in half and place 2 halves in a bag) and freeze for up to 3 months. To warm a frozen baguette, wrap it in foil and place in a 350°F (230°C) oven for 15 to 20 minutes or until warmed through.

5. *Slide baguettes onto baking stone and add water to broiler pan.* Using an oven mitt, carefully pull the middle rack of the oven out several inches. Hold the cookie sheet level with the rack so that the first row of baguettes will slide sideways onto the center of the hot stone. With a quick forward jerk of your arms, slide the baguettes from the cookie sheet to the back of the stone. Then with the same motion, slide the second row of baguettes onto the front of the stone. Push the middle rack back in place. Pull the lower rack out, pour the hot water into the broiler pan and push the lower rack back in place. Close the oven door immediately so the steam will envelop the oven.

6. *Bake.* Bake for 12 to 15 minutes or until the crust is a medium dark brown and an instant-read thermometer inserted in the center of a baguette registers at least 190°F (90°C). Wearing oven mitts, remove baguettes by hand to cool on a wire rack.

Naan

Makes 8 flatbreads

Equipment:
- Rolling pin
- Large baking sheet
- Broiler pan
- Baking stone
- Metal spatula

Brushed with melted butter or ghee before baking, puffy ovals of naan are meant to help scoop up the flavorful curries of northern India. Try these easy ones first, before going on to Traditional Naan (page 72) made with all-purpose and whole wheat flours or Peshawari Naan (page 114), with dried fruit, herbs and nuts incorporated into the dough.

¼	recipe prepared Easy Artisan Dough (page 34), about the size of a softball	¼
	Unbleached all-purpose or bread flour	
¼ cup	cornmeal	50 mL
	Melted butter or olive oil	
2 cups	hot water	500 mL

1. *Form.* Place dough on a floured surface and dust very lightly with flour. Flour your hands and the rolling pin. Working the dough as little as possible and adding flour as necessary, form the dough into an 8-inch (20 cm) cylinder. With a dough scraper, cut the dough into 1-inch (2.5 cm) slices. Roll out each slice into a 6-inch (15 cm) long oval. Lightly flour any sticky places on the dough. The dough should feel soft and smooth all over, like a baby's skin, but not at all sticky.

2. *Rest.* Sprinkle the cornmeal on the cookie sheet and place the dough ovals on the cornmeal. Cover with a tea towel and let rest at room temperature for 40 minutes.

3. *Prepare oven for artisan baking.* About 30 minutes before baking, place the broiler pan on the lower shelf and the baking stone on the middle shelf of the oven. Preheat to 450°F (230°C).

4. *Brush with melted butter.* Brush the naan with melted butter.

5. *Place naan on baking stone and add water to broiler pan.* Using an oven mitt, carefully pull the middle rack of the oven out several inches. With a metal spatula, place four naan on the hot stone. Pull the lower rack out, pour the hot water into the broiler pan and push the lower rack back in place. Close the oven door immediately so the steam will envelop the oven.

6. *Bake.* Bake for 7 to 8 minutes or until the crust is lightly blistered. Wearing oven mitts, remove the naan by hand to cool on a wire rack. Repeat the baking process with the remaining naan.

Pita Bread

Makes 4 flatbreads

Equipment:
- Rolling pin
- Baking sheet
- Broiler pan
- Baking stone
- Metal spatula

Pita bread — which rises higher than naan — is meant to scoop up hummus or other Middle Eastern spreads, or to be split in half to hold sandwich fillings.

¼	recipe prepared Easy Artisan Dough (page 34), about the size of a softball	¼
	Unbleached all-purpose flour	
¼ cup	cornmeal	50 mL
	Melted butter or olive oil	
2 cups	hot water	500 mL

1. *Form.* Place dough on a floured surface and dust very lightly with flour. Flour your hands and the rolling pin. Working the dough as little as possible and adding flour as necessary, form the dough into an 8-inch (20 cm) cylinder. With a dough scraper, cut the dough into 2-inch (5 cm) slices. Roll out each slice into a 6-inch (15 cm) round. Lightly flour any sticky places on the dough. The dough should feel soft and smooth all over, like a baby's skin, but not at all sticky.

2. *Rest.* Sprinkle the cornmeal on the cookie sheet and place the dough rounds on the cornmeal. Cover with a tea towel and let rest at room temperature for 40 minutes.

3. *Prepare oven for artisan baking.* About 30 minutes before baking, place the broiler pan on the lower shelf and the baking stone on the middle shelf of the oven. Preheat to 450°F (230°C).

4. *Brush with melted butter.* Brush the pitas with melted butter.

5. *Place flatbread on baking stone and add water to broiler pan.* Using an oven mitt, carefully pull the middle rack of the oven out several inches. With a metal spatula, place pitas on the hot stone. Pull the lower rack out, pour the hot water into the broiler pan and push the lower rack back in place. Close the oven door immediately so the steam will envelop the oven.

6. *Bake.* Bake for 6 to 8 minutes or until puffed and light brown. Wearing oven mitts, remove the pitas by hand to cool on a wire rack.

Breadsticks

Makes 8 breadsticks		

¼	recipe prepared Easy Artisan Dough (page 34), about the size of a softball	¼
	Unbleached all-purpose flour	
¼ cup	cornmeal	50 mL
2 cups	hot water	500 mL

Equipment:
- Baking sheet
- Broiler pan
- Baking stone

Serve these mellow, crusty breadsticks with soups, salads or dipping sauces.

1. *Form.* Place dough on a floured surface and dust very lightly with flour. Flour your hands. Working the dough as little as possible and adding flour as necessary, pat the dough into an 8-inch (20 cm) square. Lightly flour any sticky places on the dough. The dough should feel soft and smooth all over, like a baby's skin, but not at all sticky.

2. *Cut.* Using a pizza wheel or a sharp knife, cut the square into eight 1-inch (2.5 cm) wide strips.

3. *Rest.* Sprinkle the cornmeal on the baking sheet and place the dough strips about 2 inches (5 cm) apart on the cornmeal. Cover with a tea towel and let rest at room temperature for 40 minutes.

4. *Prepare oven for artisan baking.* About 30 minutes before baking, place the broiler pan on the lower shelf and the baking stone on the middle shelf of the oven. Preheat to 450°F (230°C).

5. *Place baking sheet on baking stone and add water to broiler pan.* Using an oven mitt, carefully pull the middle rack of the oven out several inches. Place the baking sheet of breadsticks on the hot stone. Pull the lower rack out, pour the hot water into the broiler pan and push the lower rack back in place. Close the oven door immediately so the steam will envelop the oven.

6. *Bake.* Bake for 15 to 17 minutes or until lightly browned. Transfer to a wire rack to cool.

Change It Up

Parmesan Breadsticks: After Step 1, sprinkle each dough strip with 1 tbsp (15 mL) freshly grated Parmesan cheese.

Three-Seed Breadsticks: After Step 1, brush each dough strip with olive oil, then sprinkle with a mixture of 2 tbsp (25 mL) each poppy seeds, sesame seeds and fennel seeds.

Fougasse

Equipment:
- Rolling pin
- Large baking sheet, lined with parchment paper
- Broiler pan
- Baking stone

What's focaccia to Italians is fougasse to the French — an artisan flatbread, usually with a savory flavor. The trick with fougasse is to create the diagonal slits that, when opened, make the distinctive leafy pattern in the bread.

¼	recipe prepared Easy Artisan Dough (page 34), about the size of a softball	¼
	Unbleached all-purpose flour	
1 tbsp	olive oil	15 mL
2 cups	hot water	500 mL

1. *Form.* Place dough on a floured surface and dust very lightly with flour. Flour your hands and the rolling pin. Working the dough as little as possible and adding flour as necessary, roll out the dough into a 12- by 6-inch (30 by 15 cm) oval. Lightly flour any sticky places on the dough. The dough should feel soft and smooth all over, like a baby's skin, but not at all sticky.

2. *Cut.* Using a pizza wheel or a sharp knife, cut two rows of four diagonal slashes evenly spaced along the length of the oval, about 2 to 3 inches (5 to 7.5 cm) long, that almost meet in the middle of the dough, like this: / \. Transfer the dough to the prepared baking sheet and pull the top and sides of the dough to stretch it into a larger oval with opened slits. Brush the surface of the dough with the olive oil.

3. *Rest.* Cover with a tea towel and let rest at room temperature for 40 minutes.

4. *Prepare oven for artisan baking.* About 30 minutes before baking, place the broiler pan on the lower shelf and the baking stone on the middle shelf of the oven. Preheat to 450°F (230°C).

5. *Place baking sheet on baking stone and add water to broiler pan.* Using an oven mitt, carefully pull the middle rack of the oven out several inches. Place the baking sheet on the hot stone. Push the middle rack back in place. Pull the lower rack out, pour the hot water into the broiler pan and push the lower rack back in place. Close the oven door immediately so the steam will envelop the oven.

6. *Bake.* Bake for 17 to 20 minutes or until the crust is medium brown. Transfer to a wire rack to cool.

Focaccia with Fresh Rosemary

Equipment:
- 8-inch (20 cm) square metal baking pan or dish
- Broiler pan
- Baking stone

Focaccia, the savory Italian flatbread, can be enjoyed in so many ways. Serve it as a bread to dip in olive oil at the table. Slice it in half horizontally and make sandwiches or panini. Or cut it into cubes, toss with olive oil and toast in the oven to use as croutons for a fabulous salad. What gives focaccia its distinctive flavor is the slurry of olive oil, salt and water you brush on the dough.

1/4	recipe prepared Easy Artisan Dough (page 34), about the size of a softball	1/4
	Unbleached all-purpose flour	
2 tbsp	olive oil, divided	25 mL
1/2 tsp	fine kosher or sea salt	2 mL
1 tbsp	water	15 mL
1 tbsp	fresh rosemary leaves	15 mL
2 cups	hot water	500 mL

1. *Form.* Place dough on a floured surface and dust very lightly with flour. Flour your hands. Working the dough as little as possible and adding flour as necessary, pat the dough into an 8-inch (20 cm) square. Lightly flour any sticky places on the dough. The dough should feel soft and smooth all over, like a baby's skin, but not at all sticky.

2. *Top.* Pour 1 tbsp (15 mL) of the olive oil into baking pan and brush the bottom and sides with the oil. Transfer the dough to the prepared pan and pat to fit. In a small bowl, combine the remaining oil with the salt and water to make a slurry. Brush the slurry over the dough. Sprinkle with rosemary.

3. *Rest.* Cover with a tea towel and let rest at room temperature for 40 minutes.

4. *Prepare oven for artisan baking.* About 30 minutes before baking, place the broiler pan on the lower shelf and the baking stone on the middle shelf of the oven. Preheat to 450°F (230°C).

5. *Dimple flatbread.* Using the handle of a wooden spoon, dimple the flatbread at 2-inch (5 cm) intervals.

You Can Also Use
Easy Artisan Whole-Grain Dough (page 56), made with semolina, Easy Artisan Slow-Rise Dough (page 148) or Slow-Rise Herbed Polenta Dough (page 151).

6. *Place baking pan on baking stone and add water to broiler pan.* Using an oven mitt, carefully pull the middle rack of the oven out several inches. Place the pan of focaccia on the hot stone. Push the middle rack back in place. Pull the lower rack out, pour the hot water into the broiler pan and push the lower rack back in place. Close the oven door immediately so the steam will envelop the oven.

7. *Bake.* Bake for 25 to 27 minutes or until the crust is lightly browned. Remove from pan and transfer to a wire rack to cool.

Change It Up

Roasted Sage and Onion Focaccia: Substitute 8 fresh sage leaves for the rosemary. Top with $1/2$ cup (125 mL) thinly sliced red onion and 2 thinly sliced shallots. Sprinkle with $1/2$ cup (125 mL) freshly grated Parmesan cheese and drizzle with 1 tbsp (15 mL) olive oil. Bake for 27 to 30 minutes or until the crust is lightly browned and the onion is roasted.

Flatbread with Caramelized Onions and Brie

Equipment:
- 8-inch (20 cm) square metal baking pan, greased
- Broiler pan
- Baking stone

As an entrée for a casual meal or cut into squares for an appetizer, this flatbread always gets rave reviews.

¼	recipe prepared Easy Artisan Dough (page 34), about the size of a softball	¼
	Unbleached all-purpose flour	
1 cup	Easy Caramelized Onions (page 304)	250 mL
8 oz	Brie cheese (rind on), cut into 1-inch (2.5 cm) pieces	250 g
2 cups	hot water	500 mL

1. *Form.* Place dough on a floured surface and dust very lightly with flour. Flour your hands. Working the dough as little as possible and adding flour as necessary, pat the dough into an 8-inch (20 cm) square. Lightly flour any sticky places on the dough. The dough should feel soft and smooth all over, like a baby's skin, but not at all sticky.

2. *Dimple flatbread.* Transfer the dough to the prepared pan and pat to fit. Using the handle of a wooden spoon, dimple the flatbread at 2-inch (5 cm) intervals.

3. *Top.* Using a fork, spread the caramelized onions over the top of the flatbread, then dot with Brie.

4. *Rest.* Cover with a tea towel and let rest at room temperature for 40 minutes.

5. *Prepare oven for artisan baking.* About 30 minutes before baking, place the broiler pan on the lower shelf and the baking stone on the middle shelf of the oven. Preheat to 450°F (230°C).

When you have Easy Caramelized Onions (page 304) on hand, Easy Artisan Dough in the refrigerator and a bottle of wine in the rack, you're always ready to entertain.

6. *Place baking pan on baking stone and add water to broiler pan.* Using an oven mitt, carefully pull the middle rack of the oven out several inches. Place the pan of flatbread on the hot stone. Push the middle rack back in place. Pull the lower rack out, pour the hot water into the broiler pan and push the lower rack back in place. Close the oven door immediately so the steam will envelop the oven.

7. *Bake.* Bake for 25 to 27 minutes or until the crust is lightly browned. Remove from pan and transfer to a wire rack to cool.

Change It Up

Heirloom Tomato Flatbread: After patting the flatbread into the pan, dimple the dough, then top with 8 fresh basil leaves. Arrange 1 cup (250 mL) chopped fresh heirloom tomatoes (try golden or orange heirlooms) on top of the basil. Sprinkle with ½ cup (125 mL) freshly grated Parmesan cheese and drizzle with 2 tbsp (25 mL) olive oil.

Soft Pretzels

Equipment:
- 4-cup (1 L) heatproof glass measuring cup or bowl
- Three-sided cookie sheet, flexible cutting board or baker's peel
- Tongs
- Broiler pan
- Baking stone

Once you've made breadsticks, you're ready for pretzels. What gives pretzels their distinctive flavor is lye — a dry, caustic substance also known as caustic soda or sodium hydroxide. You can find it in the plumbing aisle of hardware stores. You need only a very little, mixed into boiling water, in which to dip each pretzel dough before baking. You can omit the lye wash, but your pretzels will taste like breadsticks.

¼	recipe prepared Easy Artisan Dough (page 34), about the size of a softball	¼
	Unbleached all-purpose flour	
½ cup	cornmeal	125 mL
1 cup	boiling water	250 mL
1 tsp	lye	5 mL
	Coarse kosher salt or pretzel salt	
2 cups	hot water	500 mL

1. *Form.* Place dough on a floured surface and dust very lightly with flour. Flour your hands. Working the dough as little as possible and adding flour as necessary, pat the dough into an 8-inch (20 cm) square. Lightly flour any sticky places on the dough. The dough should feel soft and smooth all over, like a baby's skin, but not at all sticky.

2. *Cut.* Using a pizza wheel or a sharp knife, cut the square into eight 1-inch (2.5 cm) wide strips. Gently pull and squeeze each strip to lengthen it to 14 inches (35 cm). Holding an end of a strip in each hand, cross one hand over the other to form a pretzel shape. Press the ends into the body of the pretzel.

3. *Rest.* Cover with a tea towel and let rest at room temperature for 40 minutes.

4. *Prepare oven for artisan baking.* About 30 minutes before baking, place the broiler pan on the lower shelf and the baking stone on the middle shelf of the oven. Preheat to 450°F (230°C).

5. *Prepare lye bath.* Right before baking, combine the boiling water and lye in the heatproof measuring cup. Sprinkle the cornmeal on the cookie sheet. Using tongs, dip each pretzel in the hot lye mixture, let drain briefly and place about 2 inches (5 cm) apart on the cornmeal. Pour the remaining lye mixture down the drain and wash out the bowl. Sprinkle the pretzels with salt.

You Can Also Use

Easy Artisan Whole-Grain Dough (page 56), made with semolina, or Caraway Rye Dough (page 58).

6. *Slide pretzels onto baking stone and add water to broiler pan.* Using an oven mitt, carefully pull the middle rack of the oven out several inches. Hold the cookie sheet level with the rack so that the pretzels will slide onto the hot stone. With a quick forward jerk of your arms, slide the pretzels from the cookie sheet to the stone. If a pretzel lands too close to another, use a metal spatula to reposition it. Push the middle rack back in place. Pull the lower rack out, pour the hot water into the broiler pan and push the lower rack back in place. Close the oven door immediately so the steam will envelop the oven.

7. *Bake.* Bake for 17 to 19 minutes or until well browned. Wearing oven mitts, remove the pretzels by hand to cool on a wire rack.

Change It Up

Salty Caraway Pretzels: Sprinkle pretzels with caraway seeds as well as salt.

Cheddar Pretzels: Dust each pretzel with 1 tbsp (15 mL) powdered Cheddar cheese (available in bulk and online) before sprinkling with salt.

Fig and Gorgonzola Swirl Loaf

Equipment:
- Rolling pin (optional)
- Flexible cutting board, floured, or two metal spatulas
- Baking sheet, lined with parchment paper
- Broiler pan
- Baking stone

For snack breads, appetizers or accompaniments to soup and salad, this loaf, with its interior swirl of savory filling, is a great recipe to customize. And it's easy: Roll or pat out the dough, spread it with your choice of filling, roll up and bake. Because the filling oozes out and can burn on the hot baking stone, bake this loaf on a baking sheet lined with parchment paper. For alternative savory fillings beyond the variations below, try your favorite artichoke and jalapeño dip or tapenade.

1/4	recipe prepared Easy Artisan Dough (page 34), about the size of a softball	1/4
	Unbleached all-purpose flour	
1/2 cup	fig preserves	125 mL
1/2 cup	crumbled Gorgonzola or other blue cheese	125 mL
2 cups	hot water	500 mL

1. **Form and fill.** Place dough on a floured surface and dust very lightly with flour. Flour your hands and the rolling pin, if using. Working the dough as little as possible and adding flour as necessary, pat or roll out the dough into a 10- by 9-inch (25 by 23 cm) rectangle. Spread fig preserves over the dough, leaving a 1-inch (2.5 cm) perimeter. Sprinkle Gorgonzola over the preserves. Starting with a long end, roll up the dough into a cylinder. If the dough begins to stick to the surface, use a dough scraper to push flour under the dough and scrape it up. Gently press and squeeze as you're rolling, to form the dough into a solid cylinder. Pinch the ends and long seam closed. Lightly flour any sticky places on the dough. The dough should feel soft and smooth all over, like a baby's skin, but not at all sticky.

2. **Rest.** Using the cutting board or two metal spatulas, transfer the loaf to the prepared baking sheet, seam side down. Cover with a tea towel and let rest at room temperature for 40 minutes.

3. **Prepare oven for artisan baking.** About 30 minutes before baking, place the broiler pan on the lower shelf and the baking stone on the middle shelf of the oven. Preheat to 450°F (230°C).

4. **Slash loaf with serrated knife.** Using a serrated knife, make five evenly spaced diagonal slashes, about 1/2 inch (1 cm deep), across the top of the loaf, exposing the moist dough under the surface.

You Can Also Use
Easy Artisan Whole-Grain Dough (page 56), made with semolina.

5. *Place baking sheet on baking stone and add water to broiler pan.* Using an oven mitt, carefully pull the middle rack of the oven out several inches. Place the baking sheet on the hot stone. Push the middle rack back in place. Pull the lower rack out, pour the hot water into the broiler pan and push the lower rack back in place. Close the oven door immediately so the steam will envelop the oven.

6. *Bake.* Bake for 25 to 27 minutes or until the crust is dark brown and an instant-read thermometer inserted in the center of the loaf registers at least 190°F (90°C). Remove from pan and transfer to a wire rack to cool.

Change It Up

Spanish Quince and Manchego Swirl Loaf: Substitute $\frac{1}{2}$ cup (125 mL) quince preserves or paste for the fig preserves and $\frac{1}{2}$ cup (125 mL) freshly grated Manchego or Parmesan cheese for the Gorgonzola.

Garlic Herb Cream Cheese and Roasted Red Pepper Swirl Loaf: Substitute $\frac{1}{2}$ cup (125 mL) softened garlic and herb–flavored cream cheese for the fig preserves and $\frac{1}{2}$ cup (125 mL) chopped roasted red peppers for the Gorgonzola.

Caprese Swirl Rolls

Makes 12 rolls

Equipment:
- Rolling pin
- Baking sheet, lined with parchment paper
- Broiler pan
- Baking stone

Once you've tried the savory swirled bread, it's easy to go a step further and make rolls, delicious as cocktail, tailgate or casual meal fare. This version is a take on the traditional Caprese salad of fresh tomatoes, basil and mozzarella. For these rolls, you can also use the same fillings suggested in the Fig and Gorgonzola Swirl Loaf (page 48), or try some new ones.

½	recipe prepared Easy Artisan Dough (page 34), about the size of a volleyball	½
	Unbleached all-purpose flour	
½ cup	pesto	125 mL
1 cup	finely chopped tomatoes	250 mL
1 cup	finely chopped fresh mozzarella cheese (bocconcini)	250 mL
2 cups	hot water	500 mL

1. **Form and fill.** Place dough on a floured surface and dust very lightly with flour. Flour your hands and the rolling pin. Working the dough as little as possible and adding flour as necessary, roll out the dough into a 16- by 10-inch (40 by 25 cm) rectangle. Spread pesto over the dough, leaving a ½-inch (1 cm) perimeter. Scatter tomatoes and mozzarella over the pesto. Starting with a long end, roll up the dough into a cylinder. If the dough begins to stick to the surface, use a dough scraper to push flour under the dough and scrape it up. Gently press and squeeze as you're rolling, to form the dough into a solid cylinder. The cylinder will lengthen to 18 inches (45 cm). With a pastry brush, brush off any excess flour. Pinch the ends and long seam closed, then turn seam side down. With the dough scraper, slice the cylinder into twelve 1½-inch (4 cm) pieces.

2. **Rest.** Place the rolls, cut side up, about 2 inches (5 cm) apart on the prepared baking sheet. Cover with a tea towel and let rest at room temperature for 40 minutes.

3. **Prepare oven for artisan baking.** About 30 minutes before baking, place the broiler pan on the lower shelf and the baking stone on the middle shelf of the oven. Preheat to 450°F (230°C).

Easy Artisan Whole-Grain
Dough (page 56), made
with semolina.

4. *Place baking sheet on baking stone and add water to broiler pan.* Using an oven mitt, carefully pull the middle rack of the oven out several inches. Place the baking sheet on the hot stone. Push the middle rack back in place. Pull the lower rack out, pour the hot water into the broiler pan and push the lower rack back in place. Close the oven door immediately so the steam will envelop the oven.

5. *Bake.* Bake for 13 to 15 minutes or until the rolls are risen and browned. Transfer to a wire rack to cool on baking sheet.

Change It Up

Caramelized Onion and Brie Rolls: Substitute 1 cup (250 mL) Easy Caramelized Onions (page 304) and 1 cup (250 mL) finely chopped Brie cheese (with the rind on) for the pesto, tomatoes and mozzarella. This also makes a delicious savory swirl loaf (page 48).

Sicilian Swirl Rolls: Substitute 1/2 cup (125 mL) prepared pizza sauce for the pesto and 1 cup (250 mL) crumbled cooked Italian sausage for the tomatoes. This also makes a delicious savory swirl loaf (page 48).

Greek-Style Pizza

Makes 1 pizza, to serve 4

Equipment:
- Rolling pin
- 12-inch (30 cm) round perforated pizza pan
- Broiler pan
- Baking stone

All the flavors of a good Greek salad can also be had in this crisp-crusted pizza.

¼	recipe prepared Easy Artisan Dough (page 34), about the size of a softball	¼
	Unbleached all-purpose flour	
1 cup	chopped tomatoes	250 mL
½ cup	sliced pitted kalamata olives	125 mL
½ cup	crumbled feta cheese	125 mL
2 tbsp	olive oil	25 mL
2 cups	hot water	500 mL
1 cup	packed baby arugula	250 mL

1. **Form.** Place dough on a floured surface and dust very lightly with flour. Flour your hands and the rolling pin. Working the dough as little as possible and adding flour as necessary, roll out the dough into a 12-inch (30 cm) round. Lightly flour any sticky places on the dough as you roll. The dough should feel gently taut and smooth all over, like a baby's skin, but not at all sticky.

2. **Rest.** Drape the dough over the rolling pin and transfer to the pizza pan. Pat into place. Cover with a tea towel and let rest at room temperature for 40 minutes.

3. **Prepare oven for artisan baking.** About 30 minutes before baking, place the broiler pan on the lower shelf and the baking stone on the middle shelf of the oven. Preheat to 450°F (230°C).

4. **Add pizza toppings.** Sprinkle tomatoes, olives and feta over the dough, then drizzle with olive oil.

5. **Place pizza pan on baking stone and add water to broiler pan.** Place the pizza pan on the hot stone. Pull the lower rack out, pour the hot water into the broiler pan and push the lower rack back in place. Close the oven door immediately so the steam will envelop the oven.

6. **Bake.** Bake for 15 minutes or until the edges of the crust have browned. Place the arugula in the center of the pizza. To serve, cut the pizza into wedges.

Tip

When you are proficient at sliding dough onto the baking stone, you can place the unbaked pizza on a cornmeal-sprinkled baker's peel instead of using the pizza pan. With a quick forward jerk of your arms, slide the pizza from the baker's peel onto the stone.

You Can Also Use

Easy Artisan Whole-Grain Dough (page 56), made with semolina or white whole wheat flour.

Change It Up

Pizza Margherita: Prepare through Step 3. Top the dough with 3 plum (Roma) tomatoes, cut lengthwise into $1/2$-inch (1 cm) slices, 8 fresh basil leaves, cut into shreds, and 8 oz (250 g) fresh mozzarella cheese (bocconcini), cut into $1/2$-inch (1 cm) slices. Drizzle with 2 tbsp (25 mL) olive oil. Bake for 15 to 17 minutes or until lightly browned.

Pizza Funghi: Prepare through Step 3. Top the dough with 8 oz (250 g) thinly sliced portobello or cremini mushrooms, 2 tbsp (25 mL) chopped fresh flat-leaf (Italian) parsley and $1/2$ cup (125 mL) freshly grated Parmesan cheese. Drizzle with 2 tbsp (25 mL) olive oil. Bake for 15 to 17 minutes or until lightly browned.

Whole-Grain Breads

Master Recipe #2
Easy Artisan Whole-Grain Dough

Adding whole-grain flours to artisan dough increases the flavor, texture and fiber in the bread. These flours can be finely or more coarsely ground, whichever you prefer. It's easy to substitute 2 cups (500 mL) of a gluten-rich whole-grain flour (see page 57) for 2 cups (500 mL) unbleached all-purpose or bread flour in the Easy Artisan Dough recipe, as here. If you wish to use low-gluten or no-gluten flour (see page 57) for the whole-grain component, counter it by using unbleached bread flour instead of all-purpose for the regular flour component, as unbleached bread flour has more protein to make gluten (and make up for the lack of it in low-gluten flours).

Makes enough dough for bread, rolls, pizza or flatbread to serve 12 to 16

Equipment:
- Instant-read thermometer
- 16-cup (4 L) mixing bowl
- Wooden spoon or Danish dough whisk

Tip
To increase the amount of protein in unbleached all-purpose flour when using it with low-gluten or no-gluten flour, add 1 tsp (2 mL) Artisan Bread Dough Enhancer (page 294) to each cup (250 mL) all-purpose flour.

4½ cups	unbleached all-purpose or bread flour	1.125 L
2 cups	gluten-rich whole-grain flour (see page 57)	500 mL
2 tbsp	instant or bread machine yeast	25 mL
1½ tbsp	fine table or kosher salt	22 mL
3 cups	lukewarm water (about 100°F/38°C)	750 mL

1. ***Measure.*** One at a time, spoon the unbleached flour and whole-grain flour into a measuring cup, level with a knife or your finger, then dump into the mixing bowl. Combine well.

2. ***Mix.*** Add the yeast and salt to the flours. Stir together with a wooden spoon or Danish dough whisk. Pour in the water and stir together until just moistened. Beat 40 strokes, scraping the bottom and the sides of the bowl, until the dough forms a lumpy, sticky mass.

3. ***Rise.*** Cover the bowl with plastic wrap and let rise at room temperature (72°F/22°C) in a draft-free place for 2 hours or until the dough has risen nearly to the top of the bowl and has a sponge-like appearance.

4. ***Use right away or refrigerate.*** Use that day or place the dough, covered with plastic wrap, in the refrigerator for up to 3 days before baking.

Tips

Combining 1½ cups (375 mL) hot with 1½ cups (375 mL) cold tap water will result in lukewarm water of approximately 100°F (38°C).

Before storing the dough in the refrigerator, use a permanent marker to write the date on the plastic wrap, so you'll know when you made your dough — and when to use it up 3 days later.

Baking with Canadian Flour

Canadian flour has a higher protein content than some U.S. flours and therefore absorbs more water. If you are using Canadian bread flour, start by adding about ½ cup (125 mL) less than called for, and add just enough of the remaining ½ cup (125 mL) to make a thick, paste-like dough. To get the best texture from your bread, you want to avoid a dough that is too dry. You don't need to adjust the amount of all-purpose flour or whole-grain flour.

Easy Artisan Whole-Grain Breads in Minutes a Day

Day 1	Stir the dough together and let rise. Bake, or cover and chill.
Days 2–3	Remove part of the dough, form and bake.

High-Gluten Whole-Grain Flours

Atta (Indian whole wheat flour for roti, naan and chapati)

Whole wheat flour

White whole wheat flour

Graham flour (coarsely ground whole wheat)

Semolina or durum wheat flour

Sprouted whole-grain hard winter wheat flour

No-Gluten or Low-Gluten Whole-Grain Flours

Amaranth flour

Chickpea (garbanzo bean) flour

Corn flour

Millet flour

Oat flour

Quinoa flour

Rice flour (glutinous or brown)

Rye flour

Soy flour

Spelt flour

Tapioca flour

Teff flour

Caraway Rye Dough

Equipment:
- Instant-read thermometer
- 16-cup (4 L) mixing bowl
- Wooden spoon or Danish dough whisk

The classic combination of caraway seeds, rye flour and molasses makes a darker, more flavorful dough.

Baking with Canadian Flour

Canadian flour has a higher protein content than some U.S. flours and therefore absorbs more water. If you are using Canadian bread flour, start by adding about $1/2$ cup (125 mL) less than called for, and add just enough of the remaining $1/2$ cup (125 mL) to make a thick, paste-like dough. You don't need to adjust the amount of rye flour.

$4^1/_2$ cups	unbleached bread flour	1.125 L
2 cups	rye flour	500 mL
2 tbsp	instant or bread machine yeast	25 mL
2 tbsp	caraway seeds	25 mL
$1^1/_2$ tbsp	fine table or kosher salt	22 mL
$1/_3$ cup	light (fancy) molasses	75 mL
3 cups	lukewarm water (about 100°F/38°C)	750 mL

1. *Measure.* One at a time, spoon the bread flour and rye flour into a measuring cup, level with a knife or your finger, then dump into the mixing bowl. Combine well.

2. *Mix.* Add the yeast, caraway seeds and salt to the flours. Stir together with a wooden spoon or Danish dough whisk. Stir molasses into the water. Pour into the flour mixture and stir together until just moistened. Beat 40 strokes, scraping the bottom and the sides of the bowl, until the dough forms a lumpy, sticky mass.

3. *Rise.* Cover the bowl with plastic wrap and let rise at room temperature (72°F/22°C) in a draft-free place for 2 hours or until the dough has risen nearly to the top of the bowl and has a sponge-like appearance.

4. *Use right away or refrigerate.* Use that day or place the dough, covered with plastic wrap, in the refrigerator for up to 3 days before baking.

Cracked Wheat Dough

Equipment:
- Instant-read thermometer
- 16-cup (4 L) mixing bowl
- Wooden spoon or Danish dough whisk

Put your hot winter breakfast cereal to good use in this dough.

Baking with Canadian Flour

Canadian flour has a higher protein content than some U.S. flours and therefore absorbs more water. If you are using Canadian bread flour, start by adding about ½ cup (125 mL) less than called for, and add just enough of the remaining ½ cup (125 mL) to make a thick, paste-like dough. You don't need to adjust the amount of all-purpose flour.

1½ cups	uncooked cracked wheat cereal	375 mL
½ cup	liquid honey	125 mL
1½ tbsp	unsalted butter	22 mL
1½ tsp	salt	7 mL
1⅔ cups	boiling water	400 mL
4½ cups	unbleached all-purpose or bread flour	1.125 L
2 tbsp	instant or bread machine yeast	25 mL
1½ tbsp	fine table or kosher salt	22 mL
3 cups	lukewarm water (about 100°F/38°C)	750 mL

1. *Combine.* In a bowl, combine wheat cereal, honey, butter and salt. Pour in boiling water, stir and let stand for 15 minutes or until the cereal has softened and the mixture is still warm (100°F/38°C), but not hot.

2. *Measure.* Spoon the flour into a measuring cup, level with a knife or your finger, then dump the flour into the mixing bowl.

3. *Mix.* Add the wheat cereal mixture, yeast and salt to the flour. Stir together with a wooden spoon or Danish dough whisk. Pour in the water and stir together until just moistened. Beat 40 strokes, scraping the bottom and the sides of the bowl, until the dough forms a lumpy, sticky mass.

4. *Rise.* Cover the bowl with plastic wrap and let rise at room temperature (72°F/22°C) in a draft-free place for 2 hours or until the dough has risen nearly to the top of the bowl and has a sponge-like appearance.

5. *Use right away or refrigerate.* Use that day or place the dough, covered with plastic wrap, in the refrigerator for up to 3 days before baking.

Cornmeal Pepper Dough

Makes enough dough for bread, rolls, pizza or flatbread to serve 12 to 16

Equipment:
- Instant-read thermometer
- 16-cup (4 L) mixing bowl
- Wooden spoon or Danish dough whisk

Surprisingly savory, this dough makes a great appetizer bread.

Tip

Because cornmeal doesn't absorb water like other flours, the dough will be moister.

Baking with Canadian Flour

Canadian flour has a higher protein content than some U.S. flours and therefore absorbs more water. If you are using Canadian bread flour, start by adding about ½ cup (125 mL) less than called for, and add just enough of the remaining ½ cup (125 mL) to make a thick, paste-like dough. You don't need to adjust the amount of all-purpose flour.

4½ cups	unbleached bread flour	1.125 L
2 cups	cornmeal	500 mL
1 cup	unbleached all-purpose flour	250 mL
2 tbsp	instant or bread machine yeast	25 mL
1½ tbsp	fine table or kosher salt	22 mL
1 tbsp	freshly ground white pepper	15 mL
1 tbsp	freshly ground black pepper	15 mL
1 tbsp	granulated sugar	15 mL
2	eggs, beaten	2
3 cups	lukewarm water (about 100°F/38°C)	750 mL

1. *Measure.* One at a time, spoon the bread flour, cornmeal and all-purpose flour into a measuring cup, level with a knife or your finger, then dump into the mixing bowl. Combine well.

2. *Mix.* Add the yeast, salt, white pepper, black pepper and sugar to the flour mixture. Stir together with a wooden spoon or Danish dough whisk. Stir eggs into the water. Pour into the flour mixture and stir together until just moistened. Beat 40 strokes, scraping the bottom and the sides of the bowl, until the dough forms a lumpy, sticky mass.

3. *Rise.* Cover the bowl with plastic wrap and let rise at room temperature (72°F/22°C) in a draft-free place for 2 hours or until the dough has risen nearly to the top of the bowl and has a sponge-like appearance.

4. *Use right away or refrigerate.* Use that day or place the dough, covered with plastic wrap, in the refrigerator for up to 3 days before baking.

Northern Lakes Wild Rice Dough

Equipment:
- Instant-read thermometer
- 16-cup (4 L) mixing bowl
- Wooden spoon or Danish dough whisk

With flecks of dark rice, this dough makes a handsome bread.

Baking with Canadian Flour

Canadian flour has a higher protein content than some U.S. flours and therefore absorbs more water. If you are using Canadian bread flour, start by adding about ½ cup (125 mL) less than called for, and add just enough of the remaining ½ cup (125 mL) to make a thick, paste-like dough. You don't need to adjust the amount of rye flour.

4½ cups	unbleached bread flour	1.125 L
1 cup	stone-ground rye flour	250 mL
1 cup	cooked wild rice or short-grain black rice, cooled and patted dry	250 mL
2 tbsp	instant or bread machine yeast	25 mL
1½ tbsp	fine table or kosher salt	22 mL
1 tbsp	freshly ground white pepper	15 mL
⅓ cup	wildflower, clover or other pale amber liquid honey	75 mL
3 cups	lukewarm water (about 100°F/38°C)	750 mL

1. *Measure.* One at a time, spoon the bread flour and rye flour into a measuring cup, level with a knife or your finger, then dump into the mixing bowl. Combine well.

2. *Mix.* Add the wild rice, yeast, salt and pepper to the flours. Stir together with a wooden spoon or Danish dough whisk. Stir honey into the water. Pour into the flour mixture and stir together until just moistened. Beat 40 strokes, scraping the bottom and the sides of the bowl, until the dough forms a lumpy, sticky mass.

3. *Rise.* Cover the bowl with plastic wrap and let rise at room temperature (72°F/22°C) in a draft-free place for 2 hours or until the dough has risen nearly to the top of the bowl and has a sponge-like appearance.

4. *Use right away or refrigerate.* Use that day or place the dough, covered with plastic wrap, in the refrigerator for up to 3 days before baking.

Daily Grind Whole Wheat Dough

Makes enough dough for bread, rolls, pizza or flatbread to serve 12 to 16

Equipment:
- Instant-read thermometer
- 16-cup (4 L) mixing bowl
- Wooden spoon or Danish dough whisk

The nutty flavor of freshly ground wheat comes through in this dough.

Tip

Three cups (750 mL) whole wheat kernels will grind into about 7 cups (1.75 L) fine whole wheat flour.

Baking with Canadian Flour

Canadian flour has a higher protein content than some U.S. flours and therefore absorbs more water. If you are using bread flour, start by adding about 1/2 cup (125 mL) less than called for, and add just enough of the remaining 1/2 cup (125 mL) to make a thick, paste-like dough. You don't need to adjust the amount of all-purpose flour.

4 1/2 cups	unbleached all-purpose or bread flour	1.125 L
2 cups	freshly ground whole wheat kernels	500 mL
2 tbsp	instant or bread machine yeast	25 mL
1 1/2 tbsp	fine table or kosher salt	22 mL
3 cups	lukewarm water (about 100°F/38°C)	750 mL

1. **Measure.** One at a time, spoon the flour and whole wheat kernels into a measuring cup, level with a knife or your finger, then dump into the mixing bowl. Combine well.

2. **Mix.** Add the yeast and salt to the flour mixture. Stir together with a wooden spoon or Danish dough whisk. Pour in the water and stir together until just moistened. Beat 40 strokes, scraping the bottom and the sides of the bowl, until the dough forms a lumpy, sticky mass.

3. **Rise.** Cover the bowl with plastic wrap and let rise at room temperature (72°F/22°C) in a draft-free place for 2 hours or until the dough has risen nearly to the top of the bowl and has a sponge-like appearance.

4. **Use right away or refrigerate.** Use that day or place the dough, covered with plastic wrap, in the refrigerator for up to 3 days before baking.

Whole Wheat Soy Dough

Makes enough dough
for bread, rolls, pizza
or flatbread to serve
12 to 16

Equipment:
- Instant-read thermometer
- 16-cup (4 L) mixing bowl
- Wooden spoon or Danish
  dough whisk

*You can add the benefits
of soy to bread by using
this dough.*

Tip
The dough will taste
somewhat like bean sprouts,
but that flavor disappears
during baking.

Baking with Canadian Flour
Canadian flour has a
higher protein content
than some U.S. flours
and therefore absorbs
more water. If you are
using bread flour, start
by adding about $\frac{1}{2}$ cup
(125 mL) less than
called for, and add
just enough of the
remaining $\frac{1}{2}$ cup
(125 mL) to make a
thick, paste-like dough.
You don't need to
adjust the amount of
all-purpose, whole
wheat or soy flour.

4$\frac{1}{2}$ cups	unbleached all-purpose or bread flour	1.125 L
1 cup	whole wheat flour	250 mL
1 cup	soy flour	250 mL
2 tbsp	instant or bread machine yeast	25 mL
1$\frac{1}{2}$ tbsp	fine table or kosher salt	22 mL
3 cups	lukewarm water (about 100°F/38°C)	750 mL

1. *Measure.* One at a time, spoon the unbleached flour, whole wheat flour and soy flour into a measuring cup, level with a knife or your finger, then dump into the mixing bowl. Combine well.

2. *Mix.* Add the yeast and salt to the flours. Stir together with a wooden spoon or Danish dough whisk. Pour in the water and stir together until just moistened. Beat 40 strokes, scraping the bottom and the sides of the bowl, until the dough forms a lumpy, sticky mass.

3. *Rise.* Cover the bowl with plastic wrap and let rise at room temperature (72°F/22°C) in a draft-free place for 2 hours or until the dough has risen nearly to the top of the bowl and has a sponge-like appearance.

4. *Use right away or refrigerate.* Use that day or place the dough, covered with plastic wrap, in the refrigerator for up to 3 days before baking.

Granola Dough

Makes enough dough for bread, rolls, pizza or flatbread to serve 12 to 16

Equipment:
- Instant-read thermometer
- 16-cup (4 L) mixing bowl
- Wooden spoon or Danish dough whisk

Choose your favorite granola, then grind it into a coarse flour for this dough.

Tip

About 2½ cups (625 mL) prepared granola will grind in the food processor to 2 cups (500 mL) granola "flour." The dried fruit and nuts might still be in larger pieces, but that will add to the texture of the loaf.

4½ cups	unbleached all-purpose or bread flour	1.125 L
2 cups	ground granola	500 mL
2 tbsp	instant or bread machine yeast	25 mL
1½ tbsp	fine table or kosher salt	22 mL
2 tsp	ground cinnamon or apple pie spice	10 mL
3 cups	lukewarm water (about 100°F/38°C)	750 mL

1. *Measure.* One at a time, spoon the flour and granola into a measuring cup, level with a knife or your finger, then dump into the mixing bowl. Combine well.

2. *Mix.* Add the yeast, salt and cinnamon to the flour mixture. Stir together with a wooden spoon or Danish dough whisk. Pour in the water and stir together until just moistened. Beat 40 strokes, scraping the bottom and the sides of the bowl, until the dough forms a lumpy, sticky mass.

3. *Rise.* Cover the bowl with plastic wrap and let rise at room temperature (72°F/22°C) in a draft-free place for 2 hours or until the dough has risen nearly to the top of the bowl and has a sponge-like appearance.

4. *Use right away or refrigerate.* Use that day or place the dough, covered with plastic wrap, in the refrigerator for up to 3 days before baking.

Baking with Canadian Flour

Canadian flour has a higher protein content than some U.S. flours and therefore absorbs more water. If you are using Canadian bread flour, start by adding about ½ cup (125 mL) less than called for, and add just enough of the remaining ½ cup (125 mL) to make a thick, paste-like dough. You don't need to adjust the amount of all-purpose flour.

Baby Boule (page 25) and Batard (page 27)

clockwise from top: Rolls (page 28), Focaccia with
Fresh Rosemary (page 42), Breadsticks (page 40)
and Fig and Gorgonzola Swirl Loaf (page 48)

Traditional Naan (page 72)

Daily Grind Cinnamon Rolls (page 74)

Oatmeal Honey Bread (page 85)

Three-Seed Batard (page 100)

Grilled Afghan Flatbread with Cilantro and
Green Onions (variation, page 113)

Roquefort and Walnut Fougasse (page 104)

Oatmeal Honey Dough

Mellow and slightly sweet, bread made from this dough is great toasted.

4$\frac{1}{2}$ cups	unbleached bread flour	1.125 L
2 cups	large-flake (old-fashioned) rolled oats	500 mL
2 tbsp	instant or bread machine yeast	25 mL
1$\frac{1}{2}$ tbsp	fine table or kosher salt	22 mL
$\frac{1}{3}$ cup	wildflower, clover or other pale amber liquid honey	75 mL
3 cups	lukewarm water (about 100°F/38°C)	750 mL

1. *Measure.* One at a time, spoon the flour and oats into a measuring cup, level with a knife or your finger, then dump into the mixing bowl. Combine well.

2. *Mix.* Add the yeast and salt to the flour mixture. Stir together with a wooden spoon or Danish dough whisk. Stir honey into the water. Pour into the flour mixture and stir together until just moistened. Beat 40 strokes, scraping the bottom and the sides of the bowl, until the dough forms a lumpy, sticky mass.

3. *Rise.* Cover the bowl with plastic wrap and let rise at room temperature (72°F/22°C) in a draft-free place for 2 hours or until the dough has risen nearly to the top of the bowl and has a sponge-like appearance.

4. *Use right away or refrigerate.* Use that day or place the dough, covered with plastic wrap, in the refrigerator for up to 3 days before baking.

Baking with Canadian Flour

Canadian flour has a higher protein content than some U.S. flours and therefore absorbs more water. If you are using Canadian bread flour, start by adding about $\frac{1}{2}$ cup (125 mL) less than called for, and add just enough of the remaining $\frac{1}{2}$ cup (125 mL) to make a thick, paste-like dough.

Provençal Socca Dough

Makes enough dough for flatbread to serve 12 to 16

Equipment:
- Instant-read thermometer
- 16-cup (4 L) mixing bowl
- Wooden spoon or Danish dough whisk

The nutty flavor of chickpeas (garbanzo beans) comes through in this dough from the south of France.

Baking with Canadian Flour

Canadian flour has a higher protein content than some U.S. flours and therefore absorbs more water. If you are using Canadian bread flour, start by adding about ½ cup (125 mL) less than called for, and add just enough of the remaining ½ cup (125 mL) to make a thick, paste-like dough. You don't need to adjust the amount of chickpea flour.

4½ cups	unbleached bread flour	1.125 L
2 cups	chickpea (garbanzo bean) flour	500 mL
2 tbsp	instant or bread machine yeast	25 mL
1½ tbsp	fine table or kosher salt	22 mL
3 cups	lukewarm water (about 100°F/38°C)	750 mL

1. *Measure.* One at a time, spoon the bread flour and chickpea flour into a measuring cup, level with a knife or your finger, then dump into the mixing bowl. Combine well.

2. *Mix.* Add the yeast and salt to the flours. Stir together with a wooden spoon or Danish dough whisk. Pour in the water and stir together until just moistened. Beat 40 strokes, scraping the bottom and the sides of the bowl, until the dough forms a lumpy, sticky mass.

3. *Rise.* Cover the bowl with plastic wrap and let rise at room temperature (72°F/22°C) in a draft-free place for 2 hours or until the dough has risen nearly to the top of the bowl and has a sponge-like appearance.

4. *Use right away or refrigerate.* Use that day or place the dough, covered with plastic wrap, in the refrigerator for up to 3 days before baking.

Traditional Naan Dough

Equipment:
- Instant-read thermometer
- 16-cup (4 L) mixing bowl
- Wooden spoon or Danish dough whisk

Traditional naan dough is made with a combination of maida (fine all-purpose flour) and atta (whole wheat flour). Look for maida and atta at Indian grocers.

4½ cups	unbleached all-purpose flour	1.125 L
2 cups	atta (Indian whole wheat flour)	500 mL
2 tbsp	instant or bread machine yeast	25 mL
1½ tbsp	fine table or kosher salt	22 mL
1 cup	plain yogurt	250 mL
3 cups	lukewarm water (about 100°F/38°C)	750 mL

1. *Measure.* One at a time, spoon the all-purpose flour and atta into a measuring cup, level with a knife or your finger, then dump into the mixing bowl. Combine well.

2. *Mix.* Add the yeast and salt to the flours. Stir together with a wooden spoon or Danish dough whisk. Stir yogurt into the water. Pour into the flour mixture and stir together until just moistened. Beat 40 strokes, scraping the bottom and the sides of the bowl, until the dough forms a lumpy, sticky mass.

3. *Rise.* Cover the bowl with plastic wrap and let rise at room temperature (72°F/22°C) in a draft-free place for 2 hours or until the dough has risen nearly to the top of the bowl and has a sponge-like appearance.

4. *Use right away or refrigerate.* Use that day or place the dough, covered with plastic wrap, in the refrigerator for up to 3 days before baking.

Cracked Wheat Baguettes

Makes 2 baguettes, to serve 8

Equipment:
- Three-sided cookie sheet, flexible cutting board or baker's peel
- Broiler pan
- Baking stone

These baguettes have just a little more texture and heightened flavor from the cooked cracked wheat cereal added to the dough. In this recipe, you'll be sliding two baguettes onto the baking stone.

½	recipe prepared Cracked Wheat Dough (page 59), about the size of a volleyball	½
	Unbleached all-purpose or bread flour	
½ cup	cornmeal	125 mL
2 cups	hot water	500 mL

1. *Form.* Place dough on a floured surface and dust very lightly with flour. Flour your hands. Form the dough into a 12-inch (30 cm) log. Using a dough scraper, cut the dough into two equal portions. Working the dough as little as possible and adding flour as necessary, form each dough portion into a 14-inch (35 cm) cylinder. Smooth the dough with your hands to form a soft, non-sticky skin. Pinch any seams together. Pinch each end into a point. Lightly flour any sticky places on the dough. The dough should feel soft and smooth all over, like a baby's skin, but not at all sticky.

2. *Rest.* Sprinkle the cornmeal on the cookie sheet and place the baguettes on the cornmeal so that they are parallel to each other and about 6 inches (15 cm) apart. Cover with a tea towel and let rest at room temperature for 40 minutes.

3. *Prepare oven for artisan baking.* About 30 minutes before baking, place the broiler pan on the lower shelf and the baking stone on the middle shelf of the oven. Preheat to 450°F (230°C).

4. *Slash baguettes with serrated knife.* Using a serrated knife, make three evenly spaced diagonal slashes, about 1 inch (2.5 cm) deep, across each baguette, exposing the moist dough under the surface.

5. *Slide baguettes onto baking stone and add water to broiler pan.* Using an oven mitt, carefully pull the middle rack of the oven out several inches. Hold the cookie sheet level with the rack so that the first baguette will slide sideways onto the hot stone. With a quick forward jerk of your arms, slide the first baguette from the cookie sheet to the back of the stone. With another jerk, slide the second baguette onto the front of the stone. Make sure they're at least 4 inches (10 cm) apart. Push the middle rack back in place. Pull the lower rack out, pour the hot water into the broiler pan and push the lower rack back in place. Close the oven door immediately so the steam will envelop the oven.

6. *Bake.* Bake for 25 to 27 minutes or until the crust is a medium dark brown and an instant-read thermometer inserted in the center of the loaves registers at least 190°F (90°C). Wearing oven mitts, remove the loaves by hand to cool on a wire rack.

Rustic French Boule

Equipment:
- Three-sided cookie sheet, flexible cutting board or baker's peel
- Broiler pan
- Baking stone
- Plastic spray bottle of water

This recipe makes a large boule with enhanced flavor and texture. It will rise dramatically in the oven, producing a crusty loaf with a moist and tender crumb, which eight people can greedily consume. If you're new to whole-grain baking, start off with dough made with white whole wheat flour or semolina for the whole-grain component, as this will be more similar in flavor and texture to white bread — but a lot more interesting! Note that the slashes you'll make in this denser dough are twice as deep: 1 inch (2.5 cm). Spraying the boule with water during baking will promote a crispier crust.

½	recipe prepared Easy Artisan Whole-Grain Dough (page 56), about the size of a volleyball, made with white whole wheat flour or semolina	½
	Unbleached all-purpose or bread flour	
½ cup	cornmeal	125 mL
2 cups	hot water	500 mL

1. *Form.* Place dough on a floured surface and dust very lightly with flour. Flour your hands. Working the dough as little as possible and adding flour as necessary, form the dough into a 12-inch (30 cm) round. Smooth the dough with your hands to form a soft, non-sticky skin. Pinch any seams together. Lightly flour any sticky places on the dough. The dough should feel soft and smooth all over, like a baby's skin, but not at all sticky.

2. *Rest.* Sprinkle the cornmeal on the cookie sheet and place the dough round on the cornmeal. Cover with a tea towel and let rest at room temperature for 40 minutes.

3. *Prepare oven for artisan baking.* About 30 minutes before baking, place the broiler pan on the lower shelf and the baking stone on the middle shelf of the oven. Preheat to 450°F (230°C).

4. *Slash boule with serrated knife.* Using a serrated knife, make three evenly spaced slashes, about 1 inch (2.5 cm) deep, across the boule, exposing the moist dough under the surface.

5. *Slide boule onto baking stone and add water to broiler pan.* Using an oven mitt, carefully pull the middle rack of the oven out several inches. Hold the cookie sheet level with the rack so that the dough round will slide onto the center of the hot stone. With a quick forward jerk of your arms, slide the dough round from the cookie sheet to the stone. Push the middle rack back in place. Pull the lower rack out, pour the hot water into the broiler pan and push the lower rack back in place. Spray the boule with water. Close the oven door immediately so the steam will envelop the oven.

Tips

White whole wheat flour is milled from hard white spring wheat with a milder flavor and lighter color than hard red winter wheat. You can use it as you would traditional whole wheat flour. If you can't find it, use regular whole wheat flour.

If you have leftover boule, let it cool, place in a large plastic freezer bag (or cut it to fit in the bag) and freeze for up to 3 months. To warm, wrap the frozen bread in foil and place in a 350°F (180°C) oven for 15 to 20 minutes or until warmed through.

6. *Bake.* Bake for 15 minutes, then quickly open the oven door and spray the loaf with water again. Continue baking for 12 to 15 minutes or until the crust is a medium dark brown and an instant-read thermometer inserted in the center of the loaf registers at least 190°F (90°C). Wearing oven mitts, remove the loaf by hand to cool on a wire rack.

Change It Up

Instead of making slashes on the boule, try something more decorative. At the famous Poilâne, one of the best-loved artisan bakeries in Paris, boules are marked with a "P" in a simple but flowing script. Using a serrated knife, make a script initial on the top of your boule, then bake.

Traditional Naan

Makes 8 flatbreads

Equipment:
- Rolling pin
- Large baking sheet
- Broiler pan
- Baking stone
- Metal spatula

Traditional naan, the flatbread of northern India, Pakistan and Afghanistan, is usually baked on the walls of a charcoal- or wood-burning tandoor oven. A tandoor is dome-shaped and made of a hard-fired terracotta — a material much like your baking stone! Traditional naan doughs are made of a combination of maida (unbleached all-purpose flour) and atta (a whole wheat flour). A little plain yogurt is mixed into the dough for moisture. To be very authentic, brush these flatbreads with ghee or melted butter before baking, but they also taste delicious brushed with olive oil.

¼	recipe prepared Traditional Naan Dough (page 67), about the size of a softball	¼
	Unbleached all-purpose flour	
¼ cup	cornmeal	50 mL
	Melted butter or olive oil	
2 cups	hot water	500 mL

1. *Form.* Place dough on a floured surface and dust very lightly with flour. Flour your hands and the rolling pin. Working the dough as little as possible and adding flour as necessary, form the dough into an 8-inch (20 cm) cylinder. With a dough scraper, cut the dough into 1-inch (2.5 cm) slices. Roll out each slice into a 6-inch (15 cm) long oval. Lightly flour any sticky places on the dough. The dough should feel soft and smooth all over, like a baby's skin, but not at all sticky.

2. *Rest.* Sprinkle the cornmeal on the baking sheet and place the dough ovals on the cornmeal. Cover with a tea towel and let rest at room temperature for 40 minutes.

3. *Prepare oven for artisan baking.* About 30 minutes before baking, place the broiler pan on the lower shelf and the baking stone on the middle shelf of the oven. Preheat to 450°F (230°C).

4. *Brush with melted butter.* Brush the naan with melted butter.

5. *Place naan on baking stone and add water to broiler pan.* Using an oven mitt, carefully pull the middle rack of the oven out several inches. With a metal spatula, place four naan on the hot stone. Push the middle rack back in place. Pull the lower rack out, pour the hot water into the broiler pan and push the lower rack back in place. Close the oven door immediately so the steam will envelop the oven.

6. *Bake.* Bake for 7 to 8 minutes or until the crust is lightly blistered. Wearing oven mitts, remove the naan by hand to cool on a wire rack. Repeat the baking process with the remaining naan.

Change It Up

Grilled Naan: Prepare a hot fire in your barbecue grill or heat a ridged grill pan indoors. Brush both sides of the naan with melted butter or olive oil and grill, turning once, until they have good grill marks, about 1 minute per side.

Daily Grind Cinnamon Rolls

Makes 8 rolls

Equipment:
- Rolling pin
- 8-inch (20 cm) round cake pan, buttered
- Broiler pan
- Baking stone

With freshly ground wheat as part of the dough, these cinnamon rolls put a healthier spin on a classic recipe. Increased fiber from the wheat bran, vitamins E and B from the wheat germ, blood sugar–lowering cinnamon and anti-bacterial/fungal/viral honey make these rolls good for you as well as delicious. Many grocery or health food stores sell wheat kernels, or berries, in bulk and offer a grain mill so you can grind your own wheat right at the store and take it home. If you really get into whole-grain baking, you can buy a grain mill for home use. Once you taste freshly ground wheat, with its slightly nutty, delicious flavor, you'll be a convert.

½	recipe prepared Daily Grind Whole Wheat Dough (page 62), about the size of a volleyball	½
	Unbleached all-purpose or bread flour	
¼ cup	unsalted butter, softened	50 mL
¼ cup	liquid honey	50 mL
2 tsp	ground cinnamon	10 mL
2 cups	hot water	500 mL
	Easy Artisan Glaze (page 302)	

1. ***Form and fill.*** Place dough on a floured surface and dust very lightly with flour. Flour your hands and the rolling pin. Working the dough as little as possible and adding flour as necessary, roll out the dough into a 12- by 8-inch (30 by 20 cm) rectangle. Spread butter over the dough with a spatula or knife, leaving a ½-inch (1 cm) perimeter. In a small bowl, combine honey and cinnamon; spread over the dough, leaving a ½-inch (1 cm) perimeter. Starting with a short end, roll up dough into a cylinder. If the dough begins to stick to the surface, use a dough scraper to push flour under the dough and scrape it up. Gently press and squeeze as you're rolling to form the dough into a solid cylinder. With a pastry brush, brush off any excess flour. With the dough scraper, slice the cylinder into 1-inch (2 cm) pieces.

2. ***Rest.*** Place the rolls, cut side up, in the prepared pan so that they are almost touching. Cover with a tea towel and let rest at room temperature for 40 minutes.

3. ***Prepare oven for artisan baking.*** About 30 minutes before baking, place the broiler pan on the lower shelf and the baking stone on the middle shelf of the oven. Preheat to 400°F (200°C).

Tip

Three cups (750 mL) whole wheat kernels will grind into about 7 cups (1.75 L) fine whole wheat flour.

You Can Also Use

Easy Artisan Whole-Grain Dough (page 56), made with whole wheat flour or semolina.

4. *Place cake pan on baking stone and add water to broiler pan.* Using an oven mitt, carefully pull the middle rack of the oven out several inches. Place the cake pan on the hot stone. Push the middle rack back in place. Pull the lower rack out, pour the hot water into the broiler pan and push the lower rack back in place. Close the oven door immediately so the steam will envelop the oven.

5. *Bake.* Bake for 23 to 24 minutes or until an instant-read thermometer inserted in the center of the rolls registers at least 190°F (90°C). Transfer to a wire rack to cool in pan. Once cool, drizzle with glaze.

Change It Up

Daily Grind Cinnamon Swirl Loaf: Roll the dough into a cylinder, but do not cut into slices. Place the dough, seam side down, on a baking sheet lined with parchment paper. Bake at 400°F (200°C) for 27 to 30 minutes or until an instant-read thermometer inserted in the center of the loaf registers at least 190°F (90°C). Let cool on pan on a wire rack. Once cool, drizzle with glaze.

Cornmeal Pepper Mini Loaves

Makes 2 or 4 small loaves, to serve 12 to 16 for appetizers

Equipment:
- Four 10³/₄-oz (or 284 mL) clean, empty soup cans or two 8¹/₂- by 4¹/₂-inch (21 by 11 cm) loaf pans, oiled
- Broiler pan
- Baking stone

Savory Cornmeal Pepper Dough makes fabulous boules, baguettes and batards to slather in Artisan Butter (page 295). But it really shines as the base for crostini. Top the rounds (from the soup cans) or the rectangles (from the loaf pans) with goat cheese, arugula and roasted red pepper; unsalted butter, prosciutto and melon; crumbled cooked chorizo, a dollop of sour cream and chopped green onion; or whatever toppings you choose. Use a whole batch of dough and bake ahead for a party.

Tips

Because the cornmeal doesn't absorb the water like other flours, the dough will be moister.

To make crostini, slice the bread into ¹/₂-inch (1 cm) slices and toast on a baking sheet in a 350°F (180°C) oven for 10 to 15 minutes or until lightly browned. Top with the ingredients of your choice.

¹/₂	recipe prepared Cornmeal Pepper Dough (page 60), about the size of a volleyball	¹/₂
	Unbleached bread flour	
2 cups	hot water	500 mL

1. *Form.* Place dough on a floured surface and dust very lightly with flour. Flour your hands. Working the dough as little as possible and adding flour as necessary, form the dough into a 12-inch (30 cm) cylinder. Smooth the dough with your hands to form a soft, non-sticky skin. With a dough scraper, slice the dough into four equal portions if you're using soup cans, two equal portions if you're using loaf pans.

2. *Rest.* Place a portion of dough in each bread mold (soup can or loaf pan). Cover with tea towels and let rest at room temperature for 40 minutes.

3. *Prepare oven for artisan baking.* About 30 minutes before baking, place the broiler pan on the lower shelf and the baking stone on the middle shelf of the oven. Preheat to 450°F (230°C).

4. ***Place bread molds on baking stone and add water to broiler pan.*** Using an oven mitt, carefully pull the middle rack of the oven out several inches. Place the bread molds, open side up, on the baking stone. Push the middle rack back in place. Pull the lower rack out, pour the hot water into the broiler pan and push the lower rack back in place. Close the oven door immediately so the steam will envelop the oven.

5. *Bake.* Bake the loaf pans for 20 to 22 minutes and the soup cans for 25 to 27 minutes or until the crust is a medium dark brown and an instant-read thermometer inserted in the center of the bread registers at least 190°F (90°C). Run a thin spatula or knife around each bread mold to loosen the breads and invert onto wire racks, removing pans or cans, to cool.

Roggenbrot

Equipment:
- Three-sided cookie sheet, flexible cutting board or baker's peel
- Broiler pan
- Baking stone

This German rye bread, in the batard shape, is a rustic-looking peasant loaf with a moist crumb, a crisp dark crust and a wonderful mellow flavor — with just enough texture from the rye flour and enough flavor from the caraway seeds to make it interesting. Slice and serve this bread with Artisan Butter (page 295). You can also use it to make the classic Reuben sandwich or a ham on rye.

¹⁄₂	recipe prepared Caraway Rye Dough (page 58), about the size of a volleyball	¹⁄₂
	Unbleached bread flour	
¹⁄₂ cup	cornmeal	125 mL
2 cups	hot water	500 mL

1. *Form.* Place dough on a floured surface and dust very lightly with flour. Flour your hands. Working the dough as little as possible and adding flour as necessary, form the dough into a 14-inch (35 cm) cylinder. Smooth the dough with your hands to form a soft, non-sticky skin. Pinch any seams together. Pinch each end into a point. Lightly flour any sticky places on the dough. The dough should feel soft and smooth all over, like a baby's skin, but not at all sticky.

2. *Rest.* Sprinkle the cornmeal on the cookie sheet and place the batard on the cornmeal. Cover with a tea towel and let rest at room temperature for 40 minutes.

3. *Prepare oven for artisan baking.* About 30 minutes before baking, place the broiler pan on the lower shelf and the baking stone on the middle shelf of the oven. Preheat to 450°F (230°C).

4. *Slash batard with serrated knife.* Using a serrated knife, make five evenly spaced diagonal slashes, about 1 inch (2 cm) deep, across the batard, exposing the moist dough under the surface.

5. *Slide batard onto baking stone and add water to broiler pan.* Using an oven mitt, carefully pull the middle rack of the oven out several inches. Hold the cookie sheet level with the rack so that the loaf will slide sideways onto the center of the hot stone. With a quick forward jerk of your arms, slide the batard from the cookie sheet to the stone. Push the middle rack back in place. Pull the lower rack out, pour the hot water into the broiler pan and push the lower rack back in place. Close the oven door immediately so the steam will envelop the oven.

6. *Bake.* Bake for 27 to 29 minutes or until the crust is a medium dark brown and an instant-read thermometer inserted in the center of the loaf registers at least 190°F (90°C). Wearing oven mitts, remove the loaf by hand to cool on a wire rack.

Northern Lakes Wild Rice Crescent Rolls

Makes 12 rolls

Equipment:
- Rolling pin
- Pizza wheel
- Large baking sheet, lined with parchment paper
- Broiler pan
- Baking stone

An egg wash gives a shiny finish to these handsome, dark-flecked crescent rolls, which have a savory flavor, a moist crumb and a somewhat crispy crust. Serve them as part of your dinner roll basket, or use them to make mini ham or turkey sandwiches.

You Can Also Use
Caraway Rye Dough (page 58), Easy Artisan Dough (page 34) or Easy Artisan Whole-Grain Dough (page 56), made with white whole wheat flour.

½	recipe prepared Northern Lakes Wild Rice Dough (page 61), about the size of a volleyball	½
	Unbleached bread flour	
1	egg	1
1 tbsp	water	15 mL
	Coarse kosher or pretzel salt	
2 cups	hot water	500 mL

1. **Form.** Place dough on a floured surface and dust very lightly with flour. Flour your hands and the rolling pin. Working the dough as little as possible and adding flour as necessary, roll out the dough into a 12-inch (40 cm) circle. Using the pizza wheel, cut the dough into quarters. Cut each quarter into thirds. Starting with a thick end, roll up each triangle of dough. Gently pull the rolled dough to lengthen it, then shape into a crescent.

2. **Rest.** Place the rolls 2 inches (5 cm) apart on the prepared baking sheet. Cover with a tea towel and let rest at room temperature for 40 minutes.

3. **Prepare oven for artisan baking.** About 30 minutes before baking, place the broiler pan on the lower shelf and the baking stone on the middle shelf of the oven. Preheat to 450°F (230°C).

4. **Add topping.** Five minutes before baking, beat egg and water in a small bowl. Brush the top of each roll with egg wash and sprinkle with salt.

5. **Place baking sheet on baking stone and add water to broiler pan.** Using an oven mitt, carefully pull the middle rack of the oven out several inches. Place the baking sheet on the hot stone. Push the middle rack back in place. Pull the lower rack out, pour the hot water into the broiler pan and push the lower rack back in place. Close the oven door immediately so the steam will envelop the oven.

6. **Bake.** Bake for 17 to 20 minutes or until the rolls are a medium reddish-brown and the crust is somewhat crisp when tapped with a finger. Transfer to a wire rack to cool.

Provençal Socca with Roasted Shallots and Garlic

Equipment:
- Rolling pin
- Baking sheet
- Broiler pan
- Baking stone

Traditional Provençal socca is a thin crêpe made from chickpea (garbanzo bean) flour — a street food specialty of Van Gogh's town of Arles. This artisan version is just the thing to serve with a glass of wine for a sophisticated appetizer. Chickpea flour is available in the specialty flour section of well-stocked grocery stores.

¼	recipe prepared Provençal Socca Dough (page 66), about the size of a softball	¼
	Unbleached bread flour	
¼ cup	cornmeal	50 mL
2 cups	Caramelized Shallots and Garlic with Red Wine (page 305)	500 mL
1 tbsp	fresh rosemary leaves	15 mL
2 cups	hot water	500 mL

1. *Form.* Place dough on a floured surface and dust very lightly with flour. Flour your hands and the rolling pin. Working the dough as little as possible and adding flour as necessary, roll out the dough into a 12- by 9-inch (30 by 23 cm) oval. Lightly flour any sticky places on the dough. The dough should feel soft and smooth all over, like a baby's skin, but not at all sticky.

2. *Dimple flatbread.* Sprinkle the cornmeal on the baking sheet and place the dough oval on the cornmeal. Using the handle of a wooden spoon, dimple the flatbread at 2-inch (5 cm) intervals.

3. *Add topping.* Spread the caramelized shallots and garlic over the top of the flatbread, then sprinkle with rosemary.

4. *Rest.* Cover with a tea towel and let rest at room temperature for 40 minutes.

5. *Prepare oven for artisan baking.* About 30 minutes before baking, place the broiler pan on the lower shelf and the baking stone on the middle shelf of the oven. Preheat to 450°F (230°C).

6. *Place baking sheet on baking stone and add water to broiler pan.* Using an oven mitt, carefully pull the middle rack of the oven out several inches. Place the baking sheet on the hot stone. Push the middle rack back in place. Pull the lower rack out, pour the hot water into the broiler pan and push the lower rack back in place. Close the oven door immediately so the steam will envelop the oven.

7. *Bake.* Bake for 20 to 25 minutes or until the crust is lightly browned. Transfer to a wire rack to cool.

Caraway Rye Tart with Ham and Gruyère

Makes 1 tart, to serve 6 to 8

Equipment:
- Rolling pin
- 8-inch (20 cm) round baking pan
- Broiler pan
- Baking stone

This savory tart, perfect for a casual meal, is a cross between a deep-dish pizza and a quiche. A slice of it goes well with a frosty mug of beer and a green salad. Make this tart more Alsatian with ham and Gruyère, or more Italian with sausage and Asiago.

1/4	recipe prepared Caraway Rye Dough (page 58), about the size of a softball	1/4
	Unbleached bread flour	
2	eggs, beaten	2
1 cup	heavy or whipping (35%) cream	250 mL
8 oz	ham, diced, or Italian sausage, cooked and crumbled	250 g
1/2 cup	finely chopped green onions	125 mL
1/2 cup	shredded Gruyère or Asiago cheese	125 mL
2 cups	hot water	500 mL

1. **Form.** Place dough on a floured surface and dust very lightly with flour. Flour your hands and the rolling pin. Working the dough as little as possible and adding flour as necessary, roll out the dough into a 10-inch (25 cm) circle. Lightly flour any sticky places on the dough as you roll. The dough should feel gently taut and smooth all over, like a baby's skin, but not at all sticky.

2. **Rest.** Drape the dough over the rolling pin and transfer to the baking pan. Fit the dough into the bottom and up the sides of the pan. Cover with a tea towel and let rest at room temperature for 40 minutes.

3. **Prepare oven for artisan baking.** About 30 minutes before baking, place the broiler pan on the lower shelf and the baking stone on the middle shelf of the oven. Preheat to 450°F (230°C).

4. **Make tart filling.** Five minutes before baking, whisk together eggs and cream in a small bowl. Scatter ham and green onions over the tart crust and pour in the egg mixture. Sprinkle with Gruyère.

Change It Up

Sauerkraut and Bratwurst Tart: Instead of the tart filling, spread Dijon mustard over the dough. Top with 2 cups (500 mL) drained sauerkraut, 2 sliced cooked bratwurst, $\frac{1}{2}$ cup (125 mL) green onions and $\frac{1}{2}$ cup (125 mL) shredded Gruyère cheese.

5. *Place baking pan on baking stone and add water to broiler pan.* Using an oven mitt, carefully pull the middle rack of the oven out several inches. Place the baking pan on the hot stone. Push the middle rack back in place. Pull the lower rack out, pour the hot water into the broiler pan and push the lower rack back in place. Close the oven door immediately so the steam will envelop the oven.

6. *Bake.* Bake for 17 to 20 minutes or until the filling has browned and the crust has turned a medium reddish-brown. Transfer to a wire rack to cool.

Amish Pinwheel Bread

Makes 1 large loaf, to serve 8 to 10

Equipment:
- Rolling pin (optional)
- Three-sided cookie sheet, flexible cutting board or baker's peel
- Baking stone
- Broiler pan

Adapted from an Amish bread recipe from northern Ohio, this two-color bread looks as good as it tastes, with an interior swirl of contrasting cream and tan. To get this effect, you can use two whole-grain doughs of different colors or pair the softer Easy Artisan Dough with Easy Artisan Whole-Grain Dough, as here.

¼	recipe prepared Easy Artisan Dough (page 34), about the size of a softball	¼
¼	recipe prepared Easy Artisan Whole-Grain Dough (page 56), about the size of a softball, made with a darker flour	¼
	Unbleached all-purpose or bread flour	
½ cup	cornmeal	125 mL
2 cups	hot water	500 mL

1. **Form.** Place dough portions on a floured surface and dust very lightly with flour. Flour your hands. Working the dough as little as possible and adding flour as necessary, roll out or pat each dough portion into a 10- by 9-inch (25 by 23 cm) rectangle. Stack one rectangle on top of the other. Starting with a long end, roll up the dough into a cylinder. If the dough begins to stick to the surface, use a dough scraper to push flour under the dough and scrape it up. Gently press and squeeze as you're rolling to form the dough into a solid cylinder. With a pastry brush, brush off any excess flour. Pinch the ends and long seam closed. Lightly flour any sticky places on the dough. The dough should feel soft and smooth all over, like a baby's skin, but not at all sticky.

2. **Rest.** Sprinkle the cornmeal on the cookie sheet and place the dough, seam side down, on the cornmeal. Cover with a tea towel and let rest at room temperature for 40 minutes.

3. **Prepare oven for artisan baking.** About 30 minutes before baking, place the broiler pan on the lower shelf and the baking stone on the middle shelf of the oven. Preheat to 450°F (230°C).

4. **Slash loaf with serrated knife.** Using a serrated knife, make five evenly spaced diagonal slashes, about 1 inch (2 cm) deep, across the loaf, exposing the moist dough under the surface.

You Can Also Use

Easy Artisan Dough paired with any darker dough, such as Caraway Rye (page 58), Granola (page 64) or Northern Lakes Wild Rice (page 61), for contrast.

5. *Slide loaf onto baking stone and add water to broiler pan.* Using an oven mitt, carefully pull the middle rack of the oven out several inches. Hold the cookie sheet level with the rack so that the loaf will slide sideways onto the center of the hot stone. With a quick forward jerk of your arms, slide the loaf from the cookie sheet to the stone. Push the middle rack back in place. Pull the lower rack out, pour the hot water into the broiler pan and push the lower rack back in place. Close the oven door immediately so the steam will envelop the oven.

6. *Bake.* Bake for 27 to 29 minutes or until the crust is a medium dark brown and an instant-read thermometer inserted in the center of the loaf registers at least 190°F (90°C). Wearing oven mitts, remove the loaf by hand to cool on a wire rack.

Great Plains Granola Bread

Equipment:
- Two 9- by 5-inch (23 by 12.5 cm) loaf pans, greased
- Broiler pan
- Baking stone

I like this bread baked in a pan so that it's easy to slice, toast and slather with Artisan Butter (page 295) in the morning. Its mellow, slightly spicy flavor is a result of all the goodies in the granola you grind and use to make the dough.

1	recipe prepared Granola Dough (page 64)	1
	Unbleached all-purpose or bread flour	
2 cups	hot water	500 mL

1. *Form.* Place dough on a floured surface and dust very lightly with flour. Divide it in half with a serrated knife and dough scraper. Flour your hands. Working the dough as little as possible and adding flour as necessary, form each portion into an 8-inch (20 cm) cylinder. Smooth the dough with your hands to form a soft, non-sticky skin. Pinch any seams together. Lightly flour any sticky places on the dough. The dough should feel soft and smooth all over, like a baby's skin, but not at all sticky.

2. *Rest.* Place each cylinder in a prepared loaf pan. Cover with tea towels and let rest at room temperature for 40 minutes.

3. *Prepare oven for artisan baking.* About 30 minutes before baking, place the broiler pan on the lower shelf and the baking stone on the middle shelf of the oven. Preheat to 400°F (200°C).

4. *Place loaf pans on baking stone and add water to broiler pan.* Using an oven mitt, carefully pull the middle rack of the oven out several inches. Place the loaf pans at least 3 inches (7.5 cm) apart on the hot stone. Push the middle rack back in place. Pull the lower rack out, pour the hot water into the broiler pan and push the lower rack back in place. Close the oven door immediately so the steam will envelop the oven.

5. *Bake.* Bake for 27 to 30 minutes or until the crust is a medium dark brown and an instant-read thermometer inserted in the center of the loafs registers at least 190°F (90°C). Transfer to a wire rack to cool in pans for 10 minutes. Remove from pans and let cool on rack.

Oatmeal Honey Bread

Makes 2 loaves, to serve 16

Equipment:
- Two 9- by 5-inch (23 by 12.5 cm) loaf pans, greased
- Broiler pan
- Baking stone

This is another bread I prefer baked in a pan so it's easy to slice and toast in the morning.

1	recipe prepared Oatmeal Honey Dough (page 65)	1
	Unbleached bread flour	
2 cups	hot water	500 mL

1. *Form.* Place dough on a floured surface and dust very lightly with flour. Divide it in half with a serrated knife and dough scraper. Flour your hands. Working the dough as little as possible and adding flour as necessary, form each portion into an 8-inch (20 cm) cylinder. Smooth the dough with your hands to form a soft, non-sticky skin. Pinch any seams together. Lightly flour any sticky places on the dough. The dough should feel soft and smooth all over, like a baby's skin, but not at all sticky.

2. *Rest.* Place each cylinder in a prepared loaf pan. Cover with tea towels and let rest at room temperature for 40 minutes.

3. *Prepare oven for artisan baking.* About 30 minutes before baking, place the broiler pan on the lower shelf and the baking stone on the middle shelf of the oven. Preheat to 400°F (200°C).

4. *Place loaf pans on baking stone and add water to broiler pan.* Using an oven mitt, carefully pull the middle rack of the oven out several inches. Place the loaf pans at least 3 inches (7.5 cm) apart on the hot stone. Push the middle rack back in place. Pull the lower rack out, pour the hot water into the broiler pan and push the lower rack back in place. Close the oven door immediately so the steam will envelop the oven.

5. *Bake.* Bake for 27 to 30 minutes or until the crust is a medium dark brown and an instant-read thermometer inserted in the center of the loafs registers at least 190°F (90°C). Transfer to a wire rack to cool in pans for 10 minutes. Remove from pans and let cool on rack.

White Whole Wheat Pizza with Grilled Vegetables

Makes 1 pizza, to serve 4

Equipment:
- Rolling pin
- 12-inch (30 cm) round perforated pizza pan
- Broiler pan
- Baking stone

This artisan-style pizza features a crisp whole-grain crust and simple grilled toppings, but it can be customized with the toppings of your choice (see tip, opposite).

Tip

When you are proficient at sliding dough onto the baking stone, you can place the unbaked pizza on a cornmeal-sprinkled baker's peel instead of using the pizza pan. With a quick forward jerk of your arms, slide the pizza from the baker's peel onto the stone.

¼	recipe prepared Easy Artisan Whole-Grain Dough (page 56), about the size of a softball, made with white whole wheat flour	¼
	Unbleached all-purpose or bread flour	
1 cup	chopped tomatoes	250 mL
1 cup	chopped grilled vegetables, such as onion, zucchini and bell pepper	250 mL
½ cup	freshly grated Parmesan or shredded Asiago cheese	125 mL
2 tbsp	olive oil	25 mL
2 cups	hot water	500 mL
1 cup	packed baby arugula	250 mL

1. *Form.* Place dough on a floured surface and dust very lightly with flour. Flour your hands and the rolling pin. Working the dough as little as possible and adding flour as necessary, roll out the dough into a 12-inch (30 cm) circle. Lightly flour any sticky places on the dough as you roll. The dough should feel gently taut and smooth all over, like a baby's skin, but not at all sticky.

2. *Rest.* Drape the dough over the rolling pin and transfer to the pizza pan. Pat into place. Cover with a tea towel and let rest at room temperature for 40 minutes.

3. *Prepare oven for artisan baking.* About 30 minutes before baking, place the broiler pan on the lower shelf and the baking stone on the middle shelf of the oven. Preheat to 450°F (230°C).

4. *Add pizza toppings.* Sprinkle tomatoes, grilled vegetables and Parmesan over the dough, then drizzle with olive oil.

Tip

This type of thin-crust pizza is not meant for heavy sauce, cheese and meat toppings. Instead, use toppings that add bold flavor without bulk, such as thinly sliced onion, prosciutto or crisp-cooked pancetta, grated aged cheeses, chèvre, feta or blue cheese crumbles, olives, pesto, roasted red pepper, cooked Italian sausage crumbles, thinly sliced mushrooms, fresh herbs, fresh tomatoes, oil-packed sun-dried tomatoes or thin asparagus stalks.

You Can Also Use

Easy Artisan Dough (page 34) or Easy Artisan Whole-Grain Dough made with semolina or whole wheat flour.

5. *Place pizza pan on baking stone and add water to broiler pan.* Place the pizza pan on the hot stone. Pull the lower rack out, pour the hot water into the broiler pan and push the lower rack back in place. Close the oven door immediately so the steam will envelop the oven.

6. *Bake.* Bake for 15 minutes or until the edges of the crust have browned. Place the arugula in the center of the pizza. To serve, cut the pizza into wedges.

Seeded Breads and Filled Breads

Master Recipe #3
Easy Artisan Seeded and Filled Dough

Adding a coating or filling to a prepared dough is the next step in making artisan breads. Once you've mastered this step — which is more about a new technique than a new recipe — you can customize just about any dough with your own fillings or coatings. Instead of a moist inner filling that is spread on the dough, as in Fig and Gorgonzola Swirl Loaf (page 48), these dry filling ingredients will be dispersed throughout the dough with a rolling pin. For the outer coating, you'll brush a loaf with lightly beaten egg white, then sprinkle and pat on the topping. The topping on the bread usually either hints at its flavor (grated cheese, rolled oats, herbs) or is decorative (seeds).

Makes enough dough for bread, rolls, pizza or flatbread to serve 12 to 16

Equipment:
- Rolling pin
- Three-sided cookie sheet, flexible cutting board or baker's peel

½	recipe prepared Easy Artisan Dough (page 34), about the size of a volleyball	½
	Unbleached all-purpose or bread flour	
½ cup	cornmeal	125 mL

Filling

1 cup	dried fruit, snipped into small pieces, toasted chopped nuts, chopped oil-cured olives, dried or chopped fresh herbs and/or seeds	250 mL

Topping

1	egg white, lightly beaten	1
½ cup	seeds, such as sesame, poppy, fennel, nigella or a mixture	125 mL

1. *Fill.* Place dough on a floured surface and dust very lightly with flour. Flour your hands and the rolling pin. Working the dough as little as possible and adding flour as necessary, roll out the dough into a 16-inch (40 cm) long oval. Sprinkle one-quarter of the filling on the upper half of the dough oval and press into the dough with your hands. Fold the other half over the filling. Turn the dough a quarter turn. Working the dough as little as possible and adding flour as necessary, roll out the dough into an oval. Sprinkle another quarter of the filling on the upper half of the oval and press into the dough with your hands. Fold the other half over the filling. Turn the dough a quarter turn. Working the dough as little as possible and adding flour as necessary, roll out the dough into an oval. Repeat this process twice more, until all of the filling has been incorporated into the dough.

You Can Also Use

Easy Artisan Whole-Grain Dough (page 56), Easy Artisan Flavored Dough (page 120) or Easy Artisan Slow-Rise Dough (page 148).

2. *Form.* Form the dough into a flatbread, batard, boule, baguettes or whatever shape you like.

3. *Rest.* Sprinkle the cornmeal on the cookie sheet and place the formed loaf on the cornbread. Cover with a tea towel and let rest at room temperature for 40 minutes.

4. *Top.* Brush the formed loaf with egg white. Sprinkle and pat on the seeds.

5. *Slash dough with serrated knife.* Follow the directions for an earlier recipe, based on the shape of loaf you've formed and the type of dough you used.

6. *Bake.* Follow the directions for an earlier recipe, based on the shape of loaf you've formed and the type of dough you used.

Top Seeds

Seed	How Used	Flavor
Anise	Rolled into dough	Licorice
Caraway	Rolled into dough; patted on crust	Caraway
Cardamom	Crushed, stirred into sweet dough	Cardamom
Cumin	Rolled into dough; patted on crust	Cumin
Dill	Rolled into dough; patted on crust	Dill
Fennel	Rolled into dough; patted on crust	Licorice
Pepita (pumpkin)	Patted on crust	Nutty
Poppy	Rolled into dough; patted on crust	Sweet
Millet	Rolled into dough; patted on crust	Mildly nutty
Nigella	Rolled into dough; patted on crust	Onion
Sesame	Patted on crust	Sesame
Sunflower	Rolled into dough; patted on crust	Nutty

Sesame Semolina Boule

Equipment:
- Three-sided cookie sheet, flexible cutting board or baker's peel
- Broiler pan
- Baking stone

This classic artisan loaf has a slightly more honeycombed crumb and mellow yellow color — from the high-protein semolina flour — as well as a patterned crust from the sesame seeds. And you made it!

1/2	recipe prepared Easy Artisan Whole-Grain Dough (page 56), about the size of a volleyball, made with semolina	1/2
	Unbleached all-purpose or bread flour	
1/2 cup	cornmeal	125 mL
1	egg white, lightly beaten	1
1/2 cup	sesame seeds	125 mL
2 cups	hot water	500 mL

1. *Form.* Place dough on a floured surface and dust very lightly with flour. Flour your hands. Working the dough as little as possible and adding flour as necessary, form the dough into a 12-inch (30 cm) round. Smooth the dough with your hands to form a soft, non-sticky skin. Pinch any seams together. Lightly flour any sticky places on the dough. The dough should feel soft and smooth all over, like a baby's skin, but not at all sticky.

2. *Rest.* Sprinkle the cornmeal on the cookie sheet and place the dough round on the cornmeal. Cover with a tea towel and let rest at room temperature for 40 minutes.

3. *Prepare oven for artisan baking.* About 30 minutes before baking, place the broiler pan on the lower shelf and the baking stone on the middle shelf of the oven. Preheat to 450°F (230°C).

4. *Top.* Brush the boule with egg white. Sprinkle and pat on the seeds.

5. *Slash boule with serrated knife.* Using a serrated knife, make three evenly spaced slashes, about 1 inch (2.5 cm) deep, across the boule, exposing the moist dough under the surface.

Tip

For higher drama, use black sesame seeds instead of golden sesame seeds.

6. *Slide boule onto baking stone and add water to broiler pan.* Using an oven mitt, carefully pull the middle rack of the oven out several inches. Hold the cutting board level with the rack so that the dough round will slide onto the center of the hot stone. With a quick forward jerk of your arms, slide the dough round from the cookie sheet to the stone. Push the middle rack back in place. Pull the lower rack out, pour the hot water into the broiler pan and push the lower rack back in place. Close the oven door immediately so the steam will envelop the oven.

7. *Bake.* Bake for 27 to 30 minutes or until the crust is a medium dark brown and an instant-read thermometer inserted in the center of the loaf registers at least 190°F (90°C). Wearing oven mitts, remove the loaf by hand to cool on a wire rack.

Change It Up

Oatmeal Honey Boule: Use Oatmeal Honey Dough (page 65) and top with $1/2$ cup (125 mL) rolled oats.

Whole Wheat Cheddar Boule

Equipment:
- Rolling pin
- Three-sided cookie sheet, flexible cutting board or baker's peel
- Broiler pan
- Baking stone

For maximum flavor, use an aged Cheddar to stand up to the robust whole wheat. You'll fill and top this bread with cheese.

½	recipe prepared Easy Artisan Whole-Grain Dough (page 56), about the size of a volleyball, made with semolina	½
	Unbleached all-purpose or bread flour	
1½ cups	shredded aged Cheddar cheese	375 mL
½ cup	cornmeal	125 mL
1	egg white, lightly beaten	1
2 cups	hot water	500 mL

1. *Fill.* Place dough on a floured surface and dust very lightly with flour. Flour your hands and the rolling pin. Working the dough as little as possible and adding flour as necessary, roll out the dough into a 16-inch (40 cm) long oval. Reserve 2 tbsp (25 mL) of the cheese for topping. Sprinkle one-quarter of the remaining cheese on the upper half of the dough oval and press into the dough with your hands. Fold the other half over the cheese. Turn the dough a quarter turn. Working the dough as little as possible and adding flour as necessary, roll out the dough into an oval. Sprinkle another quarter of the cheese on the upper half of the oval and press into the dough with your hands. Fold the other half over the cheese. Turn the dough a quarter turn. Working the dough as little as possible and adding flour as necessary, roll out the dough into an oval. Repeat this process twice more, until of the cheese has been incorporated into the dough.

2. *Form.* Working the dough as little as possible and adding flour as necessary, form the dough into a 12-inch (30 cm) round. Smooth the dough with your hands to form a soft, non-sticky skin. Pinch any seams together. Lightly flour any sticky places on the dough. The dough should feel soft and smooth all over, like a baby's skin, but not at all sticky.

3. *Rest.* Sprinkle the cornmeal on the cookie sheet and place the dough round on the cornmeal. Cover with a tea towel and let rest at room temperature for 40 minutes.

Tip

Instead of making slashes on the boule, try something more decorative. At the famous Poilâne, one of the best-loved artisan bakeries in Paris, boules are marked with a "P" in a simple but flowing script. Using a serrated knife, make a script initial on the top of your boule, then bake.

4. *Prepare oven for artisan baking.* About 30 minutes before baking, place the broiler pan on the lower shelf and the baking stone on the middle shelf of the oven. Preheat to 450°F (230°C).

5. *Top.* Brush the boule with egg white. Sprinkle and pat on the reserved cheese.

6. *Slash boule with serrated knife.* Using a serrated knife, make three evenly spaced slashes, about 1 inch (2.5 cm) deep, across the boule, exposing the moist dough under the surface.

7. *Slide boule onto baking stone and add water to broiler pan.* Using an oven mitt, carefully pull the middle rack of the oven out several inches. Hold the cutting board level with the rack so that the dough round will slide onto the center of the hot stone. With a quick forward jerk of your arms, slide the dough round from the cookie sheet to the stone. Push the middle rack back in place. Pull the lower rack out, pour the hot water into the broiler pan and push the lower rack back in place. Close the oven door immediately so the steam will envelop the oven.

8. *Bake.* Bake for 27 to 30 minutes or until the crust is a medium dark brown and an instant-read thermometer inserted in the center of the loaf registers at least 190°F (90°C). Wearing oven mitts, remove the loaf by hand to cool on a wire rack.

Change It Up

Italian Asiago Boule: Substitute coarsely shredded Asiago for the Cheddar.

Swiss Rye Boule

Look for cave-aged cheeses to use in this dough — they have a nuttier and bolder flavor than unaged cheese.

¹⁄₂	recipe prepared Caraway Rye Dough (page 58), about the size of a volleyball	¹⁄₂
	Unbleached all-purpose or bread flour	
1¹⁄₂ cups	coarsely shredded cave-aged Swiss or Gruyère cheese	375 mL
¹⁄₂ cup	cornmeal	125 mL
1	egg white, lightly beaten	1
2 cups	hot water	500 mL

1. *Fill.* Place dough on a floured surface and dust very lightly with flour. Flour your hands and the rolling pin. Working the dough as little as possible and adding flour as necessary, roll out the dough into a 16-inch (40 cm) long oval. Reserve 2 tbsp (25 mL) of the cheese for topping. Sprinkle one-quarter of the remaining cheese on the upper half of the dough oval and press into the dough with your hands. Fold the other half over the cheese. Turn the dough a quarter turn. Working the dough as little as possible and adding flour as necessary, roll out the dough into an oval. Sprinkle another quarter of the cheese on the upper half of the oval and press into the dough with your hands. Fold the other half over the cheese. Turn the dough a quarter turn. Working the dough as little as possible and adding flour as necessary, roll out the dough into an oval. Repeat this process twice more, until of the cheese has been incorporated into the dough.

2. *Form.* Working the dough as little as possible and adding flour as necessary, form the dough into a 12-inch (30 cm) round. Smooth the dough with your hands to form a soft, non-sticky skin. Pinch any seams together. Lightly flour any sticky places on the dough. The dough should feel soft and smooth all over, like a baby's skin, but not at all sticky.

3. *Rest.* Sprinkle the cornmeal on the cookie sheet and place the dough round on the cornmeal. Cover with a tea towel and let rest at room temperature for 40 minutes.

Tip

Instead of making slashes on the boule, try something more decorative. At the famous Poilâne, one of the best-loved artisan bakeries in Paris, boules are marked with a "P" in a simple but flowing script. Using a serrated knife, make a script initial on the top of your boule, then bake.

4. *Prepare oven for artisan baking.* About 30 minutes before baking, place the broiler pan on the lower shelf and the baking stone on the middle shelf of the oven. Preheat to 450°F (230°C).

5. *Top.* Brush the boule with egg white. Sprinkle and pat on the reserved cheese.

6. *Slash boule with serrated knife.* Using a serrated knife, make three evenly spaced slashes, about 1 inch (2.5 cm) deep, across the boule, exposing the moist dough under the surface.

7. *Slide boule onto baking stone and add water to broiler pan.* Using an oven mitt, carefully pull the middle rack of the oven out several inches. Hold the cutting board level with the rack so that the dough round will slide onto the center of the hot stone. With a quick forward jerk of your arms, slide the dough round from the cookie sheet to the stone. Push the middle rack back in place. Pull the lower rack out, pour the hot water into the broiler pan and push the lower rack back in place. Close the oven door immediately so the steam will envelop the oven.

8. *Bake.* Bake for 27 to 30 minutes or until the crust is a medium dark brown and an instant-read thermometer inserted in the center of the loaf registers at least 190°F (90°C). Wearing oven mitts, remove the loaf by hand to cool on a wire rack.

Rosemary Walnut Boule

Makes 1 large round loaf, or boule, to serve 8

Equipment:
- Rolling pin
- Three-sided cookie sheet, flexible cutting board or baker's peel
- Broiler pan
- Baking stone

Savory Rosemary Walnuts (page 297) are delicious for snacking, but are equally good as a filling for artisan bread.

½	recipe prepared Easy Artisan Dough (page 34), about the size of a volleyball	½
	Unbleached all-purpose or bread flour	
½	recipe Rosemary Walnuts (page 297), coarsely chopped	½
½ cup	cornmeal	125 mL
2 cups	hot water	500 mL

1. *Fill.* Place dough on a floured surface and dust very lightly with flour. Flour your hands and the rolling pin. Working the dough as little as possible and adding flour as necessary, roll out the dough into a 16-inch (40 cm) long oval. Sprinkle one-quarter of the walnuts on the upper half of the dough oval and press into the dough with your hands. Fold the other half over the walnuts. Turn the dough a quarter turn. Working the dough as little as possible and adding flour as necessary, roll out the dough into an oval. Sprinkle another quarter of the walnuts on the upper half of the oval and press into the dough with your hands. Fold the other half over the walnuts. Turn the dough a quarter turn. Working the dough as little as possible and adding flour as necessary, roll out the dough into an oval. Repeat this process twice more, until all of the walnuts have been incorporated into the dough.

2. *Form.* Working the dough as little as possible and adding flour as necessary, form the dough into a 10-inch (25 cm) round. Smooth the dough with your hands to form a soft, non-sticky skin. Pinch any seams together. Lightly flour any sticky places on the dough. The dough should feel soft and smooth all over, like a baby's skin, but not at all sticky.

3. *Rest.* Sprinkle the cornmeal on the cookie sheet and place the dough round on the cornmeal. Cover with a tea towel and let rest at room temperature for 40 minutes.

4. *Prepare oven for artisan baking.* About 30 minutes before baking, place the broiler pan on the lower shelf and the baking stone on the middle shelf of the oven. Preheat to 450°F (230°C).

You Can Also Use
Easy Artisan Whole-Grain Dough (page 56). Make the slashes 1 inch (2.5 cm) deep.

5. *Slash boule with serrated knife.* Using a serrated knife, make three evenly spaced slashes, about $\frac{1}{2}$ inch (1 cm) deep, across the boule, exposing the moist dough under the surface.

6. *Slide boule onto baking stone and add water to broiler pan.* Using an oven mitt, carefully pull the middle rack of the oven out several inches. Hold the cutting board level with the rack so that the dough round will slide onto the center of the hot stone. With a quick forward jerk of your arms, slide the dough round from the cookie sheet to the stone. Push the middle rack back in place. Pull the lower rack out, pour the hot water into the broiler pan and push the lower rack back in place. Close the oven door immediately so the steam will envelop the oven.

7. *Bake.* Bake for 27 to 30 minutes or until the crust is a medium dark brown and an instant-read thermometer inserted in the center of the loaf registers at least 190°F (90°C). Wearing oven mitts, remove the loaf by hand to cool on a wire rack.

Three-Seed Batard

Makes 1 large loaf, to serve 8 to 10

Equipment:
- Rolling pin
- Three-sided cookie sheet
- Flexible cutting board, floured, or two metal spatulas
- Broiler pan
- Baking stone

In this bread, the topping is a clue to what you'll find inside: delicious flavor and texture from the seeds.

½	recipe prepared Easy Artisan Dough (page 34), about the size of a volleyball	½
	Unbleached all-purpose or bread flour	
6 tbsp	mixed poppy, millet and fennel seeds	90 mL
½ cup	cornmeal	50 mL
1	egg white, lightly beaten	1
2 cups	hot water	500 mL

1. *Fill.* Place dough on a floured surface and dust very lightly with flour. Flour your hands and the rolling pin. Working the dough as little as possible and adding flour as necessary, roll out the dough into a 16-inch (40 cm) long oval. Reserve 2 tbsp (25 mL) of the seeds for topping. Sprinkle one-quarter of the remaining seeds on the upper half of the dough oval and press into the dough with your hands. Fold the other half over the seeds. Turn the dough a quarter turn. Working the dough as little as possible and adding flour as necessary, roll out the dough into an oval. Sprinkle another quarter of the seeds on the upper half of the oval and press into the dough with your hands. Fold the other half over the seeds. Turn the dough a quarter turn. Working the dough as little as possible and adding flour as necessary, roll out the dough into an oval. Repeat this process twice more, until all of the seeds have been incorporated into the dough.

2. *Form.* Working the dough as little as possible and adding flour as necessary, form the dough into a 14-inch (35 cm) cylinder. Pinch the ends and any seams closed. Lightly flour any sticky places on the dough. The dough should feel soft and smooth all over, like a baby's skin, but not at all sticky.

3. *Rest.* Sprinkle the cornmeal on the cookie sheet. Using the cutting board or two metal spatulas, transfer the loaf to the cookie sheet. Cover with a tea towel and let rest at room temperature for 40 minutes.

4. *Prepare oven for artisan baking.* About 30 minutes before baking, place the broiler pan on the lower shelf and the baking stone on the middle shelf of the oven. Preheat to 450°F (230°C).

You Can Also Use
Easy Artisan Whole-Grain Dough (page 56). Make the slashes 1 inch (2.5 cm) deep.

5. *Top.* Brush the batard with egg white. Sprinkle and pat on the reserved seeds.

6. *Slash batard with serrated knife.* Using a serrated knife, make five slashes, about $\frac{1}{2}$ inch (1 cm) deep, diagonally across the top of the loaf, exposing the moist dough under the surface.

7. *Slide batard onto baking stone and add water to broiler pan.* Using an oven mitt, carefully pull the middle rack of the oven out several inches. Hold the cookie sheet level with the rack so that the loaf will slide sideways onto the hot stone. With a quick forward jerk of your arms, slide the loaf from the cookie sheet to the stone. If necessary, use a metal spatula to reposition the loaf. Push the middle rack back in place. Pull the lower rack out, pour the hot water into the broiler pan and push the lower rack back in place. Close the oven door immediately so the steam will envelop the oven.

8. *Bake.* Bake for 25 to 27 minutes or until the crust is dark brown and an instant-read thermometer inserted in the center of the loaf registers at least 190°F (90°C). Wearing oven mitts, remove the loaf by hand to cool on a wire rack.

Change It Up

Six-Seed Batard: Use 6 tbsp (90 mL) of mixed poppy, fennel, millet, sesame and finely chopped roasted pepitas and sunflower seeds.

Orchard Batard

Makes 1 large loaf, to serve 8 to 10

Equipment:
- Rolling pin
- Three-sided cookie sheet
- Flexible cutting board, floured, or two metal spatulas
- Broiler pan
- Baking stone

Filled with succulent dried fruit, this bread is delicious toasted, spread with cream cheese and drizzled with wildflower or clover honey. There is no topping, but the brush of egg white produces a glistening crust.

½	recipe prepared Easy Artisan Dough (page 34), about the size of a volleyball	½
	Unbleached all-purpose or bread flour	
1 cup	mixed dried fruit, such as snipped apricots, figs, dates, dried cherries and golden raisins	250 mL
½ cup	cornmeal	50 mL
1	egg white, lightly beaten	1
2 cups	hot water	500 mL

1. *Fill.* Place dough on a floured surface and dust very lightly with flour. Flour your hands and the rolling pin. Working the dough as little as possible and adding flour as necessary, roll out the dough into a 16-inch (40 cm) long oval. Sprinkle one-quarter of the fruit on the upper half of the dough oval and press into the dough with your hands. Fold the other half over the fruit. Turn the dough a quarter turn. Working the dough as little as possible and adding flour as necessary, roll out the dough into an oval. Sprinkle another quarter of the fruit on the upper half of the oval and press into the dough with your hands. Fold the other half over the fruit. Turn the dough a quarter turn. Working the dough as little as possible and adding flour as necessary, roll out the dough into an oval. Repeat this process twice more, until all of the fruit has been incorporated into the dough.

2. *Form.* Working the dough as little as possible and adding flour as necessary, form the dough into a 14-inch (35 cm) cylinder. Pinch the ends and any seams closed. Lightly flour any sticky places on the dough. The dough should feel soft and smooth all over, like a baby's skin, but not at all sticky.

3. *Rest.* Sprinkle the cornmeal on the cookie sheet. Using the cutting board or two metal spatulas, transfer the loaf to the cookie sheet. Cover with a tea towel and let rest at room temperature for 40 minutes.

4. *Prepare oven for artisan baking.* About 30 minutes before baking, place the broiler pan on the lower shelf and the baking stone on the middle shelf of the oven. Preheat to 450°F (230°C).

You Can Also Use

Easy Artisan Whole-Grain
Dough (page 56). Make the
slashes 1 inch (2.5 cm) deep.

5. *Top.* Brush the batard with egg white.

6. *Slash batard with serrated knife.* Using a serrated knife, make five cross-hatch slashes, about $\frac{1}{2}$ inch (1 cm) deep, diagonally across the top of the loaf, exposing the moist dough under the surface.

7. *Slide batard onto baking stone and add water to broiler pan.* Using an oven mitt, carefully pull the middle rack of the oven out several inches. Hold the cookie sheet level with the rack so that the loaf will slide sideways onto the hot stone. With a quick forward jerk of your arms, slide the loaf from the cookie sheet to the stone. If necessary, use a metal spatula to reposition the loaf. Push the middle rack back in place. Pull the lower rack out, pour the hot water into the broiler pan and push the lower rack back in place. Close the oven door immediately so the steam will envelop the oven.

8. *Bake.* Bake for 25 to 27 minutes or until the crust is dark brown and an instant-read thermometer inserted in the center registers at least 190°F (90°C). Wearing oven mitts, remove the loaf by hand to cool on a wire rack.

Change It Up

Use a mixture of dried fruits and nuts, such as whole pistachios or chopped walnuts, pecans or almonds. Just keep the total amount to 1 cup (250 mL).

Roquefort and Walnut Fougasse

Equipment:
- Rolling pin
- Large baking sheet, lined
  with parchment paper
- Broiler pan
- Baking stone

*While Italians pile their
fillings on top of focaccia, the
French like to incorporate
theirs into the dough itself,
as in this fougasse recipe.
This recipe makes a thicker,
more bread-like fougasse,
impressive on a buffet table
for brunch or cocktails, or
as part of a casual meal. For
a thinner, smaller, crispier
version, see Fougasse (page
41) or Fougasse aux Grattons
(page 108).*

1½ cups	crumbled Roquefort or other good-quality blue cheese (about 12 oz/375 g)	375 mL
1 cup	toasted walnuts, chopped	250 mL
½	recipe prepared Easy Artisan Dough (page 34), about the size of a volleyball	½
1 tbsp	olive oil	15 mL
2 cups	hot water	500 mL

1. *Combine.* In a small bowl, combine blue cheese and walnuts.

2. *Form.* Place dough on a floured surface and dust very lightly with flour. Flour your hands and the rolling pin. Working the dough as little as possible and adding flour as necessary, roll out the dough into a 12- by 6-inch (30 by 15 cm) oval. Lightly flour any sticky places on the dough. The dough should feel soft and smooth all over, like a baby's skin, but not at all sticky.

3. *Fill.* Arrange one-quarter of the filling on the upper half of the dough and press into the dough with your hands. Fold the other half over the filling. Turn the dough a quarter turn. Working the dough as little as possible and adding flour as necessary, roll out the dough into an oval. Arrange another quarter of the filling on the upper half of the oval and press into the dough with your hands. Fold the other half over the filling. Turn the dough a quarter turn. Working the dough as little as possible and adding flour as necessary, roll out the dough into an oval. Repeat this process twice more, until all of the filling has been incorporated into the dough.

4. *Cut.* Using a pizza wheel or a sharp knife, cut two rows of four diagonal slashes evenly spaced along the length of the oval, about 2 to 3 inches (5 to 7.5 cm) long, that almost meet in the middle of the dough, like this: /\. Transfer the dough to the prepared baking sheet and pull the top and sides of the dough to stretch it into a larger oval with opened slits. Brush the surface of the dough with the olive oil.

5. *Rest.* Cover with a tea towel and let rest at room temperature for 40 minutes.

6. *Prepare oven for artisan baking.* About 30 minutes before baking, place the broiler pan on the lower shelf and the baking stone on the middle shelf of the oven. Preheat to 450°F (230°C).

7. *Place baking sheet on baking stone and add water to broiler pan.* Using an oven mitt, carefully pull the middle rack of the oven out several inches. Place the baking sheet on the hot stone. Push the middle rack back in place. Pull the lower rack out, pour the hot water into the broiler pan and push the lower rack back in place. Close the oven door immediately so the steam will envelop the oven.

8. *Bake.* Bake for 35 to 40 minutes or until the crust is medium brown. Transfer to a wire rack to cool.

Goat Cheese and Dried Fruit Fougasse

Makes 1 large flatbread, to serve 8 to 12

Equipment:
- Rolling pin
- Large baking sheet, lined with parchment paper
- Broiler pan
- Baking stone

For a delicious pairing, serve this appetizer fougasse with a dry rosé.

Tip

Snip the dried fruit into small pieces, using kitchen shears. If the blades of the shears get sticky, dip them in hot water.

1 cup	snipped dried fruit (apricots, figs, plums, etc.)	250 mL
½ cup	warm brandy, cognac or sherry	125 mL
1 cup	crumbled fresh chèvre or goat cheese	250 mL
½	recipe prepared Easy Artisan Dough (page 34), about the size of a volleyball	½
1 tbsp	olive oil	15 mL
2 cups	hot water	500 mL

1. *Combine.* Place dried fruit in a bowl, add brandy and let stand for 30 minutes or until plump. Drain. Add chèvre and combine well.

2. *Form.* Place dough on a floured surface and dust very lightly with flour. Flour your hands and the rolling pin. Working the dough as little as possible and adding flour as necessary, roll out the dough into a 12- by 6-inch (30 by 15 cm) oval. Lightly flour any sticky places on the dough. The dough should feel soft and smooth all over, like a baby's skin, but not at all sticky.

3. *Fill.* Arrange one-quarter of the filling on the upper half of the dough and press into the dough with your hands. Fold the other half over the filling. Turn the dough a quarter turn. Working the dough as little as possible and adding flour as necessary, roll out the dough into an oval. Arrange another quarter of the filling on the upper half of the oval and press into the dough with your hands. Fold the other half over the filling. Turn the dough a quarter turn. Working the dough as little as possible and adding flour as necessary, roll out the dough into an oval. Repeat this process twice more, until all of the filling has been incorporated into the dough.

4. *Cut.* Using a pizza wheel or a sharp knife, cut two rows of four diagonal slashes evenly spaced along the length of the oval, about 2 to 3 inches (5 to 7.5 cm) long, that almost meet in the middle of the dough, like this: /\. Transfer the dough to the prepared baking sheet and pull the top and sides of the dough to stretch it into a larger oval with opened slits. Brush the surface of the dough with the olive oil.

5. *Rest.* Cover with a tea towel and let rest at room temperature for 40 minutes.

6. *Prepare oven for artisan baking.* About 30 minutes before baking, place the broiler pan on the lower shelf and the baking stone on the middle shelf of the oven. Preheat to 450°F (230°C).

7. *Place baking sheet on baking stone and add water to broiler pan.* Using an oven mitt, carefully pull the middle rack of the oven out several inches. Place the baking sheet on the hot stone. Push the middle rack back in place. Pull the lower rack out, pour the hot water into the broiler pan and push the lower rack back in place. Close the oven door immediately so the steam will envelop the oven.

8. *Bake.* Bake for 35 to 40 minutes or until the crust is medium brown. Transfer to a wire rack to cool.

Fougasse aux Grattons

Equipment:
- Rolling pin
- Large baking sheet, lined with parchment paper
- Broiler pan
- Baking stone

Popular in the south of France, "grattons," or "gratelons," are crispy, fried pieces of pork belly or bacon. Here, they're slowly rendered in a little dry white wine, then folded into artisan dough.

Once you're made fougasse, with its leaf-like perforations, you'll want to make many different kinds. This one would be delicious as an appetizer with a cocktail or glass of wine, with a hearty soup, with a brunch casserole or, as they do in Provence, with a bitter green salad of endive or dandelion greens.

½ cup	dry white wine	125 mL
8	slices smoked bacon or 8 oz (250 g) pancetta, finely chopped	8
¼	recipe prepared Easy Artisan Dough (page 34), about the size of a softball	¼
2 cups	hot water	500 mL

1. **Combine.** In a skillet, bring wine and bacon to a boil over medium heat. Reduce heat to low and simmer for 35 to 40 minutes or until the fat is rendered and bacon is browned. Using a slotted spoon, transfer bacon to a plate lined with paper towels to drain. Reserve the melted fat in the skillet.

2. **Form.** Place dough on a floured surface and dust very lightly with flour. Flour your hands and the rolling pin. Working the dough as little as possible and adding flour as necessary, roll out the dough into a 12- by 6-inch (30 by 15 cm) oval. Lightly flour any sticky places on the dough. The dough should feel soft and smooth all over, like a baby's skin, but not at all sticky.

3. **Fill.** Arrange one-quarter of the grattons on the upper half of the dough and press into the dough with your hands. Fold the other half over the grattons. Turn the dough a quarter turn. Working the dough as little as possible and adding flour as necessary, roll out the dough into an oval. Arrange another quarter of the grattons on the upper half of the dough and press into the dough with your hands. Fold the other half over the grattons. Turn the dough a quarter turn. Working the dough as little as possible and adding flour as necessary, roll out the dough into an oval. Repeat this process twice more, until all of the grattons have been incorporated into the dough.

4. **Cut.** Using a pizza wheel or a sharp knife, cut two rows of four diagonal slashes evenly spaced along the length of the oval, about 2 to 3 inches (5 to 7.5 cm) long, that almost meet in the middle of the dough, like this: /\. Transfer the dough to the prepared baking sheet and pull the top and sides of the dough to stretch it into a larger oval with opened slits. Brush the surface of the dough with the melted bacon fat.

Tip

For the best bacon flavor in your leftover bread, wrap bread in foil and warm it in a 350°F (180°C) oven before serving.

You Can Also Use

Easy Artisan Whole-Grain Dough (page 56), made with white whole wheat flour, buckwheat flour or chickpea (garbanzo bean) flour.

5. *Rest.* Cover with a tea towel and let rest at room temperature for 40 minutes.

6. *Prepare oven for artisan baking.* About 30 minutes before baking, place the broiler pan on the lower shelf and the baking stone on the middle shelf of the oven. Preheat to 450°F (230°C).

7. *Place baking sheet on baking stone and add water to broiler pan.* Using an oven mitt, carefully pull the middle rack of the oven out several inches. Place the baking sheet on the hot stone. Push the middle rack back in place. Pull the lower rack out, pour the hot water into the broiler pan and push the lower rack back in place. Close the oven door immediately so the steam will envelop the oven.

8. *Bake.* Bake for 22 to 25 minutes or until the crust is medium brown. Transfer to a wire rack to cool.

Rosemary and Black Olive Fougasse

Makes 1 flatbread, to serve 4 to 6

Equipment:
- Rolling pin
- Large baking sheet, lined with parchment paper
- Broiler pan
- Baking stone

Pair this savory fougasse with a rich Burgundy or Merlot.

1 cup	chopped oil-cured pitted black olives	250 mL
1 tbsp	fresh rosemary leaves	15 mL
¼	recipe prepared Easy Artisan Dough (page 34), about the size of a softball	¼
	Olive oil	
2 cups	hot water	500 mL

1. *Combine.* In a bowl, combine olives and rosemary.

2. *Form.* Place dough on a floured surface and dust very lightly with flour. Flour your hands and the rolling pin. Working the dough as little as possible and adding flour as necessary, roll out the dough into a 12- by 6-inch (30 by 15 cm) oval. Lightly flour any sticky places on the dough. The dough should feel soft and smooth all over, like a baby's skin, but not at all sticky.

3. *Fill.* Arrange one-quarter of the filling on the upper half of the dough and press into the dough with your hands. Fold the other half over the filling. Turn the dough a quarter turn. Working the dough as little as possible and adding flour as necessary, roll out the dough into an oval. Arrange another quarter of the filling on the upper half of the dough and press into the dough with your hands. Fold the other half over the filling. Turn the dough a quarter turn. Working the dough as little as possible and adding flour as necessary, roll out the dough into an oval. Repeat this process twice more, until all of the filling has been incorporated into the dough.

4. *Cut.* Using a pizza wheel or a sharp knife, cut two rows of four diagonal slashes evenly spaced along the length of the oval, about 2 to 3 inches (5 to 7.5 cm) long, that almost meet in the middle of the dough, like this: / \. Transfer the dough to the prepared baking sheet and pull the top and sides of the dough to stretch it into a larger oval with opened slits. Brush the surface of the dough with olive oil.

You Can Also Use
Easy Artisan Whole-Grain Dough (page 56), made with white whole wheat flour, buckwheat flour or chickpea (garbanzo bean) flour.

5. *Rest.* Cover with a tea towel and let rest at room temperature for 40 minutes.

6. *Prepare oven for artisan baking.* About 30 minutes before baking, place the broiler pan on the lower shelf and the baking stone on the middle shelf of the oven. Preheat to 450°F (230°C).

7. *Place baking sheet on baking stone and add water to broiler pan.* Using an oven mitt, carefully pull the middle rack of the oven out several inches. Place the baking sheet on the hot stone. Push the middle rack back in place. Pull the lower rack out, pour the hot water into the broiler pan and push the lower rack back in place. Close the oven door immediately so the steam will envelop the oven.

8. *Bake.* Bake for 22 to 25 minutes or until the crust is medium brown. Transfer to a wire rack to cool.

Afghan Flatbread with Cilantro and Green Onions

Makes 4 flatbreads

Equipment:
- Rolling pin
- Large baking sheet
- Broiler pan
- Baking stone
- Metal spatula

A specialty of Kabul, these half-moon-shaped flatbreads are stuffed with cilantro and green onions, and the dough halves are pressed — not rolled — together. Then these flatbreads are brushed with oil and baked or grilled. They're a fresh-tasting and traditional accompaniment to grilled beef kabobs or roast lamb.

¼	recipe prepared Traditional Naan Dough (page 67), about the size of a softball	¼
1 cup	finely chopped fresh cilantro	250 mL
1 cup	finely chopped green onions, with some of the green	250 mL
	Unbleached all-purpose or bread flour	
¼ cup	cornmeal	50 mL
	Olive oil	
2 cups	hot water	500 mL

1. *Form.* Place dough on a floured surface and dust very lightly with flour. Flour your hands and the rolling pin. Working the dough as little as possible and adding flour as necessary, form the dough into an 8-inch (20 cm) cylinder. With a dough scraper, cut the dough into 2-inch (5 cm) slices. Roll out each slice into an 8-inch (20 cm) long oval. Lightly flour any sticky places on the dough. The dough should feel soft and smooth all over, like a baby's skin, but not at all sticky.

2. *Fill.* Sprinkle ¼ cup (50 mL) each cilantro and green onions on the upper half of each dough oval and press into the dough with your hands. Fold the other half over the filling and press the edges of the dough together. Turn the dough a quarter turn. Working the dough as little as possible and adding flour as necessary, roll out the dough into a 8-inch (20 cm) oval.

3. *Rest.* Sprinkle the cornmeal on the baking sheet and place the dough ovals on the cornmeal. Cover with a tea towel and let rest at room temperature for 40 minutes.

4. *Prepare oven for artisan baking.* About 30 minutes before baking, place the broiler pan on the lower shelf and the baking stone on the middle shelf of the oven. Preheat to 450°F (230°C).

Tip

Look for maida, atta and other naan ingredients at Indian grocers.

5. *Brush with oil.* Brush the flatbreads with olive oil.

6. *Place flatbreads on baking stone and add water to broiler pan.* Using an oven mitt, carefully pull the middle rack of the oven out several inches. With a metal spatula, place two flatbreads on the hot stone. Pull the lower rack out, pour the hot water into the broiler pan and push the lower rack back in place. Close the oven door immediately so the steam will envelop the oven.

7. *Bake.* Bake for 7 to 8 minutes or until the crust is lightly blistered. Wearing oven mitts, remove the flatbreads by hand to cool on a wire rack. Repeat the baking process with the remaining flatbreads.

Change It Up

Grilled Afghan Flatbread with Cilantro and Green Onions: Prepare a hot fire in your barbecue grill or heat a ridged grill pan indoors. Brush both sides of the flatbread with olive oil and grill, turning once, until they have good grill marks, about 1 minute per side.

Peshawari Naan

Makes 8 flatbreads

Equipment:
- Rolling pin
- Large baking sheet
- Broiler pan
- Baking stone
- Metal spatula

Peshawar is a city in northern Pakistan just east of Kabul, Afghanistan, and the Khyber Pass. It's a town known for its naan stuffed with locally grown goodies — different kinds of raisins, herbs and roasted nuts such as pistachios, almonds and cashews.

1 tbsp	roasted salted cashews	15 mL
1 tbsp	roasted salted pistachios	15 mL
1 tbsp	golden raisins	15 mL
1 tsp	fennel seeds	5 mL
¼	recipe prepared Traditional Naan Dough (page 67), about the size of a softball	¼
	Unbleached all-purpose or bread flour	
¼ cup	cornmeal	50 mL
	Melted butter or olive oil	
2 cups	hot water	500 mL

1. **Combine.** In a food processor or mini chopper, combine cashews, pistachios, raisins and fennel seeds; process until finely ground.

2. **Form.** Place dough on a floured surface and dust very lightly with flour. Flour your hands and the rolling pin. Working the dough as little as possible and adding flour as necessary, form the dough into an 8-inch (20 cm) cylinder. With a dough scraper, cut the dough into 1-inch (2.5 cm) slices. Roll out each slice into a 6-inch (15 cm) long oval. Lightly flour any sticky places on the dough. The dough should feel soft and smooth all over, like a baby's skin, but not at all sticky.

3. **Fill.** Sprinkle one-eighth of the filling on the upper half of each dough oval and press into the dough with your hands. Fold the other half over the filling. Turn the dough a quarter turn. Working the dough as little as possible and adding flour as necessary, roll out the dough into a 6-inch (15 cm) oval.

4. **Rest.** Sprinkle the cornmeal on the baking sheet and place the dough ovals on the cornmeal. Cover with a tea towel and let rest at room temperature for 40 minutes.

Tip
Look for maida, atta and other naan ingredients at Indian grocers.

5. *Prepare oven for artisan baking.* About 30 minutes before baking, place the broiler pan on the lower shelf and the baking stone on the middle shelf of the oven. Preheat to 450°F (230°C).

6. *Brush with melted butter.* Brush the naan with melted butter.

7. *Place naan on baking stone and add water to broiler pan.* Using an oven mitt, carefully pull the middle rack of the oven out several inches. With a metal spatula, place four naan on the hot stone. Pull the lower rack out, pour the hot water into the broiler pan and push the lower rack back in place. Close the oven door immediately so the steam will envelop the oven.

8. *Bake.* Bake for 7 to 8 minutes or until the crust is lightly blistered. Wearing oven mitts, remove the naan by hand to cool on a wire rack. Repeat the baking process with the remaining naan.

Change It Up

Grilled Peshawari Naan: Prepare a hot fire in your barbecue grill or heat a ridged grill pan indoors. Brush both sides of the naan with melted butter or olive oil and grill, turning once, until they have good grill marks, about 1 minute per side.

Nigella Naan

Equipment:
- Rolling pin
- Large baking sheet
- Broiler pan
- Baking stone
- Metal spatula

Nigella seeds are small, pointed black seeds that have a smoky, onion-like flavor. They're also known as charnuska *(in Russian baking), black cumin seeds and onion seeds. You can find them at Indian or Pakistani grocers, or online. The seeds are softened a bit first in hot water, then rolled into the dough. You could also make this flatbread with cumin seeds — without softening in water first — another traditional naan flavoring.*

1 tbsp	nigella seeds	15 mL
1/2 cup	boiling water	125 mL
1/4	recipe prepared Traditional Naan Dough (page 67), about the size of a softball	1/4
	Unbleached all-purpose or bread flour	
1/4 cup	cornmeal	50 mL
	Melted butter or olive oil	
2 cups	hot water	500 mL

1. **Combine.** In a small bowl, combine nigella seeds and boiling water. Let stand until cool, then drain and pat the seeds dry.

2. **Form.** Place dough on a floured surface and dust very lightly with flour. Flour your hands and the rolling pin. Working the dough as little as possible and adding flour as necessary, form the dough into an 8-inch (20 cm) cylinder. With a dough scraper, cut the dough into 1-inch (2.5 cm) slices. Roll out each slice into a 6-inch (15 cm) long oval. Lightly flour any sticky places on the dough. The dough should feel soft and smooth all over, like a baby's skin, but not at all sticky.

3. **Fill.** Sprinkle 1/2 tsp (2 mL) nigella seeds on the upper half of each dough oval and press into the dough with your hands. Fold the other half over the seeds. Turn the dough a quarter turn. Working the dough as little as possible and adding flour as necessary, roll out the dough into a 6-inch (15 cm) oval.

4. **Rest.** Sprinkle the cornmeal on the baking sheet and place the dough ovals on the cornmeal. Cover with a tea towel and let rest at room temperature for 40 minutes.

5. **Prepare oven for artisan baking.** About 30 minutes before baking, place the broiler pan on the lower shelf and the baking stone on the middle shelf of the oven. Preheat to 450°F (230°C).

Look for maida, atta, nigella seeds and other naan ingredients at Indian grocers.

6. *Brush with melted butter.* Brush the naan with melted butter.

7. *Place naan on baking stone and add water to broiler pan.* Using an oven mitt, carefully pull the middle rack of the oven out several inches. With a metal spatula, place four naan on the hot stone. Pull the lower rack out, pour the hot water into the broiler pan and push the lower rack back in place. Close the oven door immediately so the steam will envelop the oven.

8. *Bake.* Bake for 7 to 8 minutes or until the crust is lightly blistered. Wearing oven mitts, remove the naan by hand to cool on a wire rack. Repeat the baking process with the remaining naan.

Change It Up

Grilled Nigella Naan: Prepare a hot fire in your barbecue grill or heat a ridged grill pan indoors. Brush both sides of the naan with melted butter or olive oil and grill, turning once, until they have good grill marks, about 1 minute per side.

Flavored Breads

Master Recipe #4
Easy Artisan Flavored Dough

In this master recipe, we substitute flavoring liquids for some of the water and stir in dried herbs, spices and other boldly flavored ingredients to create customized breads.

Makes enough dough for bread, rolls, pizza or flatbread to serve 12 to 16

Equipment:
- Instant-read thermometer
- 16-cup (4 L) mixing bowl
- Wooden spoon or Danish dough whisk

Tip

For the liquid component, you can use milk, buttermilk, beer, juice, applesauce or puréed squash or pumpkin in addition to water. Milk, juice and beer can be substituted 1 cup for 1 cup (250 mL) for up to 2 cups (750 mL) of the water, keeping the total liquid at 3 cups (750 mL). But puréed squash and pumpkin, applesauce and buttermilk are more dense, so you can replace them 1 cup for 1 cup (250 mL) for up to 2 cups (500 mL) of the water, but to compensate, you'll need to stir in additional water to equal 4 cups (1 L) liquid. You can also add up to ¼ cup (50 mL) liquid honey without decreasing the amount of the other liquids.

6½ cups	unbleached all-purpose or bread flour	1.625 L
2 tbsp	instant or bread machine yeast	25 mL
1½ tbsp	fine kosher salt	22 mL
	Dried herbs, spices or other flavoring ingredients (optional, see page 121 for suggestions and amounts)	
3 to 4 cups	lukewarm liquid (see tip, at left), about 100°F (38°C)	750 mL to 1 L

1. *Measure.* Spoon the flour into a measuring cup, level with a knife or your finger, then dump the flour into the mixing bowl.

2. *Mix.* Add the yeast and salt to the flour. Add optional ingredients, if desired. Stir together with a wooden spoon or Danish dough whisk. Pour in the liquids and stir together until just moistened. Beat 40 strokes, scraping the bottom and the sides of the bowl, until the dough forms a lumpy, sticky mass.

3. *Rise.* Cover the bowl with plastic wrap and let rise at room temperature (72°F/22°C) in a draft-free place for 2 hours or until the dough has risen nearly to the top of the bowl and has a sponge-like appearance.

4. *Use right away or refrigerate.* Use that day or place the dough, covered with plastic wrap, in the refrigerator for up to 3 days before baking.

Baking with Canadian Flour

Canadian flour has a higher protein content than some U.S. flours and therefore absorbs more water. If you are using Canadian bread flour, start by adding about ½ cup (125 mL) less than called for, and add just enough of the remaining ½ cup (125 mL) to make a thick, paste-like dough. You don't need to adjust the amount of all-purpose flour.

Tip

Before storing the dough in the refrigerator, use a permanent marker to write the date on the plastic wrap, so you'll know when you made your dough — and when to use it up 3 days later.

Easy Artisan Flavored Breads in Minutes a Day

Day 1	Stir the dough together and let rise. Bake, or cover and chill.
Days 2–3	Remove part of the dough, form and bake.

Flavor Up

Flavoring	Amount to Add	How to Use
Chocolate chips	1 to 2 cups (250 to 500 mL)	Stir into flour mixture
Citrus zest or oil ingredients	1 to 2 tsp (5 to 10 mL)	Stir into liquid
Dried fruits	1 to 2 cups (250 to 500 mL)	Steep in liquid ingredients for 15 minutes
Herbs, dried	1 to 2 tbsp (15 to 25 mL)	Stir into flour mixture
Garlic, roasted and mashed	Up to 1 bulb	Stir into flour mixture
Onion, chopped and sautéed	1 cup (250 mL)	Stir into flour mixture or fold into dough after it has risen
Pesto	1 cup (250 mL)	Fold into dough after it has risen
Saffron	1 to 2 tsp (5 to 10 mL)	Steep in liquid ingredients for 30 minutes
Seeds	1 cup (250 mL)	Stir into flour mixture or fold into dough after it has risen
Spices	1 to 2 tbsp (15 to 25 mL)	Stir into flour mixture
Sun-dried tomatoes	$1/2$ cup (125 mL)	Finely chop and stir into liquid ingredients

Brewhouse Dough

Equipment:
- Instant-read thermometer
- 16-cup (4 L) mixing bowl
- Wooden spoon or Danish dough whisk
- 4-cup (1 L) glass measuring cup

Breads made from this dough are delicious with artisan cheeses and charcuterie.

6½ cups	unbleached all-purpose or bread flour	1.625 L
2 tbsp	instant or bread machine yeast	25 mL
1½ tbsp	fine kosher salt	22 mL
2 cups	good-quality lager beer or ale	500 mL
1 cup	hot water	250 mL
¼ cup	liquid honey	50 mL

1. **Measure.** Spoon the flour into a measuring cup, level with a knife or your finger, then dump the flour into the mixing bowl.

2. **Mix.** Add the yeast and salt to the flour. Stir together with a wooden spoon or Danish dough whisk. In the glass measuring cup, combine beer, hot water and honey. Pour into the flour mixture and stir together until just moistened. Beat 40 strokes, scraping the bottom and the sides of the bowl, until the dough forms a lumpy, sticky mass.

3. **Rise.** Cover the bowl with plastic wrap and let rise at room temperature (72°F/22°C) in a draft-free place for 2 hours or until the dough has risen nearly to the top of the bowl and has a sponge-like appearance.

4. **Use right away or refrigerate.** Use that day or place the dough, covered with plastic wrap, in the refrigerator for up to 3 days before baking.

Baking with Canadian Flour

Canadian flour has a higher protein content than some U.S. flours and therefore absorbs more water. If you are using Canadian bread flour, start by adding about ½ cup (125 mL) less than called for, and add just enough of the remaining ½ cup (125 mL) to make a thick, paste-like dough. To get the best texture from your bread, you want to avoid a dough that is too dry. You don't need to adjust the amount of all-purpose flour.

Black and Tan Dough

Equipment:
- Instant-read thermometer
- 16-cup (4 L) mixing bowl
- Wooden spoon or Danish dough whisk
- 4-cup (1 L) glass measuring cup

Try a flatbread made with this dough and topped with smoked sausage and Havarti cheese.

6 1/2 cups	unbleached all-purpose or bread flour	1.625 L
2 tbsp	instant or bread machine yeast	25 mL
1 1/2 tbsp	fine kosher salt	22 mL
1 cup	pale ale	250 mL
1 cup	dark beer (such as stout or porter)	250 mL
1 cup	hot water	250 mL
1/4 cup	liquid honey	50 mL

1. *Measure.* Spoon the flour into a measuring cup, level with a knife or your finger, then dump the flour into the mixing bowl.

2. *Mix.* Add the yeast and salt to the flour. Stir together with a wooden spoon or Danish dough whisk. In the glass measuring cup, combine pale ale, dark beer, hot water and honey. Pour into the flour mixture and stir together until just moistened. Beat 40 strokes, scraping the bottom and the sides of the bowl, until the dough forms a lumpy, sticky mass.

3. *Rise.* Cover the bowl with plastic wrap and let rise at room temperature (72°F/22°C) in a draft-free place for 2 hours or until the dough has risen nearly to the top of the bowl and has a sponge-like appearance.

4. *Use right away or refrigerate.* Use that day or place the dough, covered with plastic wrap, in the refrigerator for up to 3 days before baking.

Baking with Canadian Flour

Canadian flour has a higher protein content than some U.S. flours and therefore absorbs more water. If you are using Canadian bread flour, start by adding about 1/2 cup (125 mL) less than called for, and add just enough of the remaining 1/2 cup (125 mL) to make a thick, paste-like dough. To get the best texture from your bread, you want to avoid a dough that is too dry. You don't need to adjust the amount of all-purpose flour.

Shaker Buttermilk Dough

Makes enough dough for bread, rolls, pizza or flatbread to serve 12 to 16

Equipment:
- Instant-read thermometer
- 16-cup (4 L) mixing bowl
- Wooden spoon or Danish dough whisk
- 4-cup (1 L) glass measuring cup

Shaker religious communities throughout the eastern United States were known for the quality of their homemade foods, including this dough.

6½ cups	unbleached all-purpose or bread flour	1.625 L
2 tbsp	instant or bread machine yeast	25 mL
1½ tbsp	fine kosher salt	22 mL
2 cups	buttermilk	500 mL
2 cups	hot water	500 mL

1. *Measure.* Spoon the flour into a measuring cup, level with a knife or your finger, then dump the flour into the mixing bowl.

2. *Mix.* Add the yeast and salt to the flour. Stir together with a wooden spoon or Danish dough whisk. In the glass measuring cup, combine buttermilk and hot water. Pour into the flour mixture and stir together until just moistened. Beat 40 strokes, scraping the bottom and the sides of the bowl, until the dough forms a lumpy, sticky mass.

3. *Rise.* Cover the bowl with plastic wrap and let rise at room temperature (72°F/22°C) in a draft-free place for 2 hours or until the dough has risen nearly to the top of the bowl and has a sponge-like appearance.

4. *Use right away or refrigerate.* Use that day or place the dough, covered with plastic wrap, in the refrigerator for up to 3 days before baking.

Baking with Canadian Flour

Canadian flour has a higher protein content than some U.S. flours and therefore absorbs more water. If you are using Canadian bread flour, start by adding about ½ cup (125 mL) less than called for, and add just enough of the remaining ½ cup (125 mL) to make a thick, paste-like dough. To get the best texture from your bread, you want to avoid a dough that is too dry. You don't need to adjust the amount of all-purpose flour.

Sun-Dried Tomato Dough

Makes enough dough for bread, rolls, pizza or flatbread to serve 12 to 16

Equipment:
- Instant-read thermometer
- 16-cup (4 L) mixing bowl
- Wooden spoon or Danish dough whisk
- 4-cup (1 L) glass measuring cup

Adding sun-dried tomatoes to dough is an easy way to get vibrant color and flavor.

Tip

Snip the sun-dried tomatoes into small pieces using kitchen shears.

6½ cups	unbleached all-purpose or bread flour	1.625 L
2 tbsp	instant or bread machine yeast	25 mL
1½ tbsp	fine kosher salt	22 mL
3 cups	hot water	750 mL
½ cup	snipped oil-packed sun-dried tomatoes	125 mL

1. *Measure.* Spoon the flour into a measuring cup, level with a knife or your finger, then dump the flour into the mixing bowl.

2. *Mix.* Add the yeast and salt to the flour. Stir together with a wooden spoon or Danish dough whisk. In the glass measuring cup, combine hot water, tomatoes and their oil. Pour into the flour mixture and stir together until just moistened. Beat 40 strokes, scraping the bottom and the sides of the bowl, until the dough forms a lumpy, sticky mass.

3. *Rise.* Cover the bowl with plastic wrap and let rise at room temperature (72°F/22°C) in a draft-free place for 2 hours or until the dough has risen nearly to the top of the bowl and has a sponge-like appearance.

4. *Use right away or refrigerate.* Use that day or place the dough, covered with plastic wrap, in the refrigerator for up to 3 days before baking.

Baking with Canadian Flour

Canadian flour has a higher protein content than some U.S. flours and therefore absorbs more water. If you are using Canadian bread flour, start by adding about ½ cup (125 mL) less than called for, and add just enough of the remaining ½ cup (125 mL) to make a thick, paste-like dough. To get the best texture from your bread, you want to avoid a dough that is too dry. You don't need to adjust the amount of all-purpose flour.

Hamburger Bun Dough

Makes enough dough for buns to serve 12 to 16

Equipment:
- Instant-read thermometer
- 16-cup (4 L) mixing bowl
- Wooden spoon or Danish dough whisk
- 4-cup (1 L) glass measuring cup

The addition of sugar and milk to the dough makes a soft bun with a good crust.

6½ cups	unbleached all-purpose or bread flour	1.625 L
2 tbsp	instant or bread machine yeast	25 mL
1½ tbsp	fine kosher salt	22 mL
1 cup	granulated sugar	250 mL
1½ cups	2% milk	375 mL
1½ cups	hot water	375 mL

1. *Measure.* Spoon the flour into a measuring cup, level with a knife or your finger, then dump the flour into the mixing bowl.

2. *Mix.* Add the yeast and salt to the flour. Stir together with a wooden spoon or Danish dough whisk. In the glass measuring cup, combine sugar, milk and hot water. Pour into the flour mixture and stir together until just moistened. Beat 40 strokes, scraping the bottom and the sides of the bowl, until the dough forms a lumpy, sticky mass.

3. *Rise.* Cover the bowl with plastic wrap and let rise at room temperature (72°F/22°C) in a draft-free place for 2 hours or until the dough has risen nearly to the top of the bowl and has a sponge-like appearance.

4. *Use right away or refrigerate.* Use that day or place the dough, covered with plastic wrap, in the refrigerator for up to 3 days before baking.

Baking with Canadian Flour
Canadian flour has a higher protein content than some U.S. flours and therefore absorbs more water. If you are using Canadian bread flour, start by adding about ½ cup (125 mL) less than called for, and add just enough of the remaining ½ cup (125 mL) to make a thick, paste-like dough. To get the best texture from your bread, you want to avoid a dough that is too dry. You don't need to adjust the amount of all-purpose flour.

Squash or Pumpkin Dough

Makes enough dough for bread, rolls, pizza or flatbread to serve 12 to 16

Equipment:
- Instant-read thermometer
- 16-cup (4 L) mixing bowl
- Wooden spoon or Danish dough whisk
- 4-cup (1 L) glass measuring cup

Enjoy Thanksgiving leftovers on bread made with this dough.

6½ cups	unbleached all-purpose or bread flour	1.625 L
2 tbsp	instant or bread machine yeast	25 mL
1½ tbsp	fine kosher salt	22 mL
2 cups	puréed cooked squash or pumpkin	500 mL
2 cups	hot water	500 mL
¼ cup	liquid honey	50 mL
1 tbsp	pumpkin pie spice	15 mL

1. *Measure.* Spoon the flour into a measuring cup, level with a knife or your finger, then dump the flour into the mixing bowl.

2. *Mix.* Add the yeast and salt to the flour. Stir together with a wooden spoon or Danish dough whisk. In the glass measuring cup, combine squash, hot water, honey and pumpkin pie spice. Pour into the flour mixture and stir together until just moistened. Beat 40 strokes, scraping the bottom and the sides of the bowl, until the dough forms a lumpy, sticky mass.

3. *Rise.* Cover the bowl with plastic wrap and let rise at room temperature (72°F/22°C) in a draft-free place for 2 hours or until the dough has risen nearly to the top of the bowl and has a sponge-like appearance.

4. *Use right away or refrigerate.* Use that day or place the dough, covered with plastic wrap, in the refrigerator for up to 3 days before baking.

Baking with Canadian Flour

Canadian flour has a higher protein content than some U.S. flours and therefore absorbs more water. If you are using Canadian bread flour, start by adding about ½ cup (125 mL) less than called for, and add just enough of the remaining ½ cup (125 mL) to make a thick, paste-like dough. To get the best texture from your bread, you want to avoid a dough that is too dry. You don't need to adjust the amount of all-purpose flour.

Honey Spice Applesauce Dough

Makes enough dough for bread, rolls, pizza or flatbread to serve 12 to 16

Equipment:
- Instant-read thermometer
- 16-cup (4 L) mixing bowl
- Wooden spoon or Danish dough whisk
- 4-cup (1 L) glass measuring cup

Honey Spice Applesauce helps make a moist and flavorful dough.

6½ cups	unbleached all-purpose or bread flour	1.625 L
2 tbsp	instant or bread machine yeast	25 mL
1½ tbsp	fine kosher salt	22 mL
2 cups	Honey Spice Applesauce (page 296)	500 mL
2 cups	hot unsweetened apple cider	500 mL

1. *Measure.* Spoon the flour into a measuring cup, level with a knife or your finger, then dump the flour into the mixing bowl.

2. *Mix.* Add the yeast and salt to the flour. Stir together with a wooden spoon or Danish dough whisk. In the glass measuring cup, combine applesauce and apple cider. Pour into the flour mixture and stir together until just moistened. Beat 40 strokes, scraping the bottom and the sides of the bowl, until the dough forms a lumpy, sticky mass.

3. *Rise.* Cover the bowl with plastic wrap and let rise at room temperature (72°F/22°C) in a draft-free place for 2 hours or until the dough has risen nearly to the top of the bowl and has a sponge-like appearance.

4. *Use right away or refrigerate.* Use that day or place the dough, covered with plastic wrap, in the refrigerator for up to 3 days before baking.

Baking with Canadian Flour

Canadian flour has a higher protein content than some U.S. flours and therefore absorbs more water. If you are using Canadian bread flour, start by adding about ½ cup (125 mL) less than called for, and add just enough of the remaining ½ cup (125 mL) to make a thick, paste-like dough. To get the best texture from your bread, you want to avoid a dough that is too dry. You don't need to adjust the amount of all-purpose flour.

Shaker Buttermilk Bread

Makes 2 loaves, to serve 16

Equipment:
- Two 9- by 5-inch (23 by 12.5 cm) loaf pans, greased
- Broiler pan
- Baking stone
- Instant-read thermometer

A celibate religious sect known for their medicinal herbs, clean-lined architecture and furniture, and the fine table their North American communities kept, the Shakers believed that eating bread hot out of the oven stirred up passions that were best left unstirred. I have to confess, however, that I can't resist the toasty aroma and moist crumb of this bread, still warm and slathered with Artisan Butter (page 295).

½	recipe prepared Shaker Buttermilk Dough (page 124), about the size of a volleyball	½
	Unbleached all-purpose or bread flour	
2 cups	hot water	500 mL

1. *Form.* Divide the dough in half. Transfer one half to a floured surface and dust very lightly with flour. Flour your hands. Working the dough as little as possible and adding flour as necessary, form the dough into an 8-inch (20 cm) cylinder. Smooth the dough with your hands to form a soft, non-sticky skin. Pinch any seams together. Lightly flour any sticky places on the dough. The dough should feel soft and smooth all over, like a baby's skin, but not at all sticky. Repeat with the remaining dough.

2. *Rest.* Place each cylinder in a prepared loaf pan. Cover with tea towels and let rest at room temperature for 40 minutes.

3. *Prepare oven for artisan baking.* About 30 minutes before baking, place the broiler pan on the lower shelf and the baking stone on the middle shelf of the oven. Preheat to 425°F (220°C).

4. *Place loaf pans onto baking stone and add water to broiler pan.* Using an oven mitt, carefully pull the middle rack of the oven out several inches. Place the loaf pans at least 3 inches (7.5 cm) apart on the hot stone. Push the middle rack back in place. Pull the lower rack out, pour the hot water into the broiler pan and push the lower rack back in place. Close the oven door immediately so the steam will envelop the oven.

5. *Bake.* Bake for 27 to 30 minutes or until the crust is a medium dark brown and an instant-read thermometer inserted in the center of the loaf registers at least 190°F (90°C). Remove from pans and transfer to a wire rack to cool.

Change It Up

Shaker Buttermilk Herb Bread: Stir 2 tbsp (25 mL) dried herbs, such as rosemary, fennel or dillweed, into the dry ingredients when first making the dough.

Honey Spice Applesauce Bread: Substitute Honey Spice Applesauce Dough (page 128).

Brewhouse Baguettes

Equipment:
- Three-sided cookie sheet, flexible cutting board or baker's peel
- Broiler pan
- Baking stone

These crusty baguettes have tons of flavor from the beer or ale used in place of some of the water in the dough. A touch of honey makes up for the slight bitterness of the brew. These are delicious with hearty soups, aged cheeses, a savory soufflé or beef stew.

$1/2$	recipe prepared Brewhouse Dough (page 122), about the size of a volleyball	$1/2$
	Unbleached all-purpose or bread flour	
$1/2$ cup	cornmeal	125 mL
2 cups	hot water	500 mL

1. *Form.* Divide the dough in half. Transfer one half to a floured surface and dust very lightly with flour. Flour your hands. Working the dough as little as possible and adding flour as necessary, form the dough into a 14-inch (35 cm) cylinder. Smooth the dough with your hands to form a soft, non-sticky skin. Pinch any seams together. Pinch each end into a point. Lightly flour any sticky places on the dough. The dough should feel soft and smooth all over, like a baby's skin, but not at all sticky. Repeat with the remaining dough.

2. *Rest.* Sprinkle the cornmeal on the cookie sheet and place baguettes about 6 inches (15 cm) apart on the cornmeal. Cover with tea towels and let rest at room temperature for 40 minutes.

3. *Prepare oven for artisan baking.* About 30 minutes before baking, place the broiler pan on the lower shelf and the baking stone on the middle shelf of the oven. Preheat to 450°F (230°C).

4. *Slash baguettes with serrated knife.* Using a serrated knife, make three evenly spaced diagonal slashes, about $1/2$ inch (1 cm) deep, across each baguette, exposing the moist dough under the surface.

You Can Also Use

Easy Artisan Whole-Grain Dough (page 56) or any of its variations. Make the slashes 1 inch (2.5 cm) deep.

5. *Slide baguettes onto baking stone and add water to broiler pan.* Using an oven mitt, carefully pull the middle rack of the oven out several inches. Hold the cookie sheet level with the rack so that the first baguette will slide sideways onto the hot stone. With a quick forward jerk of your arms, slide the first baguette from the cookie sheet to the back of the stone. With another jerk, slide the second baguette onto the front of the stone. Push the middle rack back in place. Pull the lower rack out, pour the hot water into the broiler pan and push the lower rack back in place. Close the oven door immediately so the steam will envelop the oven.

6. *Bake.* Bake for 25 minutes or until the crust is a medium dark brown and an instant-read thermometer inserted in the center of the baguettes registers at least 190°F (90°C). Wearing oven mitts, remove baguettes by hand to cool on a wire rack.

Black and Tan Boule

Makes 1 large round loaf, or boule, to serve 8

Equipment:
- Three-sided cookie sheet, flexible cutting board or baker's peel
- Broiler pan
- Baking stone
- Plastic spray bottle of water

This boule has a dark and mysteriously yeasty flavor from the combination of pale ale and stout or porter. It makes a fabulous ham or grilled cheese sandwich, but it's also delicious with Brie and cave-aged Gruyère.

Tip
Spraying the boule with water during baking helps create a blistered crust.

½	recipe prepared Black and Tan Dough (page 123), about the size of a volleyball	½
	Unbleached all-purpose or bread flour	
½ cup	cornmeal	125 mL
2 cups	hot water	500 mL

1. *Form.* Place dough on a floured surface and dust very lightly with flour. Flour your hands. Working the dough as little as possible and adding flour as necessary, form the dough into a 10-inch (25 cm) round. Smooth the dough with your hands to form a soft, non-sticky skin. Pinch any seams together. Lightly flour any sticky places on the dough. The dough should feel soft and smooth all over, like a baby's skin, but not at all sticky.

2. *Rest.* Sprinkle the cornmeal on the cookie sheet and place the dough round on the cornmeal. Cover with a tea towel and let rest at room temperature for 40 minutes.

3. *Prepare oven for artisan baking.* About 30 minutes before baking, place the broiler pan on the lower shelf and the baking stone on the middle shelf of the oven. Preheat to 450°F (230°C).

4. *Slash boule with serrated knife.* Using a serrated knife, make three evenly spaced slashes, about ½ inch (1 cm) deep, across the boule, exposing the moist dough under the surface.

5. *Slide boule onto baking stone and add water to broiler pan.* Using an oven mitt, carefully pull the middle rack of the oven out several inches. Hold the cutting board level with the rack so that the dough round will slide onto the center of the hot stone. With a quick forward jerk of your arms, slide the dough round from the cookie sheet to the stone. Push the middle rack back in place. Pull the lower rack out, pour the hot water into the broiler pan and push the lower rack back in place. Spray the boule with water. Close the oven door immediately so the steam will envelop the oven.

Tip

When you are proficient at sliding the dough onto the baking stone, you can bake two boules at one time, if it's big enough to allow enough space between them. Place the boules on the prepared cookie sheet so that they are parallel to each other and about 4 inches (10 cm) apart. Then hold the cookie sheet level with the rack so that the boules will slide onto the hot baking stone. With a quick forward jerk of your arms, slide the boules from the cookie sheet to each side of the stone.

You Can Also Use

Easy Artisan Flavored Dough (page 120) or any of its variations.

6. *Bake.* Bake for 15 minutes, then quickly open the oven door and spray the loaf with water again. Continue baking for 12 to 15 minutes or until the crust is a medium dark brown and an instant-read thermometer inserted in the center of the loaf registers at least 190°F (90°C). Wearing oven mitts, remove the loaf by hand to cool on a wire rack.

Change It Up

Instead of making slashes on the boule, try something more decorative. At the famous Poilâne, one of the best-loved artisan bakeries in Paris, boules are marked with a "P" in a simple but flowing script. Using a serrated knife, make a script initial on the top of your boule, then bake.

Buttermilk Chive Rolls

Makes 8 rolls

Equipment:
- Rolling pin
- 2 large baking sheets, lined with parchment paper
- Broiler pan
- Baking stone

These savory artisan rolls are delicious with soups and stews, prime rib and roast chicken. They're also fabulous as a base for artisan sandwiches. Slice in half and slather with your favorite aïoli, then top with grilled chicken or a juicy burger.

½	recipe prepared Shaker Buttermilk Dough (page 124), about the size of a volleyball	½
2 tbsp	dried chives	25 mL
	Unbleached all-purpose or bread flour	
1	egg, beaten with 1 tbsp (15 mL) water	1
2 cups	hot water	500 mL

1. *Form and fill.* Place dough on a floured surface and dust very lightly with flour. Flour your hands and the rolling pin. Working the dough as little as possible and adding flour as necessary, roll out the dough into a 16- by 10-inch (40 by 25 cm) rectangle. Sprinkle with chives. Starting with a long end, roll up the dough into a cylinder. If the dough begins to stick to the surface, use a dough scraper to push flour under the dough and scrape it up. Gently press and squeeze as you're rolling, to form the dough into a solid cylinder. With a pastry brush, brush off any excess flour. With the dough scraper, slice the cylinder into eight 2-inch (5 cm) pieces. Pinch the cut sides closed and coax each piece into a 4-inch (10 cm) round. Pinch any seams together.

2. *Rest.* Place the rolls about 2 inches (5 cm) apart on the prepared baking sheets. Cover with tea towels and let rest at room temperature for 40 minutes.

3. *Prepare oven for artisan baking.* About 30 minutes before baking, place the broiler pan on the lower shelf and the baking stone on the middle shelf of the oven. Preheat to 450°F (230°C).

4. *Slash rolls with serrated knife.* Using a serrated knife, make two cross-hatch slashes, about ½ inch (1 cm) deep, in the top center of each roll, exposing the moist dough under the surface. Brush the top of each roll with egg wash.

Master Recipes #1 through
#5 and all their variations.
If you use a whole-grain
dough, make the slashes
1 inch (2.5 cm) deep.

5. *Place a baking sheet on baking stone and add water to broiler pan.* Using an oven mitt, carefully pull the middle rack of the oven out several inches. Place one of the baking sheets on the hot stone. Push the middle rack back in place. Pull the lower rack out, pour the hot water into the broiler pan and push the lower rack back in place. Close the oven door immediately so the steam will envelop the oven.

6. *Bake.* Bake for 15 to 17 minutes or until the rolls are risen and very lightly browned and an instant-read thermometer inserted in the center of a roll registers at least 190°F (90°C). Remove from pan and transfer to a wire rack to cool. Repeat the baking process with the remaining rolls.

Mini Hamburger Buns

Makes 32 miniature buns

Equipment:
- 2 large baking sheets, lined with parchment paper
- Broiler pan
- Baking stone

A little milk and sugar in the dough contribute to a brown crust and a soft crumb, perfect for a juicy lamb, beef or meatball "slider." But why stop there? What about a gourmet sausage, grilled chicken or toasted cheese sandwich? These miniature buns make great cocktail fare — perhaps a Kobe beef burger topped with Easy Caramelized Onions (page 304).

1	recipe prepared Hamburger Bun Dough (page 126)	1
	Unbleached all-purpose or bread flour	
1	egg, beaten with 1 tbsp (15 mL) water	1
2 cups	hot water	500 mL

1. **Form.** Divide the dough in half. Transfer one half to a floured surface and dust very lightly with flour. Flour your hands. Working the dough as little as possible and adding flour as necessary, form the dough into a 16-inch (40 cm) cylinder. With the dough scraper, slice the cylinder into eight 2-inch (5 cm) pieces. Cut each piece in half. Pinch the cut sides closed and coax each piece into a 2-inch (5 cm) round. Pinch any seams together. Repeat with the remaining dough.

2. **Rest.** Place the buns about 1 inch (2.5 cm) apart on the prepared baking sheets. Cover with tea towels and let rest at room temperature for 40 minutes.

3. **Prepare oven for artisan baking.** About 30 minutes before baking, place the broiler pan on the lower shelf and the baking stone on the middle shelf of the oven. Preheat to 400°F (200°C).

4. **Brush with egg wash.** Brush the top of each bun with egg wash.

5. **Place a baking sheet on baking stone and add water to broiler pan.** Using an oven mitt, carefully pull the middle rack of the oven out several inches. Place one of the baking sheets on the hot stone. Push the middle rack back in place. Pull the lower rack out, pour the hot water into the broiler pan and push the lower rack back in place. Close the oven door immediately so the steam will envelop the oven.

Tips

These rolls are baked at a slightly lower temperature so the tops stay smooth.

Make the whole batch of rolls, then freeze for up to 3 months in plastic freezer bags.

You Can Also Use

Master Recipes #1 through #5 and all their variations.

6. *Bake.* Bake for 15 to 17 minutes or until the buns are domed and lightly browned and an instant-read thermometer inserted in the center of a bun registers at least 190°F (90°C). Remove from pan and transfer to a wire rack to cool. Repeat the baking with the remaining buns.

Change It Up

Large Hamburger Buns: Slice each cylinder into eight 2-inch (5 cm) pieces and coax each piece into a 4-inch (10 cm) round. Proceed with the recipe. They take the same time to bake, 15 to 17 minutes at 400°F (200°C).

Orange and Fennel Fougasse

Equipment:
- Instant-read thermometer
- 16-cup (4 L) mixing bowl
- Wooden spoon or Danish dough whisk
- Rolling pin
- Large baking sheet, lined with parchment paper
- Baking stone
- Broiler pan

In Provence, fougasse is usually a savory flatbread. But it can also be sweet, often flavored with fresh orange zest, orange flower water and fennel. This slightly sweet fougasse is usually baked for Les Treize Desserts (the Thirteen Desserts), part of the Christmas Eve feast. But why not make these, one at a time, as a fabulous hostess or holiday gift from your kitchen?

Tip

Orange flower water, which gives a very slightly perfumed quality to the bread, is available at gourmet and baking shops and online.

6½ cups	unbleached all-purpose or bread flour	1.625 L
1½ tbsp	instant or bread machine yeast	22 mL
1½ tbsp	fine kosher salt	22 mL
½ cup	granulated sugar	125 mL
¼ cup	fennel seeds	50 mL
1 tbsp	grated orange zest	15 mL
1 tbsp	orange flower water (optional)	15 mL
3 cups	lukewarm water (about 100°F/38°C)	750 mL
2 tbsp	olive oil	25 mL
2 cups	hot water	500 mL

1. *Measure.* Spoon the flour into a measuring cup, level with a knife or your finger, then dump the flour into the mixing bowl.

2. *Mix.* Add the yeast and salt to the flour. Add the sugar and fennel seeds. Stir together with a wooden spoon or Danish dough whisk. Add the orange zest and orange flower water to the lukewarm water and stir to combine. Pour into the flour mixture and stir together just until moistened. Beat 40 strokes, scraping the bottom and the sides of the bowl, until the dough forms a lumpy, sticky mass.

3. *Rise.* Cover the bowl with plastic wrap and let rise at room temperature (72°F/22°C) in a draft-free place for 2 hours or until the dough has risen nearly to the top of the bowl and has a sponge-like appearance.

4. *Use right away or refrigerate.* Use that day or place the dough, covered with plastic wrap, in the refrigerator for up to 3 days before baking.

5. *Form.* For each flatbread, remove one-quarter of the dough (about the size of a softball) with a serrated knife and a dough scraper. Transfer the dough to a floured surface and dust very lightly with flour. Flour your hands and the rolling pin. Working the dough as little as possible and adding flour as necessary, roll out the dough into a 12- by 6-inch (30 by 15 cm) oval. Lightly flour any sticky places on the dough. The dough should feel soft and smooth all over, like a baby's skin, but not at all sticky.

6. *Cut.* Using a pizza wheel or a sharp knife, cut two rows of four diagonal slashes evenly spaced along the length of the oval, about 2 to 3 inches (5 to 7.5 cm) long, that almost meet in the middle of the dough, like this: / \. Transfer the dough to the prepared baking sheet and pull the top and sides of the dough to stretch it into a larger oval with opened slits. Brush the surface of the dough with the olive oil.

7. *Prepare oven for artisan baking.* About 30 minutes before baking, place the broiler pan on the lower shelf and the baking stone on the middle shelf of the oven. Preheat to 450°F (230°C).

8. *Place baking sheet on baking stone and add water to broiler pan.* Using an oven mitt, carefully pull the middle rack of the oven out several inches. Place the baking sheet on the hot stone. Push the middle rack back in place. Pull the lower rack out, pour the hot water into the broiler pan and push the lower rack back in place. Close the oven door immediately so the steam will envelop the oven.

9. *Bake.* Bake for 17 to 20 minutes or until the crust is medium brown. Transfer to a wire rack to cool.

Chocolate Swirl Bread

Makes 2 loaves, each to serve 8

Equipment:
- Instant-read thermometer
- 16-cup (4 L) mixing bowl
- Wooden spoon or Danish dough whisk
- Rolling pin
- Flexible cutting board, floured, or two metal spatulas
- Large baking sheet, lined with parchment paper
- Baking stone
- Broiler pan

This version of Easy Artisan Flavored Dough has too many tweaks for a simple variation, but it mixes the same way as the master recipe. The chocolate chips melt and add depth of flavor to this delicious bread. Try the Chocolate Pull-Aparts with Coconut Cream Cheese Filling (variation, opposite) if you're feeling even the tiniest bit glum — they will cheer you right up.

6½ cups	unbleached all-purpose or bread flour	1.625 L
2 tbsp	instant or bread machine yeast	25 mL
1 tbsp	fine kosher salt	15 mL
½ cup	granulated sugar	125 mL
¼ cup	unsweetened cocoa powder	50 mL
1 cup	mini semisweet chocolate chips	250 mL
3 tbsp	vegetable oil	45 mL
4 cups	lukewarm water (about 100°F/38°C)	1 L
1	recipe Sweet Cream Cheese Filling (page 300)	1
2 cups	hot water	500 mL
	Easy Artisan Glaze (page 302)	

1. *Measure.* Spoon the flour into a measuring cup, level with a knife or your finger, then dump the flour into the mixing bowl.

2. *Mix.* Add the yeast and salt to the flour. Add the sugar and cocoa. Stir together with a wooden spoon or Danish dough whisk. Stir in the chocolate chips. Add the oil to the lukewarm water and stir to combine. Pour into the flour mixture and stir together just until moistened. Beat 40 strokes, scraping the bottom and the sides of the bowl, until the dough forms a lumpy, sticky mass.

3. *Rise.* Cover the bowl with plastic wrap and let rise at room temperature (72°F/22°C) in a draft-free place for 2 hours or until the dough has risen nearly to the top of the bowl and has a sponge-like appearance.

4. *Use right away or refrigerate.* Use that day or place the dough, covered with plastic wrap, in the refrigerator for up to 3 days before baking.

5. *Form.* For each loaf, remove half the dough (about the size of a volleyball) with a serrated knife and a dough scraper. Transfer the dough to a floured surface and dust very lightly with flour. Flour your hands and the rolling pin. Working the dough as little as possible and adding flour as necessary, roll out the dough into a 12- by 8-inch (30 by 20 cm) rectangle. Spread half the cream cheese filling over the dough, leaving a 1-inch (2.5 cm) perimeter. Starting with a long end, roll up the dough

Tip

Try making decadent French toast with leftovers of this bread.

Baking with Canadian Flour

Canadian flour has a higher protein content than some U.S. flours and therefore absorbs more water. If you are using Canadian bread flour, start by adding about $\frac{1}{2}$ cup (125 mL) less than called for, and add just enough of the remaining $\frac{1}{2}$ cup (125 mL) to make a thick, paste-like dough. To get the best texture from your bread, you want to avoid a dough that is too dry. You don't need to adjust the amount of all-purpose flour.

into a cylinder. If the dough begins to stick to the surface, use a dough scraper to push flour under the dough and scrape it up. Gently press and squeeze as you're rolling, to form the dough into a solid cylinder. Pinch the ends and long seam closed. Lightly flour any sticky places on the dough. The dough should feel soft and smooth all over, like a baby's skin, but not at all sticky.

6. *Rest.* Using the cutting board or two metal spatulas, transfer the loaf to the prepared baking sheet, seam side down. Cover with a tea towel and let rest at room temperature for 40 minutes.

7. *Prepare oven for artisan baking.* About 30 minutes before baking, place the broiler pan on the lower shelf and the baking stone on the middle shelf of the oven. Preheat to 400°F (200°C).

8. *Place baking sheet on baking stone and add water to broiler pan.* Using an oven mitt, carefully pull the middle rack of the oven out several inches. Place the baking sheet on the hot stone. Push the middle rack back in place. Pull the lower rack out, pour the hot water into the broiler pan and push the lower rack back in place. Close the oven door immediately so the steam will envelop the oven.

9. *Bake.* Bake for 27 to 30 minutes or until the crust is dark brown and an instant-read thermometer inserted in the center of the loaf registers at least 190°F (90°C). Remove from pan and transfer to a rack placed over a baking sheet to cool. Once cool, drizzle or brush with half the glaze.

Change It Up

Chocolate Pull-Aparts with Coconut Cream Cheese Filling: Substitute Coconut Cream Cheese Filling (variation, page 300). Cut the cylinder into 1-inch (2.5 cm) slices. Place the slices, cut side up, in a buttered 8-inch (20 cm) round cake pan so that they are almost touching. Bake for 30 to 34 minutes or until risen and browned and an instant-read thermometer inserted in the center of the rolls registers at least 190°F (90°C). Transfer to a wire rack to cool in pan. Once cool, drizzle with glaze.

Sun-Dried Tomato and Pesto Batard

Equipment:
- Rolling pin
- Baking sheet, lined with parchment paper
- Broiler pan
- Baking stone

The flavor is in the bread, so all you need is good-quality extra virgin olive oil for dipping.

¹⁄₂	recipe prepared Sun-Dried Tomato Dough (page 125), about the size of a volleyball	¹⁄₂
	Unbleached all-purpose or bread flour	
¹⁄₂ cup	prepared basil pesto	125 mL
2 cups	hot water	500 mL

1. *Form and fill.* Place dough on a floured surface and dust very lightly with flour. Flour your hands and the rolling pin. Working the dough as little as possible and adding flour as necessary, roll out the dough into a 16- by 10-inch (40 by 25 cm) rectangle. Spread pesto over the dough, leaving a ¹⁄₂-inch (1 cm) perimeter. Starting with a long end, roll up the dough into a cylinder. If the dough begins to stick to the surface, use a dough scraper to push flour under the dough and scrape it up. Gently press and squeeze as you're rolling, to form the dough into a solid cylinder. Pinch the ends and long seam closed. Lightly flour any sticky places on the dough. The dough should feel soft and smooth all over, like a baby's skin, but not at all sticky.

2. *Rest.* Place the batard on the prepared baking sheet, seam side down. Cover with a tea towel and let rest at room temperature for 40 minutes.

3. *Prepare oven for artisan baking.* About 30 minutes before baking, place the broiler pan on the lower shelf and the baking stone on the middle shelf of the oven. Preheat to 450°F (230°C).

4. *Slash batard with serrated knife.* Using a serrated knife, make five evenly spaced diagonal slashes, about ¹⁄₂ inch (1 cm) deep, across the batard, exposing the moist dough under the surface.

Cut leftover bread into cubes, then toast on a baking sheet in the oven to make croutons. They're delicious on vegetable soups and in salads. Store the croutons in a sealable plastic bag for up to 1 week.

5. *Place baking sheet on baking stone and add water to broiler pan.* Using an oven mitt, carefully pull the middle rack of the oven out several inches. Place the baking sheet on the hot stone. Push the middle rack back in place. Pull the lower rack out, pour the hot water into the broiler pan and push the lower rack back in place. Close the oven door immediately so the steam will envelop the oven.

6. *Bake.* Bake for 25 to 27 minutes or until the crust is dark brown and an instant-read thermometer inserted in the center of the loaf registers at least 190°F (90°C). Remove from pan and transfer to a wire rack to cool.

Change It Up

Semolina Pesto Bread: Substitute Easy Artisan Whole-Grain Dough (page 56), made with semolina. Make the slashes 1 inch (2.5 cm) deep.

Easy Artisan Pesto Bread: Substitute Easy Artisan Dough (page 34).

Sun-Dried Tomato and Feta Flatbread

Equipment:
- Rolling pin
- Large baking sheet, lined with parchment paper
- Broiler pan
- Baking stone
- ¼ cup (50 mL) fine dry hardwood chips, such as mesquite or apple, moistened with 2 tbsp (25 mL) water (optional)

This golden, puffy flatbread makes a great appetizer or tapas selection, and works well with any casual meal. For even more flavor, and to simulate a Tuscan wood-burning oven, smolder fine wood chips next to the broiler pan as this bakes — a "kiss of smoke" technique often used by barbecuers.

½	recipe prepared Sun-Dried Tomato Dough (page 125), about the size of a volleyball	½
	Unbleached all-purpose or bread flour	
1 cup	prepared basil pesto	250 mL
8 oz	feta cheese, crumbled	250 g
½ cup	chopped fresh flat-leaf (Italian) parsley	125 mL
	Olive oil	
2 cups	hot water	500 mL

1. **Form.** Place dough on a floured surface and dust very lightly with flour. Flour your hands and the rolling pin. Working the dough as little as possible and adding flour as necessary, roll out the dough into a 12- by 10-inch (30 by 25 cm) rectangle. Lightly flour any sticky places on the dough. The dough should feel soft and smooth all over, like a baby's skin, but not at all sticky.

2. **Top.** Transfer the dough to the prepared baking sheet. Spread pesto over the dough. Sprinkle feta and parsley over the pesto, leaving a 1-inch (2.5 cm) perimeter.

3. **Rest.** Cover with a tea towel and let rest at room temperature for 40 minutes.

4. **Prepare oven for artisan baking.** About 30 minutes before baking, place the broiler pan on the lower shelf and the baking stone on the middle shelf of the oven. Preheat to 450°F (230°C). For the wood-burning oven technique, place the moistened wood chips in a small metal pan next to the broiler pan on the lower shelf. They will start to smolder and release wisps of smoke.

You Can Also Use

Easy Artisan Dough (page 34), Easy Artisan Whole-Grain Dough (page 56), made with white whole wheat flour, Easy Artisan Slow-Rise Dough (page 148) or Easy Artisan Naturally Leavened Dough (page 230).

5. *Drizzle with oil.* Drizzle the flatbread with olive oil.

6. *Place baking sheet on baking stone and add water to broiler pan.* Using an oven mitt, carefully pull the middle rack of the oven out several inches. Place the baking sheet on the hot stone. Push the middle rack back in place. Pull the lower rack out, pour the hot water into the broiler pan and push the lower rack back in place. Close the oven door immediately so the steam will envelop the oven.

7. *Bake.* Bake for 20 to 22 minutes or until the crust is puffed and golden brown. Remove from pan and transfer to a wire rack to cool. Remove the smoldering wood chips from the oven, let cool completely, then discard.

Slow-Rise Breads

Master Recipe #5
Easy Artisan Slow-Rise Dough

Decreasing the amount of yeast and allowing for a longer rising time turns Easy Artisan Dough into a slow-rise dough — and teaches the artisan baker a valuable lesson in patience. Good things come to those who wait. With less yeast and a longer rise, you get a bread with a more developed flavor and the bigger holes of a honeycomb crumb. You also end up with a golden brown, somewhat blistered crust (a hallmark of slow-rise artisan bread). Spraying the loaves with water before and during baking helps promote that blistered crust effect.

This master recipe, which calls for filtered or bottled spring water in the dough, gets you ready for making and baking naturally leavened doughs in Part 3: Master Baking. You'll want to use filtered or spring water because it's more pure than tap water, and this helps the bread rise better. Because of the long, slow rise, the gluten in the flour has more time to make a fibrous network, so the dough will seem moist, yet stringy. And as you work the dough and form the loaves, you'll see and feel air bubbles, part of what will make the honeycomb crumb in the finished bread. This sticky dough is not as easy to divide into small portions, so all the recipes will use half the dough, for larger loaves and flatbreads.

Makes enough dough for bread, rolls or flatbreads to serve 12 to 16

Equipment:
- 16-cup (4 L) mixing bowl
- Wooden spoon or Danish dough whisk

Now that we're in the intermediate phase of artisan bread, we'll switch to a baker's peel (of course, you can still use a three-sided cookie sheet, flexible cutting board or whatever you have).

4½ cups	unbleached bread flour	1.125 L
1 cup	whole-grain flour (see page 57)	250 mL
1½ tbsp	fine kosher salt	22 mL
1	recipe prepared Biga (page 150)	1
3 cups	filtered or bottled spring water, at room temperature	750 mL

1. **Measure.** Spoon the flour into a measuring cup, level with a knife or your finger, then dump the flour into the mixing bowl, combining unbleached and whole-grain flours well.

2. **Mix.** Add the salt to the flour. Stir together with a wooden spoon or Danish dough whisk. Add the biga and water and stir together until just moistened. Beat 40 strokes, scraping the bottom and the sides of the bowl, until the dough forms a thick, spongy mass.

3. **Ferment.** Cover the bowl with plastic wrap and let ferment at room temperature (72°F/22°C) in a draft-free place for 12 to 18 hours or until it almost reaches the top of the bowl.

4. **Use right away or refrigerate.** Use right away or place the bowl, covered with plastic wrap, in the refrigerator for up to 3 days before baking.

You Can Also Use
Easy Artisan Naturally Leavened Starter (page 228) in place of the biga.

Baking with Canadian Flour

Canadian flour has a higher protein content than some U.S. flours and therefore absorbs more water. If you are using Canadian bread flour, start by adding about $1/2$ cup (125 mL) less than called for, and add just enough of the remaining $1/2$ cup (125 mL) to make a thick, paste-like dough. To get the best texture from your bread, you want to avoid a dough that is too dry. You don't need to adjust the amount of whole-grain flour.

Easy Artisan Slow-Rise Breads in Minutes a Day

Day 1	Make the biga. Let ferment.
Day 2	Wrap and chill biga or make into a dough.
Days 2–4	Form and rest dough, bake bread.

Biga

Biga is the Italian name for a pre-ferment, starter or sponge used to make slow-rise breads. You'll mix a tiny amount of yeast with flour and water, then set it aside to ferment at room temperature. After it has fermented, you will add prepared biga to other dough ingredients to make slow-rise bread. Bigas can be thicker or more moist. This one falls in the moister category, so it works with our Easy Artisan Master Dough recipes.

Mix up the biga and let it ferment at room temperature for 6 to 24 hours before making the dough. Biga is an active culture, and it's easy to tell when it's good and when it's not. When it domes in the bowl and you can see bubbles rising and breaking on the surface, it's ready to use. After the biga has domed, cover it and keep it in the refrigerator for up to 3 days before baking. When the biga deflates, its rising power has gone.

Makes about 2 cups (500 mL)

Equipment:
- 6-cup (1.5 L) bowl
- Wooden spoon or Danish dough whisk

3½ cups	unbleached all-purpose flour	875 mL
¼ tsp	instant or bread machine yeast	1 mL
1 cup	filtered or bottled spring water, at room temperature	250 mL

1. **Measure.** Spoon the flour into a measuring cup, level with a knife or your finger, then dump the flour into a mixing bowl.

2. **Mix.** Add the yeast to the flour. Stir together with a wooden spoon or Danish dough whisk. Pour in the water and stir together until just moistened. Beat 40 strokes, scraping the bottom and the sides of the bowl, until the dough forms a lumpy, sticky mass.

3. **Rise.** Cover the bowl with plastic wrap and let rise at room temperature (72°F/22°C) in a draft-free place for 6 to 24 hours. At first, the biga will look lumpy and shaggy. After several hours, it will look creamy and frothy, with small bubbles that form and rise to the surface. Eventually, it will have a smooth, domed skin, with large, wide bubbles that rise lazily to the surface.

4. **Use right away or refrigerate.** Use right away or place the bowl, covered with plastic wrap, in the refrigerator for up to 3 days before baking. If it stays domed, it's ready to go. If it's deflated, it's lost its power, so discard it.

Slow-Rise Herbed Polenta Dough

Makes enough dough for bread, rolls or flatbreads to serve 12 to 16

Equipment:
- 16-cup (4 L) mixing bowl
- Wooden spoon or Danish dough whisk

Use this pale yellow dough for Tuscan-style breads.

Tip

Because cornmeal doesn't absorb water like other flours, the dough will be very moist.

4½ cups	unbleached bread flour	1.125 L
1 cup	cornmeal	250 mL
1½ tbsp	fine kosher salt	22 mL
1 tbsp	dried rosemary	15 mL
1 tbsp	dried basil	15 mL
1	recipe prepared Biga (page 150)	1
3 cups	filtered or bottled spring water, at room temperature	750 mL

1. *Measure.* One at a time, spoon the flour and cornmeal into a measuring cup, level with a knife or your finger, then dump into the mixing bowl. Combine well.

2. *Mix.* Add the salt, rosemary and basil to the flour mixture. Stir together with a wooden spoon or Danish dough whisk. Add the biga and water and stir together until just moistened. Beat 40 strokes, scraping the bottom and the sides of the bowl, until the dough forms a thick, spongy mass.

3. *Ferment.* Cover the bowl with plastic wrap and let ferment at room temperature (72°F/22°C) in a draft-free place for 12 to 18 hours or until it almost reaches the top of the bowl.

4. *Use right away or refrigerate.* Use right away or place the bowl, covered with plastic wrap, in the refrigerator for up to 3 days before baking.

Baking with Canadian Flour

Canadian flour has a higher protein content than some U.S. flours and therefore absorbs more water. If you are using Canadian bread flour, start by adding about ½ cup (125 mL) less than called for, and add just enough of the remaining ½ cup (125 mL) to make a thick, paste-like dough. To get the best texture from your bread, you want to avoid a dough that is too dry.

Slow-Rise Sour Graham Dough

Equipment:
- 16-cup (4 L) mixing bowl
- Wooden spoon or Danish dough whisk

Tip
Graham flour is available in the specialty baking aisle.

4½ cups	unbleached bread flour	1.125 L
1 cup	graham flour (coarsely ground whole wheat)	250 mL
1½ tbsp	fine kosher salt	22 mL
½ cup	non-fat plain yogurt	125 mL
3 cups	filtered or bottled spring water, at room temperature	750 mL
1	recipe prepared Biga (page 150)	1

1. *Measure.* One at a time, spoon the bread flour and graham flour into a measuring cup, level with a knife or your finger, then dump into the mixing bowl. Combine well.

2. *Mix.* Add the salt to the flours. Stir together with a wooden spoon or Danish dough whisk. Stir yogurt into the water. Pour into the flour mixture, add the biga and stir together until just moistened. Beat 40 strokes, scraping the bottom and the sides of the bowl, until the dough forms a thick, spongy mass.

3. *Ferment.* Cover the bowl with plastic wrap and let ferment at room temperature (72°F/22°C) in a draft-free place for 12 to 18 hours or until it almost reaches the top of the bowl.

4. *Use right away or refrigerate.* Use right away or place the bowl, covered with plastic wrap, in the refrigerator for up to 3 days before baking.

Baking with Canadian Flour
Canadian flour has a higher protein content than some U.S. flours and therefore absorbs more water. If you are using Canadian bread flour, start by adding about ½ cup (125 mL) less than called for, and add just enough of the remaining ½ cup (125 mL) to make a thick, paste-like dough. To get the best texture from your bread, you want to avoid a dough that is too dry. You don't need to adjust the amount of graham flour.

Slow-Rise Sour Rye Dough

Tangy yogurt gives this dough just the right amount of sourness.

4½ cups	unbleached bread flour	1.125 L
1 cup	rye flour	250 mL
1½ tbsp	fine kosher salt	22 mL
½ cup	non-fat plain yogurt	125 mL
3 cups	filtered or bottled spring water, at room temperature	750 mL
1	recipe prepared Biga (page 150)	1

1. *Measure.* One at a time, spoon the bread flour and rye flour into a measuring cup, level with a knife or your finger, then dump into the mixing bowl. Combine well.

2. *Mix.* Add the salt to the flours. Stir together with a wooden spoon or Danish dough whisk. Stir yogurt into the water. Pour into the flour mixture, add the biga and stir together until just moistened. Beat 40 strokes, scraping the bottom and the sides of the bowl, until the dough forms a thick, spongy mass.

3. *Ferment.* Cover the bowl with plastic wrap and let ferment at room temperature (72°F/22°C) in a draft-free place for 12 to 18 hours or until it almost reaches the top of the bowl.

4. *Use right away or refrigerate.* Use right away or place the bowl, covered with plastic wrap, in the refrigerator for up to 3 days before baking.

Baking with Canadian Flour

Canadian flour has a higher protein content than some U.S. flours and therefore absorbs more water. If you are using Canadian bread flour, start by adding about ½ cup (125 mL) less than called for, and add just enough of the remaining ½ cup (125 mL) to make a thick, paste-like dough. To get the best texture from your bread, you want to avoid a dough that is too dry. You don't need to adjust the amount of rye flour.

Slow-Rise Rustic French Boule

Equipment:
- Baker's peel
- Broiler pan
- Baking stone
- Plastic spray bottle of water

Start with this classic shape to get the feel of the dough and continue practicing patience, as this loaf needs to rest and ferment for 4 hours before baking (you can bake it after a 40-minute rest, but it won't rise as high). This recipe makes a medium-size boule, which will rise dramatically in the oven, producing a crusty loaf with a honeycombed crumb. Spraying the loaf with water contributes to the formation of a medium golden brown, blistered crust. Deliciously easy!

½	recipe prepared Easy Artisan Slow-Rise Dough (page 148), about the size of a volleyball	½
	Unbleached bread flour	
½ cup	cornmeal (approx.)	125 mL
2 cups	hot water	500 mL

1. *Form.* Place dough on a floured surface and dust very lightly with flour. Flour your hands. Working the dough as little as possible and adding flour as necessary, form the dough into an 8-inch (20 cm) round. Smooth the dough with your hands to form a soft, non-sticky skin. Pinch any seams together. Lightly flour any sticky places on the dough. The dough should feel soft and smooth all over, like a baby's skin, but not at all sticky.

2. *Rest.* Sprinkle the cornmeal on the baker's peel and place the dough round on the cornmeal. Cover with plastic wrap and let rest at room temperature for 4 hours or until slightly risen.

3. *Prepare oven for artisan baking.* About 30 minutes before baking, place the broiler pan on the lower shelf and the baking stone on the middle shelf of the oven. Preheat to 450°F (230°C).

4. *Slash boule with serrated knife.* Using a serrated knife, make three evenly spaced slashes, about 1 inch (2.5 cm) deep, across the boule, exposing the moist dough under the surface. With a dough scraper, gently scrape under the boule to make sure it isn't sticking to the peel. Add more cornmeal if necessary.

Tip

After baking, keep slow-rise and naturally leavened breads wrapped in a brown paper bag, to keep their crust crisp and their crumb moist.

You Can Also Use

Slow-Rise Herbed Polenta Dough (page 151).

5. *Slide boule onto baking stone and add water to broiler pan.* Using an oven mitt, carefully pull the middle rack of the oven out several inches. Hold the baker's peel level with the rack so that the dough round will slide onto the center of the hot stone. With a quick forward jerk of your arms, slide the dough round from the peel to the stone. Push the middle rack back in place. Pull the lower rack out, pour the hot water into the broiler pan and push the lower rack back in place. Spray the boule with water. Close the oven door immediately so the steam will envelop the oven.

6. *Bake.* Bake for 30 to 32 minutes, spraying the loaf with water three times during baking, until the crust is a blistered medium golden brown and an instant-read thermometer inserted in the center of the loaf registers at least 190°F (90°C). Wearing oven mitts, remove the loaf by hand to cool on a wire rack.

Slow-Rise Sour Rye and Onion Boule

Slathered with Artisan Butter (page 295), this hearty bread is delicious with soups and stews, grilled sausages, a festive spiral ham or aged cheeses. The slight tang comes from the yogurt in the dough.

3 tbsp	olive oil	45 mL
1	large onion, chopped	1
½ tsp	freshly ground white pepper	2 mL
½ tsp	garlic salt	2 mL
½	recipe prepared Slow-Rise Sour Rye Dough (page 153), about the size of a volleyball	½
	Unbleached bread flour	
½ cup	cornmeal (approx.)	125 mL
2 cups	hot water	500 mL

1. **Prepare filling.** In a skillet, heat oil over medium-high heat. Sauté onion for 7 to 10 minutes or until transparent. Season with white pepper and garlic salt. Let cool.

2. **Turn.** Place dough on a generously floured surface and dust generously with flour. Flour your hands. Using a dough scraper, scrape the dough up and over itself, flouring and turning it as you go, for 12 to 15 turns or until the dough is soft and not sticky. Dust very lightly with flour.

3. **Fill.** Flour your hands and the rolling pin. Working the dough as little as possible and adding flour as necessary, roll out the dough into a large rectangle. Arrange one-quarter of the filling on the upper half of the dough and press into the dough with your hands. Fold the other half over the filling. Turn the dough a quarter turn. Working the dough as little as possible and adding flour as necessary, roll out the dough into a rectangle. Arrange another quarter of the filling on the upper half of the dough and press into the dough with your hands. Fold the other half over the filling. Turn the dough a quarter turn. Working the dough as little as possible and adding flour as necessary, roll out the dough into a rectangle. Repeat the process twice more, until all of the filling has been incorporated into the dough. Let rest for 5 minutes.

4. *Form.* Working the dough as little as possible and adding flour as necessary, form the dough into an 8- to 10-inch (20 to 25 cm) round. Smooth the dough with your hands to form a soft, non-sticky skin. Pinch any seams together. Lightly flour any sticky places on the dough. The dough should feel soft and smooth all over, like a baby's skin, but not at all sticky.

5. *Rest.* Sprinkle the cornmeal on the baker's peel and place the dough round on the cornmeal. Cover with plastic wrap and let rest at room temperature for 4 hours or until slightly risen.

6. *Prepare oven for artisan baking.* About 30 minutes before baking, place the broiler pan on the lower shelf and the baking stone on the middle shelf of the oven. Preheat to 450°F (230°C).

7. *Slash boule with serrated knife.* Using a serrated knife, make three evenly spaced slashes, about 1 inch (2.5 cm) deep, across the boule, exposing the moist dough under the surface. With the dough scraper, gently scrape under the boule to make sure it isn't sticking to the peel. Add more cornmeal, if necessary.

8. *Slide boule onto baking stone and add water to broiler pan.* Using an oven mitt, carefully pull the middle rack of the oven out several inches. Hold the baker's peel level with the rack so that the dough round will slide onto the center of the hot stone. With a quick forward jerk of your arms, slide the dough round from the baker's peel to the stone. Push the middle rack back in place. Pull the lower rack out, pour the hot water into the broiler pan and push the lower rack back in place. Spray the boule with water. Close the oven door immediately so the steam will envelop the oven.

9. *Bake.* Bake for 27 to 30 minutes, spraying the loaf with water three times during baking, until the crust is a blistered medium golden brown and an instant-read thermometer inserted in the center of the loaf registers at least 190°F (90°C). Wearing oven mitts, remove the loaf by hand to cool on a wire rack.

Slow-Rise Baguettes

**Makes 2 baguettes,
to serve 8 to 12**

Equipment:
- Baker's peel
- Broiler pan
- Baking stone
- Plastic spray bottle of water

When made with biga, baguettes have a fuller, more developed flavor that is truer to the classic French boulangerie. *Spraying the baguette during baking makes for a crisp, blistered crust.*

½	recipe prepared Easy Artisan Slow-Rise Dough (page 148), about the size of a volleyball	½
	Unbleached bread flour	
½ cup	cornmeal (approx.)	125 mL
2 cups	hot water	500 mL

1. **Form.** Divide the dough in half. Transfer one half to a floured surface and dust very lightly with flour. Flour your hands. Working the dough as little as possible and adding flour as necessary, form the dough into a 14-inch (35 cm) cylinder. Smooth the dough with your hands to form a soft, non-sticky skin. Pinch any seams together. Pinch each end into a point. Lightly flour any sticky places on the dough. The dough should feel soft and smooth all over, like a baby's skin, but not at all sticky. Repeat with the remaining dough.

2. **Rest.** Sprinkle the cornmeal on the baker's peel and place the baguettes on the cornmeal, spacing them about 6 inches (15 cm) apart. Cover with plastic wrap and let rest at room temperature for 2 hours or until slightly risen.

3. **Prepare oven for artisan baking.** About 30 minutes before baking, place the broiler pan on the lower shelf and the baking stone on the middle shelf of the oven. Preheat to 450°F (230°C).

4. **Slash baguettes with serrated knife.** Using a serrated knife, make three evenly spaced diagonal slashes, about 1 inch (2.5 cm) deep, across each baguette, exposing the moist dough under the surface. With a dough scraper, gently scrape under each baguette to make sure it isn't sticking to the peel. Add more cornmeal, if necessary.

5. *Slide baguettes onto baking stone and add water to broiler pan.* Using an oven mitt, carefully pull the middle rack of the oven out several inches. Hold the baker's peel level with the rack so that the first baguette will slide sideways onto the hot stone. With a quick forward jerk of your arms, slide the first baguette from the peel to the back of the stone. With another jerk, slide the second baguette onto the front of the stone. Push the middle rack back in place. Pull the lower rack out, pour the hot water into the broiler pan and push the lower rack back in place. Spray the baguettes with water. Close the oven door immediately so the steam will envelop the oven.

6. *Bake.* Bake for 15 to 17 minutes, spraying the baguettes with water three times during baking, until the crust is a blistered medium golden brown and an instant-read thermometer inserted in the center of the baguettes registers at least 190°F (90°C). Wearing oven mitts, remove baguettes by hand to cool on a wire rack.

Change It Up

Slow-Rise Baby Baguettes: Divide the dough in half. Form each half into a 12-inch (30 cm) cylinder. With the dough scraper, cut each cylinder into four 3-inch (7.5 cm) pieces. Form each piece into a baguette and proceed with the recipe. Bake on the stone, in batches, for 12 to 15 minutes.

Rustic Italian Hoagie Rolls

Makes 4 rolls

Equipment:
- Baker's peel
- Broiler pan
- Baking stone
- Plastic spray bottle of water

When you buy great ingredients for a hoagie sandwich, don't forget to make these crusty rolls.

¹⁄₂	recipe prepared Easy Artisan Slow-Rise Dough (page 148), about the size of a volleyball	¹⁄₂
	Unbleached bread flour	
¹⁄₂ cup	cornmeal (approx.)	125 mL
2 cups	hot water	500 mL

1. *Form.* Divide the dough into four portions. Place one portion on a floured surface and dust very lightly with flour. Flour your hands. Working the dough as little as possible and adding flour as necessary, form the dough into a 6-inch (15 cm) cylinder. Smooth the dough with your hands to form a soft, non-sticky skin. Pinch any seams together. Pinch each end into a point. Lightly flour any sticky places on the dough. The dough should feel soft and smooth all over, like a baby's skin, but not at all sticky. Repeat with the remaining dough.

2. *Rest.* Sprinkle the cornmeal on the baker's peel and place the rolls on the cornmeal, spacing them about 6 inches (15 cm) apart. Cover with plastic wrap and let rest at room temperature for 4 hours or until slightly risen.

3. *Prepare oven for artisan baking.* About 30 minutes before baking, place the broiler pan on the lower shelf and the baking stone on the middle shelf of the oven. Preheat to 450°F (230°C).

4. *Slash rolls with serrated knife.* Using a serrated knife, make three evenly spaced slashes, about 1 inch (2.5 cm) deep, across each roll, exposing the moist dough under the surface. With a dough scraper, gently scrape under each roll to make sure it isn't sticking to the peel. Add more cornmeal if necessary.

continued...

Buttermilk Chive Rolls
(page 134)

Chocolate Swirl Bread (page 140)

Slow-Rise Sour Rye and Onion Boule (page 156)

Leaf-Wrapped Slow-Rise Breadsticks
(page 166)

Apricot Pistachio Swirl Rolls (page 190)

Easter Babka (page 206)

Cardamom and Cinnamon–Scented
Swedish Tea Ring (page 192)

Tip

After baking, keep slow-rise and naturally leavened breads wrapped in a brown paper bag, to keep their crust crisp and their crumb moist.

You Can Also Use

Slow-Rise Herbed Polenta Dough (page 151).

5. *Slide rolls onto baking stone and add water to broiler pan.* Using an oven mitt, carefully pull the middle rack of the oven out several inches. Hold the baker's peel level with the rack so that the first two rolls will slide sideways onto the hot stone. With a quick forward jerk of your arms, slide the first two rolls from the peel to the back of the stone. With another jerk, slide the second two rolls onto the front of the stone. Push the middle rack back in place. Pull the lower rack out, pour the hot water into the broiler pan and push the lower rack back in place. Spray the rolls with water. Close the oven door immediately so the steam will envelop the oven.

6. *Bake.* Bake for 12 to 14 minutes, spraying the rolls with water three times during baking, until the crust is a blistered medium golden brown and an instant-read thermometer inserted in the center of a roll registers at least 190°F (90°C). Wearing oven mitts, remove the rolls by hand to cool on a wire rack.

Coca Mallorquina

**Makes 1 large
flatbread, to serve 12**

Equipment:
- Rolling pin
- Large baking sheet, lined
  with parchment paper
- Broiler pan
- Baking stone
- ¼ cup (50 mL) fine dry
  hardwood chips, such
  as mesquite or apple,
  moistened with 2 tbsp
  (25 mL water (optional)

*This Spanish "pizza," known
as Coca Mallorquina,
comes from Catalonia and
Mallorca. Traditionally,
this flatbread is baked in
communal wood-burning
ovens. A coca, or flatbread,
can be a meal in itself, a
snack or part of a tapas
offering — great for
entertaining. You can get the
same wood-burning oven
flavor using moistened fine
wood chips in your indoor
oven. I used my experience
as a BBQ Queen to develop
the wood-burning oven
technique.*

½	recipe prepared Easy Artisan Slow-Rise Dough (page 148), about the size of a volleyball	½
	Unbleached bread flour	
2 cups	hot water	500 mL

Topping

2	cloves garlic, minced	2
2 tsp	coarse kosher or sea salt	10 mL
6 tbsp	extra virgin olive oil	90 mL
2 tbsp	freshly squeezed lemon juice	25 mL
2 cups	diced tomatoes	500 mL
2	small zucchini, sliced paper-thin	2
¼ cup	pine nuts	50 mL
16	pitted oil-cured black olives	16

1. *Form.* Place dough on a floured surface and dust very lightly with flour. Flour your hands and the rolling pin. Working the dough as little as possible and adding flour as necessary, roll out the dough into a 12- by 10-inch (30 by 25 cm) rectangle. Lightly flour any sticky places on the dough. The dough should feel soft and smooth all over, like a baby's skin, but not at all sticky. Transfer to the prepared baking sheet.

2. *Combine.* In a small bowl, using a spoon or a fork, mash together garlic and salt. Stir in oil and lemon juice.

3. *Top.* Brush half the garlic mixture over the dough. Arrange tomatoes and zucchini over the garlic mixture, leaving a 1-inch (2.5 cm) perimeter. Sprinkle with pine nuts and olives.

4. *Rest.* Cover with plastic wrap and let rest at room temperature for 2 hours or until slightly risen.

5. *Prepare oven for artisan baking.* About 30 minutes before baking, place the broiler pan on the lower shelf and the baking stone on the middle shelf of the oven. Preheat to 450°F (230°C). For the wood-burning oven technique, place the moistened wood chips in a small metal pan next to the broiler pan on the lower shelf. They will start to smolder and release wisps of smoke.

Tips

Use a mandolin or a very sharp knife to slice the zucchini.

If using the wood chips, be sure your kitchen is well ventilated.

6. *Drizzle with garlic oil.* Drizzle flatbread with remaining garlic mixture.

7. *Place baking sheet on baking stone and add water to broiler pan.* Using an oven mitt, carefully pull the middle rack of the oven out several inches. Place the baking sheet on the hot stone. Push the middle rack back in place. Pull the lower rack out, pour the hot water into the broiler pan and push the lower rack back in place. Close the oven door immediately so the steam will envelop the oven.

9. *Bake.* Bake for 20 to 22 minutes or until the crust is puffed and golden brown. Remove from pan and transfer to a wire rack to cool. Remove the smoldering wood chips from the oven, let cool completely, then discard.

Change It Up

Coca Andalucia: Use 8 oz (250 g) thinly sliced serrano or Iberico ham and 8 oz (250 g) shaved Manchego cheese in place of the garlic mixture and vegetables. Drizzle with olive oil before baking.

Slow-Rise Ciabatta

Makes 1 large loaf, to serve 12 to 16

Equipment:
- 4-cup (1 L) bowl
- Wooden spoon or Danish dough whisk
- Baker's peel
- Flexible cutting board, floured
- Broiler pan
- Baking stone
- Plastic spray bottle of water

Ciabatta is also known as Italian slipper bread, as the shape of the bread resembles ballet shoes. Ciabatta uses both biga (or naturally leavened starter) and yeast starter, along with a touch of milk and olive oil, for a honeycombed crumb and a crisp, blistered crust. If you've made ciabatta before and beaten it with a stand mixer, you'll be surprised that you can make it this way. It's the same batter-like dough, but you have much less work — you just have to wait longer. But that's the magic of the no-knead, slow-rise method.

You'll need to spray the top of the loaf as it bakes, to make the smooth crust attain its characteristic blister. Working with slacker, looser ciabatta dough will prepare you for Master Dough #9: Easy Artisan Naturally Leavened Dough.

2 cups	unbleached bread flour	500 mL
2½ tsp	instant or bread machine yeast	12 mL
2½ tsp	fine kosher or sea salt	12 mL
1½ cups	filtered or bottled spring water, at room temperature	375 mL
1 tbsp	olive oil	15 mL
1 tbsp	milk	15 mL
½	recipe prepared Biga (page 150)	½
½ cup	cornmeal	125 mL
2 cups	hot water	500 mL

1. *Measure.* Spoon the flour into a measuring cup, level with a knife or your finger, then dump the flour into a mixing bowl.

2. *Mix.* Add the yeast and salt to the flour. Stir together with a wooden spoon or Danish dough whisk. In a measuring cup, combine water, oil and milk. Add water mixture and biga to the flour mixture and stir together until just moistened. Beat 40 strokes, scraping the bottom and the sides of the bowl, until the dough forms a thick, spongy mass.

3. *Ferment.* Cover the bowl with plastic wrap and let ferment at room temperature (72°F/22°C) in a draft-free place for 4 to 6 hours or until it almost reaches the top of the bowl.

4. *Use right away or refrigerate.* Use that day or place the bowl, covered with plastic wrap, in the refrigerator for up to 3 days before baking.

5. *Form.* Place dough on a floured surface and dust very lightly with flour. Flour your hands. Working the dough as little as possible and adding flour as necessary, scrape the dough up and over itself, flouring as you go, until the dough has settled into a 16-inch (40 cm) long oval and is not sticky. Scrape the dough up from the floured surface at intervals to make sure it isn't sticking to the surface. Add more flour when necessary. Smooth the dough with your hands to form a soft, non-sticky skin. Lightly flour any sticky places on the dough. The dough should feel soft all over, like a baby's skin, but not at all sticky.

After baking, keep slow-rise and naturally leavened breads wrapped in a brown paper bag, to keep their crust crisp and their crumb moist.

You Can Also Use

Easy Artisan Naturally Leavened Starter (page 228) in place of the biga.

Baking with Canadian Flour

Canadian flour has a higher protein content than some U.S. flours and therefore absorbs more water. If you are using Canadian bread flour, start by adding about ½ cup (125 mL) less than called for, and add just enough of the remaining ½ cup (125 mL) to make a thick, paste-like dough. To get the best texture from your bread, you want to avoid a dough that is too dry.

6. *Rest.* Leaving the dough on the floured surface, cover with plastic wrap and let rest at room temperature for 1 hour or until slightly risen.

7. *Prepare oven for artisan baking.* About 30 minutes before baking, place the broiler pan on the lower shelf and the baking stone on the middle shelf of the oven. Preheat to 450°F (230°C).

8. *Transfer ciabatta to baker's peel.* Remove the plastic wrap from the ciabatta and pinch any seams that remain. Spray with water. Sprinkle the cornmeal on the baker's peel. Using the cutting board, and adding flour to any sticky spots on the dough, transfer the ciabatta to the peel. Spray again with water.

9. *Slide ciabatta onto baking stone and add water to broiler pan.* Using an oven mitt, carefully pull the middle rack of the oven out several inches. Hold the baker's peel level with the rack so that the ciabatta will slide onto the center of the hot stone. With a quick forward jerk of your arms, slide the ciabatta from the peel to the stone. Push the middle rack back in place. Pull the lower rack out, pour the hot water into the broiler pan and push the lower rack back in place. Close the oven door immediately so the steam will envelop the oven.

10. *Bake.* Bake for 20 to 23 minutes, spraying the loaf with water three times during baking, until the crust is a blistered medium golden brown and an instant-read thermometer inserted in the center of the loaf registers at least 190°F (90°C). Wearing oven mitts, remove the loaf by hand to cool on a wire rack.

Change It Up

Ciabattini, or Ciabatta Rolls: Use a dough scraper to scrape and pat the dough, flouring as needed, into a 10-inch (25 cm) square. Using a pizza wheel or a sharp knife, cut the square into twenty-five 2-inch (5 cm) squares and place 2 inches (5 cm) apart on a large baking sheet lined with parchment paper. Cover the baking sheet with plastic wrap and let rest for 45 minutes. Spray each roll with water. Bake (without spraying) for 8 to 10 minutes or until risen and browned.

Leaf-Wrapped Slow-Rise Breadsticks

Makes 16 breadsticks

Equipment:
- 2 baking sheets, lined with parchment paper
- Broiler pan
- Baking stone

Fingers of slow-rise dough, wrapped in Swiss chard leaves, make a very rustic presentation on the dinner table. And, improbably, the chard lends the breadsticks a faint flavor of black olive. Simply offer extra virgin olive oil for dipping or Artisan Butter (page 295).

16	Swiss chard, napa or savoy cabbage leaves, rinsed and patted dry	16
1/2	recipe prepared Easy Artisan Slow-Rise Dough (page 148), about the size of a volleyball	1/2
	Unbleached bread flour	
	Olive oil	
	Kosher salt	
2 cups	hot water	500 mL

1. *Prepare leaves.* Plunge the leaves into a large pot of boiling water and blanch for 30 seconds or just until slightly wilted. Using a slotted spoon, remove to a plate lined with paper towels and pat dry. Cut out the thick inner part of each leaf if it's tough.

2. *Form.* Divide dough in half. Transfer one half to a floured surface and dust very lightly with flour. Flour your hands. Working the dough as little as possible and adding flour as necessary, pat the dough into an 8-inch (20 cm) square. Lightly flour any sticky places on the dough. The dough should feel soft and smooth all over, like a baby's skin, but not at all sticky.

3. *Cut.* Using a pizza wheel or a sharp knife, cut the square into eight 1-inch (2.5 cm) wide strips. Wrap each breadstick with a wilted Swiss chard leaf, tucking the ends under the breadstick. Repeat with the remaining dough.

4. *Rest.* Place the dough strips about 2 inches (5 cm) apart on the prepared baking sheets. Cover with plastic wrap and let rest at room temperature for 2 hours or until slightly risen.

5. *Prepare oven for artisan baking.* About 30 minutes before baking, place the broiler pan on the lower shelf and the baking stone on the middle shelf of the oven. Preheat to 450°F (230°C).

Any of the Slow-Rise Dough variations (pages 151–153).

6. *Brush with oil.* Brush wrapped breadsticks with oil and sprinkle with salt.

7. *Place a baking sheet on baking stone and add water to broiler pan.* Using an oven mitt, carefully pull the middle rack of the oven out several inches. Place one of the baking sheets on the hot stone. Push the middle rack back in place. Pull the lower rack out, pour the hot water into the broiler pan and push the lower rack back in place. Close the oven door immediately so the steam will envelop the oven.

8. *Bake.* Bake for 15 to 17 minutes or until lightly browned at the ends. Transfer to a wire rack to cool. Repeat the baking process with the remaining breadsticks.

Change It Up

Slow-Rise Asiago Breadsticks: Instead of wrapping the breadsticks with leaves, sprinkle each breadstick with 1 tbsp (15 mL) shredded Asiago cheese before baking.

Gluten-Free Breads

Master Recipe #6
Easy Artisan Gluten-Free Dough

Trying to approximate the taste, crust, crumb and interior structure of wheat bread without the gluten inherent in wheat flour takes some doing. But those who are gluten-intolerant will be glad you made the effort. For this dough, you need an assortment of gluten-free flours to get the approximate color, flavor and texture. Xanthan gum, which is made from corn and can be a little pricey, provides a framework or structure similar to that of gluten. You can find gluten-free flours and xanthan gum in the specialty baking section of the grocery or health food store, or online at www.bobsredmill.com. The eggs, vinegar, brown sugar and applesauce soften and round out the flavor of the dough.

For some people who are gluten-intolerant, even the tiniest speck of gluten can be a problem, so make sure that all ingredients you put in the dough are gluten-free. Read the labels of manufactured products to make sure nothing has been processed in a facility that also processes gluten. If you also make wheat-based doughs, run your bowls, measuring cups, dough whisk, etc., through the dishwasher again before making a gluten-free dough.

In addition, some people with gluten-intolerance are also allergic to dairy products and possibly eggs, so each recipe offers substitutes.

Makes enough dough for bread, rolls, pizza or flatbread to serve 12 to 16

Equipment:
- Instant-read thermometer
- 16-cup (4 L) mixing bowl
- Wire whisk or Danish dough whisk

Just be aware that this is a unique dough — at first, it resembles a very wet batter. After an hour, it thickens to the consistency of brownie batter. After 2 hours, it rises to about 1 inch (2.5 cm) from the top of the bowl and looks like cornbread batter or golden mashed potatoes. The raw dough doesn't taste like a yeast bread dough.

2 cups	stone-ground brown rice flour	500 mL
2 cups	tapioca flour or potato starch	500 mL
2 cups	chickpea (garbanzo bean) flour	500 mL
1 cup	cornstarch or corn flour	250 mL
2 tbsp	xanthan gum	25 mL
2 tbsp	instant or bread machine yeast	25 mL
1 tbsp	fine table or kosher salt	15 mL
6	eggs, or equivalent substitute (see tip, at right)	6
1/3 cup	packed light or dark brown sugar	75 mL
2 cups	lukewarm water (about 100°F/38°C)	500 mL
1 cup	unsweetened applesauce	250 mL
1/3 cup	vegetable oil (preferably canola)	75 mL
2 tsp	cider vinegar	10 mL

1. **Measure.** One at a time, spoon the rice flour, tapioca flour, chickpea flour and cornstarch into a measuring cup, level with a knife or your finger, then dump into the mixing bowl. Combine well.

But, magically, during baking, it makes a gluten-free white whole-grain bread with a moist and tender crumb, browned crust and mellow, yeasty flavor.

Tips

Combining 1 cup (250 mL) hot with 1 cup (250 mL) cold tap water will result in lukewarm water of approximately 100°F (38°C).

Before storing the dough in the refrigerator, use a permanent marker to write the date on the plastic wrap, so you'll know when you made your dough — and when to use it up 3 days later.

People who are gluten-intolerant are often allergic to eggs and dairy as well. This recipe is already gluten- and dairy-free; for egg-free, use the equivalent amount of liquid egg substitute for 6 eggs in place of the eggs.

2. *Mix.* Add the xanthan gum, yeast and salt to the flour mixture. Stir together with a wire whisk or Danish dough whisk. In a large bowl, lightly beat eggs. Whisk in brown sugar, water, applesauce, oil and vinegar until well combined. Pour into the flour mixture and whisk until a smooth, very loose, batter-like dough forms.

3. *Rise.* Cover the bowl with plastic wrap and let rise at room temperature (72°F/22°C) in a draft-free place for 2 hours or until the dough has risen nearly to the top of the bowl and has a thick, golden, mashed potato–like appearance.

4. *Use right away or refrigerate.* Use that day or place the dough, covered with plastic wrap, in the refrigerator for up to 3 days before baking.

Change It Up

Gluten-Free Soy Dough: Replace half or all of the chickpea flour with soy flour.

Gluten-Free Cornmeal Pepper Dough

You can get wonderful savory flavor in a gluten-free bread with this dough.

Tip

People who are gluten-intolerant are often allergic to eggs and dairy as well. This recipe is already gluten- and dairy-free; for egg-free, use the equivalent amount of liquid egg substitute for 6 eggs in place of the eggs.

2 cups	stone-ground brown rice flour	500 mL
2 cups	tapioca flour or potato starch	500 mL
2 cups	plain yellow cornmeal	500 mL
1 cup	cornstarch or corn flour	250 mL
2 tbsp	xanthan gum	25 mL
2 tbsp	instant or bread machine yeast	25 mL
1 tbsp	fine table or kosher salt	15 mL
1 tbsp	freshly ground white pepper	15 mL
1 tbsp	freshly ground black pepper	15 mL
1 tbsp	granualted sugar	15 mL
6	eggs, or equivalent substitute (see tip, at left)	6
$1/3$ cup	packed light or dark brown sugar	75 mL
2 cups	lukewarm water (about 100°F/38°C)	500 mL
1 cup	canned pumpkin pureé (not pumpkin pie mix)	250 mL
$1/3$ cup	vegetable oil (preferably canola)	75 mL
2 tsp	cider vinegar	10 mL

1. *Measure.* One at a time, spoon the rice flour, tapioca flour, cornmeal and cornstarch into a measuring cup, level with a knife or your finger, then dump into the mixing bowl. Combine well.

2. *Mix.* Add the xanthan gum, yeast, salt, white pepper, black pepper and sugar to the flour mixture. Stir together with a wire whisk or Danish dough whisk. In a large bowl, lightly beat eggs. Whisk in brown sugar, water, pumpkin purée, oil and vinegar until well combined. Pour into the flour mixture and whisk until a smooth, very loose, batter-like dough forms.

3. *Rise.* Cover the bowl with plastic wrap and let rise at room temperature (72°F/22°C) in a draft-free place for 2 hours or until the dough has risen nearly to the top of the bowl and has a thick, golden, mashed potato–like appearance.

4. *Use right away or refrigerate.* Use that day or place the dough, covered with plastic wrap, in the refrigerator for up to 3 days before baking.

Gluten-Free Caraway "Rye" Dough

Equipment:
- Instant-read thermometer
- 16-cup (4 L) mixing bowl
- Wire whisk or Danish dough whisk

Caraway, molasses and cocoa powder give the taste of rye without the rye flour.

Tip

People who are gluten-intolerant are often allergic to eggs and dairy as well. This recipe is already gluten- and dairy-free; for egg-free, use the equivalent amount of liquid egg substitute for 6 eggs in place of the eggs.

2 cups	stone-ground brown rice flour	500 mL
2 cups	tapioca flour or potato starch	500 mL
2 cups	chickpea (garbanzo bean) flour	500 mL
1 cup	cornstarch or corn flour	250 mL
2 tbsp	xanthan gum	25 mL
2 tbsp	instant or bread machine yeast	25 mL
2 tbsp	caraway seeds	25 mL
1 tbsp	fine table or kosher salt	15 mL
6	eggs, or equivalent substitute (see tip, at left)	6
½ cup	unsweetened cocoa powder	125 mL
2 cups	lukewarm water (about 100°F/38°C)	500 mL
6 tbsp	light (fancy) molasses	90 mL
⅓ cup	vegetable oil (preferably canola)	75 mL
2 tsp	cider vinegar	10 mL

1. *Measure.* One at a time, spoon the rice flour, tapioca flour, chickpea flour and cornstarch into a measuring cup, level with a knife or your finger, then dump into the mixing bowl. Combine well.

2. *Mix.* Add the xanthan gum, yeast, caraway seeds and salt to the flour mixture. Stir together with a wire whisk or Danish dough whisk. In a large bowl, lightly beat eggs. Whisk in cocoa, water, molasses, oil and vinegar until well combined. Pour into the flour mixture and whisk until a smooth, very loose, batter-like dough forms.

3. *Rise.* Cover the bowl with plastic wrap and let rise at room temperature (72°F/22°C) in a draft-free place for 2 hours or until the dough has risen nearly to the top of the bowl and has a thick, golden, mashed potato–like appearance.

4. *Use right away or refrigerate.* Use that day or place the dough, covered with plastic wrap, in the refrigerator for up to 3 days before baking.

Gluten-Free Bread

Makes 2 loaves, to serve 16

Equipment:
- Two 9- by 5-inch (23 by 12.5 cm) loaf pans, greased
- Broiler pan
- Baking stone

This moist loaf, with a tender crumb and mellow, yeasty flavor, satisfies the need for "white" bread. Use it for breakfast toast or sandwiches. It can be wrapped and stored in the refrigerator for up to 3 days.

You Can Also Use

Gluten-Free Soy Dough (variation, page 171), Gluten-Free Cornmeal Pepper Dough (page 172) or Gluten-Free Caraway "Rye" Dough (page 173).

1	recipe prepared Easy Artisan Gluten-Free Dough (page 170)	1
2 cups	hot water	500 mL

1. *Form.* Cut dough in half and place each half in a prepared loaf pan. Even out the batter-like dough and smooth the top with a dough scraper or spatula.

2. *Rest.* Cover with tea towels and let rest at room temperature for 40 minutes.

3. *Prepare oven for artisan baking.* About 30 minutes before baking, place the broiler pan on the lower shelf and the baking stone on the middle shelf of the oven. Preheat to 350°F (180°C).

4. *Place loaf pans on baking stone and add water to broiler pan.* Using an oven mitt, carefully pull the middle rack of the oven out several inches. Place the loaf pans at least 3 inches (7.5 cm) apart on the hot stone. Push the middle rack back in place. Pull the lower rack out, pour the hot water into the broiler pan and push the lower rack back in place. Close the oven door immediately so the steam will envelop the oven.

5. *Bake.* Bake for 27 to 30 minutes or until the crust is a medium dark brown and an instant-read thermometer inserted in the center of the loaves registers at least 190°F (90°C). Transfer to a wire rack to cool in pans for 10 minutes. Remove from pans and let cool on rack.

Change It Up

Seeded Gluten-Free Bread: Before baking, brush the top of each loaf with beaten egg white or an equivalent substitute and press on poppy, fennel, millet, toasted pumpkin or sunflower seeds, or a combination.

Gluten-Free Rolls

Makes 12 rolls

Equipment:
- Two 6-cup muffin tins, greased
- Broiler pan
- Baking stone

Bake these rolls for a special dinner.

You Can Also Use

Gluten-Free Soy Dough (variation, page 171), Gluten-Free Cornmeal Pepper Dough (page 172) or Gluten-Free Caraway "Rye" Dough (page 173).

½	recipe prepared Easy Artisan Gluten-Free Dough (page 170)	½
2 cups	hot water	500 mL

1. *Form.* Place about ⅓ cup (75 mL) dough in each prepared muffin cup.

2. *Rest.* Cover muffin tins with tea towels and let rest at room temperature for 40 minutes.

3. *Prepare oven for artisan baking.* About 30 minutes before baking, place the broiler pan on the lower shelf and the baking stone on the middle shelf of the oven. Preheat to 350°F (180°C).

4. *Place tins on baking stone and add water to broiler pan.* Using an oven mitt, carefully pull the middle rack of the oven out several inches. Place the muffin tins on the hot stone. Push the middle rack back in place. Pull the lower rack out, pour the hot water into the broiler pan and push the lower rack back in place. Close the oven door immediately so the steam will envelop the oven.

5. *Bake.* Bake for 22 to 25 minutes or until the crust is a medium dark brown and an instant-read thermometer inserted in the center of a roll registers at least 190°F (90°C). Transfer to a wire rack to cool in pans for 10 minutes. Remove from pans and let cool on rack.

Gluten-Free Cinnamon Rolls

With a looser dough, these rolls are a little trickier to make than those made with a wheat dough, but they're well worth the effort. Sometimes, only the comfort of a cinnamon roll will do. If dairy is a concern, make the Cinnamon Filling with dairy-free margarine and the Easy Artisan Glaze with soy milk. Make sure the vanilla you use in the glaze is labeled "gluten-free." Even the tiniest speck of gluten from a manufacturing plant that processes many different foods can prompt a reaction.

1/2	recipe prepared Easy Artisan Gluten-Free Dough (page 170)	1/2
1	recipe Cinnamon Filling (page 298)	1
2 cups	hot water	500 mL
	Easy Artisan Glaze (page 302)	

1. **Form.** Divide the dough in half. Spray the waxed paper with nonstick spray and place, sprayed side up, on a flat surface, one paper next to the other. Transfer one dough portion to a prepared paper. Using a water-moistened plastic spatula or your hands, spread the dough into a 14- by 10-inch (35 by 25 cm) rectangle. Spread with half the Cinnamon Filling. Starting with a long end, gently lift up the paper and nudge or scrape the dough so it rolls over on itself. Keep nudging and rolling until you have a cylinder. With a dough scraper, gently cut the cylinder into six 1½-inch (4 cm) pieces. Repeat the process with the remaining dough, paper and filling.

2. **Rest.** Place each piece, cut side up, in a prepared muffin cup. Cover with tea towels and let rest at room temperature for 40 minutes.

3. **Prepare oven for artisan baking.** About 30 minutes before baking, place the broiler pan on the lower shelf and the baking stone on the middle shelf of the oven. Preheat to 350°F (180°C).

4. **Place tins on baking stone and add water to broiler pan.** Using an oven mitt, carefully pull the middle rack of the oven out several inches. Place the muffin tins on the hot stone. Push the middle rack back in place. Pull the lower rack out, pour the hot water into the broiler pan and push the lower rack back in place. Close the oven door immediately so the steam will envelop the oven.

5. **Bake.** Bake for 15 to 18 minutes or until risen and lightly browned. Transfer to a wire rack to cool. Once cool, drizzle with glaze.

Gluten-Free Caramel Apple Rolls

Equipment:
- Flexible cutting board, lightly sprayed with water
- Two 20-inch (50 cm) long pieces of waxed or parchment paper
- Two 6-cup muffin tins, greased
- Broiler pan
- Baking stone

Tips

When making the Caramel Apple Filling, use dairy-free margarine if dairy is a concern.

When preparing the Almond Glaze, take care to use gluten-free almond extract, and use soy milk if dairy is a concern.

$^{1}/_{2}$	recipe prepared Easy Artisan Gluten-Free Dough (page 170)	$^{1}/_{2}$
2 cups	Caramel Apple Filling (page 298)	500 mL
2 cups	hot water	500 mL
	Almond Glaze (variation, page 302)	

1. *Form.* Divide the dough in half. Spray the waxed paper with nonstick spray and place, sprayed side up, on a flat surface, one paper next to the other. Transfer one dough portion to a prepared paper. Using a water-moistened plastic spatula or your hands, spread the dough into a 14- by 10-inch (35 by 25 cm) rectangle. Spread with half the Caramel Apple Filling. Starting with a long end, gently lift up the paper and nudge or scrape the dough so it rolls over on itself. Keep nudging and rolling until you have a cylinder. With a dough scraper, gently cut the cylinder into six 1$^{1}/_{2}$-inch (4 cm) pieces. Repeat the process with the remaining dough, paper and filling.

2. *Rest.* Place each piece, cut side up, in a prepared muffin cup. Cover with tea towels and let rest at room temperature for 40 minutes.

3. *Prepare oven for artisan baking.* About 30 minutes before baking, place the broiler pan on the lower shelf and the baking stone on the middle shelf of the oven. Preheat to 350°F (180°C).

4. *Place tins on baking stone and add water to broiler pan.* Using an oven mitt, carefully pull the middle rack of the oven out several inches. Place the muffin tins on the hot stone. Push the middle rack back in place. Pull the lower rack out, pour the hot water into the broiler pan and push the lower rack back in place. Close the oven door immediately so the steam will envelop the oven.

5. *Bake.* Bake for 15 to 18 minutes or until risen and lightly browned. Transfer to a wire rack to cool. Once cool, drizzle with glaze.

Gluten-Free Sandwich Buns

Makes 12 buns

Equipment:
- Instant-read thermometer
- 16-cup (4 L) mixing bowl
- Wire whisk or Danish dough whisk
- Twelve 4-inch (10 cm) mini pie pans, brushed with vegetable oil
- Baking stone

When you want a gluten-free bun for your sizzling burger, this is it. Make this large batch and freeze extras for up to 3 months. Because the dough is so batter-like, use 4-inch (10 cm) mini pie pans (available at kitchen shops) to form the buns.

2 cups	stone-ground brown rice flour	500 mL
2 cups	tapioca flour or potato starch	500 mL
4 tsp	xanthan gum	20 mL
1/4 cup	granulated sugar	50 mL
2 tbsp	instant or bread machine yeast	25 mL
2 tsp	fine table or kosher salt	10 mL
3	eggs, or equivalent substitute (see tip, at right)	3
1 1/2 cups	lukewarm milk or soy milk (about 100°F/38°C)	375 mL
1/2 cup	lukewarm water (about 100°F/38°C)	125 mL
1/4 cup	vegetable oil (preferably canola)	50 mL
1 tsp	cider vinegar	5 mL
1	egg white, beaten, or equivalent substitute	1
	Poppy or sesame seeds	

1. **Measure.** One at a time, spoon the rice flour and tapioca flour into a measuring cup, level with a knife or your finger, then dump into the mixing bowl. Combine well.

2. **Mix.** Add the xanthan gum, sugar, yeast and salt to the flour mixture. Stir together with a wire whisk or Danish dough whisk. In a large bowl, lightly beat eggs. Whisk in milk, water, oil and vinegar until well combined. Pour into the flour mixture and whisk until a smooth, very loose, batter-like dough forms.

3. **Rise.** Cover the bowl with plastic wrap and let rise at room temperature (72°F/22°C) in a draft-free place for 2 hours or until the dough has risen nearly to the top of the bowl and has a thick, mashed potato–like appearance.

4. **Use right away or refrigerate.** Use that day or place the dough, covered with plastic wrap, in the refrigerator for up to 3 days before baking.

5. **Form.** Spoon the dough into the prepared pans, dividing evenly.

6. **Rest.** Cover with tea towels and let rest at room temperature for 40 minutes.

Tips

Before storing the dough in the refrigerator, use a permanent marker to write the date on the plastic wrap, so you'll know when you made your dough — and when to use it up 3 days later.

To make this recipe dairy- and egg-free, use soy milk in place of cow's milk and liquid egg substitute in place of eggs and egg white.

7. *Prepare oven for artisan baking.* About 30 minutes before baking, place the baking stone on the middle shelf of the oven. Preheat to 350°F (180°C).

8. *Top.* Brush the top of the dough with beaten egg white and sprinkle with poppy seeds.

9. *Place six pans on baking stone.* Using an oven mitt, carefully pull the middle rack of the oven out several inches. Place six of the pie pans on the hot stone. Push the middle rack back in place.

10. *Bake.* Bake for 15 to 20 minutes or until an instant-read thermometer inserted in the center of a bun registers at least 190°F (90°C). Transfer to a wire rack to cool. Repeat with the remaining pans.

Gluten-Free Pizza

Makes 1 pizza, to serve 8 to 12

Equipment:
- Large baking sheet, lined with parchment paper
- Broiler pan
- Baking stone

People who are intolerant to the gluten in wheat still want to eat what everybody else does. And who can blame them? As long as the pizza toppings are also gluten-free (check the labels), there's no reason why those who are gluten-intolerant can't enjoy pizza. If dairy is a concern, use soy cheese or equivalents. This recipe makes a rectangular pizza (it's easy to spread the batter-like dough into this shape).

½	recipe prepared Easy Artisan Gluten-Free Dough (page 170)	½
1 cup	gluten-free pizza sauce	250 mL
2 cups	thinly sliced mushrooms	500 mL
2 cups	sliced pepperoni, cooked gluten-free Italian sausage or ham	500 mL
2 cups	shredded mozzarella, provolone or dairy-free cheese product	500 mL
	Olive oil	
2 cups	hot water	500 mL

1. *Form.* Place dough on the prepared baking sheet. Using a water-moistened plastic spatula or your hands, spread the dough into a 14- by 10-inch (35 by 25 cm) rectangle.

2. *Rest.* Cover with a tea towel and let rest at room temperature for 40 minutes.

3. *Prepare oven for artisan baking.* About 30 minutes before baking, place the broiler pan on the lower shelf and the baking stone on the middle shelf of the oven. Preheat to 350°F (180°C).

4. *Add pizza toppings.* Spread pizza sauce over the dough. Arrange mushrooms and pepperoni over the sauce, then sprinkle with cheese. Drizzle with olive oil.

5. *Place baking sheet on baking stone and add water to broiler pan.* Using an oven mitt, carefully pull the middle rack of the oven out several inches. Place the baking sheet on the hot stone. Push the middle rack back in place. Pull the lower rack out, pour the hot water into the broiler pan and push the lower rack back in place. Close the oven door immediately so the steam will envelop the oven.

6. *Bake.* Bake for 25 to 30 minutes or until the crust is lightly browned and the toppings are bubbling. Slice and serve.

Gluten-Free Grilled Chicken and Vegetable Pizza

Makes 1 pizza, to serve 8 to 12

Equipment:
- Large baking sheet, lined with parchment paper
- Broiler pan
- Baking stone

You can also enjoy a lighter-style pizza with a gluten-free crust.

Tip

For the fresh herbs, try flat-leaf (Italian) parsley, oregano, rosemary and/or thyme.

½	recipe prepared Easy Artisan Gluten-Free Dough (page 170)	½
¼ cup	olive oil	50 mL
1	clove garlic, minced	1
2 cups	chopped grilled chicken	500 mL
2 cups	chopped grilled red onion, zucchini and yellow summer squash	500 mL
2 cups	shredded smoked mozzarella or dairy-free mozzarella cheese product	500 mL
¼ cup	chopped fresh herbs	50 mL
2 cups	hot water	500 mL

1. *Form.* Place dough on the prepared baking sheet. Using a water-moistened plastic spatula or your hands, spread the dough into a 14- by 10-inch (35 by 25 cm) rectangle.

2. *Rest.* Cover with a tea towel and let rest at room temperature for 40 minutes.

3. *Prepare oven for artisan baking.* About 30 minutes before baking, place the broiler pan on the lower shelf and the baking stone on the middle shelf of the oven. Preheat to 350°F (180°C).

4. *Add pizza toppings.* Brush dough with olive oil and sprinkle with garlic. Arrange chicken and grilled vegetables over the dough, then sprinkle with cheese and herbs. Drizzle with olive oil.

5. *Place baking sheet on baking stone and add water to broiler pan.* Using an oven mitt, carefully pull the middle rack of the oven out several inches. Place the baking sheet on the hot stone. Push the middle rack back in place. Pull the lower rack out, pour the hot water into the broiler pan and push the lower rack back in place. Close the oven door immediately so the steam will envelop the oven.

6. *Bake.* Bake for 25 to 30 minutes or until the crust is lightly browned and the toppings are bubbling. Slice and serve.

Festive Breads

Master Recipe #7
Easy Artisan Sweet Dough

Substituting milk for the water and adding sugar, melted butter and eggs to Easy Artisan Dough transforms it into a sweet dough. With these additions, the dough is heavier, and thus needs more yeast — and stronger unbleached bread flour — to make it rise and achieve the appropriate crumb. Sweet dough recipes do best when baked on a baking sheet lined with parchment paper (sweet fillings can ooze out of the dough and blacken on your baking stone), and at a lower temperature: 400°F (200°C). With this master dough, you can produce wonderful coffee cakes, festive breads and sweet rolls with a moist, feathery crumb. The dough will last for only 3 days in the refrigerator before it turns bitter.

Makes enough dough for festive breads, coffee cakes, tea rings or sweet rolls to serve 12 to 16

Equipment:
- Instant-read thermometer
- 16-cup (4 L) mixing bowl
- 4-cup (1 L) glass measuring cup
- Wooden spoon or Danish dough whisk

Tip
Microwaving cold milk for about 2 minutes on High will result in lukewarm milk of approximately 100°F (38°C).

6½ cups	unbleached bread flour	1.625 L
2 tbsp	instant or bread machine yeast	25 mL
1½ tbsp	fine kosher salt	22 mL
2½ cups	lukewarm milk (about 100°F/38°C)	625 mL
1 cup	granulated sugar	250 mL
½ cup	unsalted butter, melted	125 mL
2	eggs	2

1. *Measure.* Spoon the flour into a measuring cup, level with a knife or your finger, then dump the flour into the mixing bowl.

2. *Mix.* Add the yeast and salt to the flour. Stir together with a wooden spoon or Danish dough whisk. In the glass measuring cup, combine milk, sugar and butter. Using a fork, beat in eggs. Pour into the flour mixture and stir together until just moistened. Beat 40 strokes, scraping the bottom and the sides of the bowl, until the dough forms a lumpy, sticky mass.

3. *Rise.* Cover the bowl with plastic wrap and let rise at room temperature (72°F/22°C) in a draft-free place for 2 hours or until the dough has risen to about 2 inches (5 cm) under the rim of the bowl and has a sponge-like appearance.

4. *Use right away or refrigerate.* Use that day or place the dough, covered with plastic wrap, in the refrigerator for up to 3 days before baking.

Tip

Before storing the dough in the refrigerator, use a permanent marker to write the date on the plastic wrap, so you'll know when you made your dough — and when to use it up 3 days later.

Baking with Canadian Flour

Canadian flour has a higher protein content than some U.S. flours and therefore absorbs more water. If you are using Canadian bread flour, start by adding about ½ cup (125 mL) less than called for, and add just enough of the remaining ½ cup (125 mL) to make a thick, paste-like dough. To get the best texture from your bread, you want to avoid a dough that is too dry.

Change It Up

Sweet Citrus-Scented Dough: Add 2 tsp (10 mL) freshly grated lemon or orange zest to the flour in Step 1.

Easy Artisan Sweet Breads in Minutes a Day

Day 1	Stir the dough together and let rise. Bake, or cover and chill.
Days 2–3	Remove part of the dough, form and bake.

Nuts!

Nut	How Used
Almonds	Ground for filling, sliced for decoration, almond extract for flavoring glazes
Hazelnuts	Ground for filling
Peanuts	Peanut butter for filling
Pecans	Ground for filling, whole halves for decoration
Pistachios	Ground for filling, roasted and shelled for decoration
Walnuts	Ground or roasted and chopped for filling

To toast whole nuts or halves, spread them on a baking sheet and toast in a 350°F (180°C) oven for 10 to 15 minutes or until golden brown.

Challah Dough

Makes enough dough for festive breads, coffee cakes or sweet rolls to serve 12 to 16

Equipment:
- Instant-read thermometer
- 16-cup (4 L) mixing bowl
- 4-cup (1 L) glass measuring cup
- Wooden spoon or Danish dough whisk

Form this dough into traditional braided or coiled loaves, or use it to make fabulous cinnamon rolls.

6½ cups	unbleached bread flour	1.625 L
2 tbsp	instant or bread machine yeast	25 mL
1½ tbsp	fine kosher salt	22 mL
2¾ cups	hot water	675 mL
1 cup	liquid honey	250 mL
¼ cup	vegetable oil	50 mL
2	eggs	2

1. *Measure.* Spoon the flour into a measuring cup, level with a knife or your finger, then dump the flour into the mixing bowl.

2. *Mix.* Add the yeast and salt to the flour. Stir together with a wooden spoon or Danish dough whisk. In the glass measuring cup, combine hot water, honey and oil. Using a fork, beat in eggs. Pour into the flour mixture and stir together until just moistened. Beat 40 strokes, scraping the bottom and the sides of the bowl, until the dough forms a lumpy, sticky mass.

3. *Rise.* Cover the bowl with plastic wrap and let rise at room temperature (72°F/22°C) in a draft-free place for 2 hours or until the dough has risen to about 2 inches (5 cm) under the rim of the bowl and has a sponge-like appearance.

4. *Use right away or refrigerate.* Use that day or place the dough, covered with plastic wrap, in the refrigerator for up to 3 days before baking.

Baking with Canadian Flour

Canadian flour has a higher protein content than some U.S. flours and therefore absorbs more water. If you are using Canadian bread flour, start by adding about ½ cup (125 mL) less than called for, and add just enough of the remaining ½ cup (125 mL) to make a thick, paste-like dough. To get the best texture from your bread, you want to avoid a dough that is too dry.

Swedish Tea Ring Dough

Equipment:
- Instant-read thermometer
- 16-cup (4 L) mixing bowl
- 4-cup (1 L) glass measuring cup
- Wooden spoon or Danish dough whisk

A hint of cardamom scents this dough, the pride of Swedish bakers.

Tip

Instead of the ground cardamom, you can purchase 24 cardamom pods and crush the seeds.

6½ cups	unbleached bread flour	1.625 L
2 tbsp	instant or bread machine yeast	25 mL
1½ tbsp	fine kosher salt	22 mL
2 tsp	ground cardamom	10 mL
2½ cups	lukewarm milk (about 100°F/38°C)	625 mL
1 cup	granulated sugar	250 mL
½ cup	unsalted butter, melted	125 mL
2	eggs	2

1. *Measure.* Spoon the flour into a measuring cup, level with a knife or your finger, then dump the flour into the mixing bowl.

2. *Mix.* Add the yeast, salt and cardamom to the flour. Stir together with a wooden spoon or Danish dough whisk. In the glass measuring cup, combine milk, sugar and butter. Using a fork, beat in eggs. Pour into the flour mixture and stir together until just moistened. Beat 40 strokes, scraping the bottom and the sides of the bowl, until the dough forms a lumpy, sticky mass.

3. *Rise.* Cover the bowl with plastic wrap and let rise at room temperature (72°F/22°C) in a draft-free place for 2 hours or until the dough has risen to about 2 inches (5 cm) under the rim of the bowl and has a sponge-like appearance.

4. *Use right away or refrigerate.* Use that day or place the dough, covered with plastic wrap, in the refrigerator for up to 3 days before baking.

Baking with Canadian Flour

Canadian flour has a higher protein content than some U.S. flours and therefore absorbs more water. If you are using Canadian bread flour, start by adding about ½ cup (125 mL) less than called for, and add just enough of the remaining ½ cup (125 mL) to make a thick, paste-like dough. To get the best texture from your bread, you want to avoid a dough that is too dry.

Chocolate Hazelnut Swirl Loaf

Makes 1 loaf, to serve 12

Equipment:
- Rolling pin (optional)
- Flexible cutting board, floured, or two metal spatulas
- Baking sheet, lined with parchment paper
- Broiler pan
- Baking stone

This rich, decadent bread can be made into a loaf or a small tea ring (see page 192 for instructions on forming a tea ring). For the best flavor, use the best dark chocolate. If you really want to gild the lily, drizzle the loaf with both Easy Artisan Glaze (page 302) and Chocolate Glaze (page 303).

½	recipe prepared Easy Artisan Sweet Dough (page 184), about the size of a volleyball	½
	Unbleached bread flour	
½ cup	Toasted Hazelnut Filling (variation, page 299)	125 mL
½ cup	finely chopped dark chocolate or chocolate chips	125 mL
2 cups	hot water	500 mL
	Easy Artisan Glaze (page 302)	

1. *Form and fill.* Place dough on a floured surface and dust very lightly with flour. Flour your hands and the rolling pin, if using. Working the dough as little as possible and adding flour as necessary, pat or roll out the dough into a 10- by 9-inch (25 by 23 cm) rectangle. Spread hazelnut filling over the dough, leaving a 1-inch (2.5 cm) perimeter. Sprinkle chocolate over the filling. Starting with a long end, roll up the dough into a cylinder. If the dough begins to stick to the surface, use a dough scraper to push flour under the dough and scrape it up. Gently press and squeeze as you're rolling, to form the dough into a solid cylinder. Pinch the ends and long seam closed. Lightly flour any sticky places on the dough. The dough should feel soft and smooth all over, like a baby's skin, but not at all sticky.

2. *Rest.* Using the cutting board or two metal spatulas, transfer the loaf to the prepared baking sheet, seam side down. Cover with a tea towel and let rest at room temperature for 40 minutes.

3. *Prepare oven for artisan baking.* About 30 minutes before baking, place the broiler pan on the lower shelf and the baking stone on the middle shelf of the oven. Preheat to 400°F (200°C).

You can use prepared chocolate hazelnut spread in place of the hazelnut filling.

You Can Also Use

Challah Dough (page 186), Easy Artisan Dough (page 34) or Easy Artisan Whole-Grain Dough (page 56), made with white whole wheat flour.

4. *Place baking sheet on baking stone and add water to broiler pan.* Using an oven mitt, carefully pull the middle rack of the oven out several inches. Place the baking sheet on the hot stone. Push the middle rack back in place. Pull the lower rack out, pour the hot water into the broiler pan and push the lower rack back in place. Close the oven door immediately so the steam will envelop the oven.

5. *Bake.* Bake for 27 to 30 minutes or until the crust is dark brown and an instant-read thermometer inserted in the center of the loaf registers at least 190°F (90°C). Remove from pan and transfer to a wire rack to cool. Once cool, drizzle with glaze.

Change It Up

Chocolate Peanut Butter Swirl Loaf: Substitute $1/2$ cup (125 mL) peanut butter for the hazelnut filling.

Raspberry Almond Swirl Loaf: Substitute $1/2$ cup (125 mL) Danish Almond Filling (page 299) or prepared almond paste for the hazelnut filling and $1/2$ cup (125 mL) good-quality seedless raspberry preserves for the chocolate. Spread the preserves over the almond filling in step 1, then proceed with the recipe.

Chocolate-Glazed Swirl Loaf: Substitute Chocolate Glaze (page 303) for the Easy Artisan Glaze.

Apricot Pistachio Swirl Rolls

Makes 12 rolls

Equipment:
- Rolling pin
- Baking sheet, lined with parchment paper
- Broiler pan
- Baking stone

Once you've tried the sweet swirled bread, it's easy to go a step further and make these fabulous rolls, delicious for breakfast or brunch. Rolling the dough up from a long side will result in smaller rolls, perfect when you're using a richer filling. For a change, you can also use the fillings suggested in the Chocolate Hazelnut Swirl Loaf recipe (page 188), or try some new ones.

½	recipe prepared Easy Artisan Sweet Dough (page 184), about the size of a volleyball	½
	Unbleached bread flour	
½ cup	Pistachio Filling (variation, page 299)	125 mL
½ cup	finely snipped dried apricots	125 mL
2 cups	hot water	500 mL
	Almond Glaze (variation, page 302)	

1. *Form and fill.* Place dough on a floured surface and dust very lightly with flour. Flour your hands and the rolling pin. Working the dough as little as possible and adding flour as necessary, roll out the dough into a 16- by 10-inch (40 by 25 cm) rectangle. Spread pistachio filling over the dough, leaving a ½-inch (1 cm) perimeter. Scatter apricots over the filling. Starting with a long end, roll up the dough into a cylinder. If the dough begins to stick to the surface, use a dough scraper to push flour under the dough and scrape it up. Gently press and squeeze as you're rolling, to form the dough into a solid cylinder. The cylinder will lengthen to 18 inches (45 cm). With a pastry brush, brush off any excess flour. Pinch the long seam closed, then turn seam side down. With the dough scraper, slice the cylinder into 1½-inch (4 cm) pieces.

2. *Rest.* Place the rolls, cut side up, about 2 inches (5 cm) apart on the prepared baking sheet. Cover with a tea towel and let rest at room temperature for 40 minutes.

3. *Prepare oven for artisan baking.* About 30 minutes before baking, place the broiler pan on the lower shelf and the baking stone on the middle shelf of the oven. Preheat to 400°F (200°C).

Tip

You can use prepared pistachio paste in place of the Pistachio Filling.

You Can Also Use

Challah Dough (page 186), Swedish Tea Ring Dough (page 187), Easy Artisan Dough (page 34) or Easy Artisan Whole-Grain Dough (page 56), made with white whole wheat flour.

4. *Place baking sheet on baking stone and add water to broiler pan.* Using an oven mitt, carefully pull the middle rack of the oven out several inches. Place the baking sheet on the hot stone. Push the middle rack back in place. Pull the lower rack out, pour the hot water into the broiler pan and push the lower rack back in place. Close the oven door immediately so the steam will envelop the oven.

5. *Bake.* Bake for 14 to 16 minutes or until the rolls are risen and browned. Transfer to a rack to cool on baking sheet. Once cool, drizzle with glaze.

Change It Up

Orange Cranberry Swirl Rolls: Substitute $1/2$ cup (125 mL) orange marmalade for the pistachio filling and $1/2$ cup (125 mL) sweetened dried cranberries for the apricots.

Cherry Almond Swirl Rolls: Substitute $1/2$ cup (125 mL) prepared almond paste or Danish Almond Filling (page 299) for the pistachio filling and $1/2$ cup (125 mL) good-quality sour cherry preserves for the apricots. Spread the preserves over the almond filling in Step 1, then proceed with the recipe.

Cardamom and Cinnamon–Scented Swedish Tea Ring

Equipment:
- Rolling pin
- Flexible cutting board, floured, or two metal spatulas
- Baking sheet, lined with parchment paper
- Broiler pan
- Baking stone

The glory of Swedish bakers, this tea ring looks as festive as it tastes. The soft, rich dough needs gentle coaxing into shape, using both hands at times, but the resulting opulent flavor is worth it. Cardamom scents the dough, and cinnamon flavors the filling. This recipe also makes wonderful cinnamon rolls (see variation, opposite).

½	recipe prepared Swedish Tea Ring Dough (page 187), about the size of a volleyball	½
	Unbleached bread flour	
½	recipe Cinnamon Filling (page 298)	½
2 cups	hot water	500 mL
	Almond Glaze (variation, page 302)	
1 cup	green candied cherries (optional)	250 mL
1 cup	red candied cherries (optional)	250 mL

1. *Form and fill.* Place dough on a floured surface and dust very lightly with flour. Flour your hands and the rolling pin. Working the dough as little as possible and adding flour as necessary, roll out the dough into an 18- by 12-inch (45 by 30 cm) rectangle. Spread cinnamon filling over the dough, leaving a 1-inch (2.5 cm) perimeter. Starting with a long end, roll up the dough into a cylinder. If the dough begins to stick to the surface, use a dough scraper to push flour under the dough and scrape it up. Gently press and squeeze as you're rolling, to form the dough into a solid cylinder. Pinch the long seam closed. Bring the ends together to form a circle and pinch closed. Lightly flour any sticky places on the dough. The dough should feel soft and smooth all over, like a baby's skin, but not at all sticky.

2. *Cut and rest.* Using the cutting board or two metal spatulas, transfer the tea ring to the prepared baking sheet, seam side down. With kitchen shears, starting from the outer rim, cut diagonal slashes in the tea ring, three-quarters of the way through the dough, at 2-inch (5 cm) intervals all around the ring. Gently fan the slices, going in the same direction, so the filling shows. Cover with a tea towel and let rest at room temperature for 40 minutes.

You Can Also Use
Easy Artisan Dough (page 34) or Easy Artisan Whole-Grain Dough (page 56), made with white whole wheat flour.

3. *Prepare oven for artisan baking.* About 30 minutes before baking, place the broiler pan on the lower shelf and the baking stone on the middle shelf of the oven. Preheat to 400°F (200°C).

4. *Place baking sheet on baking stone and add water to broiler pan.* Using an oven mitt, carefully pull the middle rack of the oven out several inches. Place the baking sheet on the hot stone. Push the middle rack back in place. Pull the lower rack out, pour the hot water into the broiler pan and push the lower rack back in place. Close the oven door immediately so the steam will envelop the oven.

5. *Bake.* Bake for 20 to 22 minutes or until risen and browned and an instant-read thermometer inserted in the center of the loaf registers at least 190°F (90°C). Remove from pan and transfer to a wire rack to cool. Once cool, drizzle with glaze. Garnish with green and red candied cherries, if desired.

Change It Up

Cardamom and Cinnamon–Scented Rolls: Cut the dough cylinder into 12 pieces. Lay each piece cut side up on the prepared baking sheet. Cover and let rise for 40 minutes, then bake for 15 minutes. Once cool, drizzle with glaze.

Classic Cinnamon Rolls

Makes 8 rolls

Equipment:
- Rolling pin
- 8-inch (20 cm) round cake pan, buttered
- Broiler pan
- Baking stone

Cinnamon rolls are true comfort food. Just the scent of them baking makes you feel good.

½	recipe prepared Easy Artisan Sweet Dough (page 184), about the size of a volleyball	½
	Unbleached bread flour	
½	recipe Cinnamon Filling (page 298)	½
2 cups	hot water	500 mL
	Easy Artisan Glaze (page 302)	

1. **Form and fill.** Place dough on a floured surface and dust very lightly with flour. Flour your hands and the rolling pin. Working the dough as little as possible and adding flour as necessary, roll out the dough into a 12- by 8-inch (30 by 20 cm) rectangle. Spread cinnamon filling over the dough, leaving a ½-inch (1 cm) perimeter. Starting with a short end, roll up the dough into a cylinder. If the dough begins to stick to the surface, use a dough scraper to push flour under the dough and scrape it up. Gently press and squeeze as you're rolling to form the dough into a solid cylinder. With a pastry brush, brush off any excess flour. Pinch the long seam closed, then turn seam side down. With the dough scraper, slice the cylinder into 1-inch (2.5 cm) pieces.

2. **Rest.** Place the rolls, cut side up, in the prepared pan so that they are almost touching. Cover with a tea towel and let rest at room temperature for 40 minutes.

3. **Prepare oven for artisan baking.** About 30 minutes before baking, place the broiler pan on the lower shelf and the baking stone on the middle shelf of the oven. Preheat to 400°F (200°C).

4. **Place cake pan on baking stone and add water to broiler pan.** Using an oven mitt, carefully pull the middle rack of the oven out several inches. Place the cake pan on the hot stone. Push the middle rack back in place. Pull the lower rack out, pour the hot water into the broiler pan and push the lower rack back in place. Close the oven door immediately so the steam will envelop the oven.

Swedish Tea Ring Dough (page 187), Easy Artisan Dough (page 34) or Easy Artisan Whole-Grain Dough (page 56), made with white whole wheat flour.

5. *Bake.* Bake for 30 to 34 minutes or until an instant-read thermometer inserted in the center of the rolls registers at least 190°F (90°C). Transfer to a wire rack to cool in pan. Once cool, drizzle with glaze.

Change It Up

Pecan Sticky Buns: In a saucepan, melt $\frac{1}{2}$ cup (125 mL) unsalted butter over medium heat. Add $\frac{1}{2}$ cup (125 mL) packed light or dark brown sugar and stir until the mixture bubbles and thickens. Pour into the prepared cake pan and set aside to cool while you form the rolls. Scatter $\frac{2}{3}$ cup (150 mL) chopped toasted pecans over the bottom of the pan. Place the rolls, cut side up, in the prepared pan and proceed with the recipe. After baking, let cool in pan briefly, then invert the rolls onto a serving plate and serve sticky side up. Omit the glaze.

Schnecken

Equipment:
- Rolling pin
- Two 9- by 5-inch (23 by 12.5 cm) loaf pans
- Broiler pan
- Baking stone

Schnecken (German for "snails," referring to the spiral filling) are large cinnamon rolls baked in a loaf pan on a bed of butter and sugar for a sticky, sweet, truly decadent treat. Tear apart into individual rolls or slice and serve.

$\frac{1}{2}$	recipe prepared Easy Artisan Sweet Dough (page 184), about the size of a volleyball	$\frac{1}{2}$
	Unbleached bread flour	
$\frac{1}{2}$	recipe Cinnamon Filling (page 298)	$\frac{1}{2}$
$\frac{1}{2}$ cup	raisins (optional)	125 mL
$\frac{1}{2}$ cup	unsalted butter, softened	125 mL
$\frac{1}{2}$ cup	granulated sugar	125 mL
2 cups	hot water	500 mL

1. *Form and fill.* Place dough on a floured surface and dust very lightly with flour. Flour your hands and the rolling pin. Working the dough as little as possible and adding flour as necessary, roll out the dough into a 12- by 8-inch (30 by 20 cm) rectangle. Spread cinnamon filling over the dough, leaving a $\frac{1}{2}$-inch (1 cm) perimeter. Scatter raisins (if using) over the filling. Starting with a long end, roll up the dough into a cylinder. If the dough begins to stick to the surface, use a dough scraper to push flour under the dough and scrape it up. Gently press and squeeze as you're rolling, to form the dough into a solid cylinder. With a pastry brush, brush off any excess flour. Pinch the long seam closed, then turn seam side down. With the dough scraper, slice the cylinder into 2-inch (5 cm) pieces.

2. *Prepare pans.* Using your fingers or a rubber spatula, spread half the butter in the bottom of each loaf pan and sprinkle each with half the sugar.

3. *Rest.* Place the rolls, cut side up, in the prepared pans. Cover with tea towels and let rest at room temperature for 40 minutes.

4. *Prepare oven for artisan baking.* About 30 minutes before baking, place the broiler pan on the lower shelf and the baking stone on the middle shelf of the oven. Preheat to 400°F (200°C).

You Can Also Use

Swedish Tea Ring Dough (page 187), Easy Artisan Dough (page 34) or Easy Artisan Whole-Grain Dough (page 56), made with white whole wheat flour.

5. *Place loaf pans on baking stone and add water to broiler pan.* Using an oven mitt, carefully pull the middle rack of the oven out several inches. Place the loaf pans at least 3 inches (7.5 cm) apart on the hot stone. Push the middle rack back in place. Pull the lower rack out, pour the hot water into the broiler pan and push the lower rack back in place. Close the oven door immediately so the steam will envelop the oven.

6. *Bake.* Bake for 13 to 17 minutes or until risen and browned and an instant-read thermometer inserted in the center of the rolls registers at least 190°F (90°C). Let cool in pans briefly, then invert onto a serving plate and serve warm.

Cider-Glazed Cinnamon Apple Rolls

Makes 8 rolls

Equipment:
- Rolling pin
- 8-inch (20 cm) round cake pan, buttered
- Broiler pan
- Baking stone

This recipe takes the classic cinnamon roll one step further with the tart crunch of apple and a cider-spiked glaze.

1/2 cup	packed light or dark brown sugar	125 mL
1 tbsp	ground cinnamon	15 mL
1/2	recipe prepared Easy Artisan Sweet Dough (page 184), about the size of a volleyball	1/2
	Unbleached bread flour	
1/2 cup	finely chopped apple	125 mL
2 cups	hot water	500 mL
	Cider Glaze (variation, page 302)	

1. *Combine.* In a small bowl, combine brown sugar and cinnamon.

2. *Form and fill.* Place dough on a floured surface and dust very lightly with flour. Flour your hands and the rolling pin. Working the dough as little as possible and adding flour as necessary, roll out the dough into a 12- by 8-inch (30 by 20 cm) rectangle. Sprinkle brown sugar mixture over the dough, leaving a 1/2-inch (1 cm) perimeter. Scatter apple over the filling. Starting with a short end, roll up the dough into a cylinder. If the dough begins to stick to the surface, use a dough scraper to push flour under the dough and scrape it up. Gently press and squeeze as you're rolling to form the dough into a solid cylinder. With a pastry brush, brush off any excess flour. Pinch the ends and long seam closed, then turn seam side down. With the dough scraper, slice the cylinder into 1-inch (2.5 cm) pieces.

3. *Rest.* Place the rolls, cut side up, in the prepared pan so that they are almost touching. Cover with a tea towel and let rest at room temperature for 40 minutes.

You Can Also Use

Swedish Tea Ring Dough (page 187), Easy Artisan Dough (page 34) or Easy Artisan Whole-Grain Dough (page 56), made with white whole wheat flour.

4. *Prepare oven for artisan baking.* About 30 minutes before baking, place the broiler pan on the lower shelf and the baking stone on the middle shelf of the oven. Preheat to 400°F (200°C).

5. *Place cake pan on baking stone and add water to broiler pan.* Using an oven mitt, carefully pull the middle rack of the oven out several inches. Place the cake pan on the hot stone. Push the middle rack back in place. Pull the lower rack out, pour the hot water into the broiler pan and push the lower rack back in place. Close the oven door immediately so the steam will envelop the oven.

6. *Bake.* Bake for 30 to 34 minutes or until an instant-read thermometer inserted in the center of the rolls registers at least 190°F (90°C). Transfer to a wire rack to cool in pan. Once cool, drizzle with glaze.

Cheese Pocket Coffee Cake

Equipment:
- Rolling pin
- Two 8-inch (20 cm) square baking pans, buttered
- Broiler pan
- Baking stone

Known in German as Schmierkuchen, *this easy coffee cake is the essence of home baking. Sweet and yeasty, with a mellow filling, a piece of this drizzled with a tart berry syrup is a good reason to wake up in the morning.*

You Can Also Use
Challah Dough (page 186).

¹⁄₂	recipe prepared Easy Artisan Sweet Dough (page 184), about the size of a volleyball	¹⁄₂
	Unbleached bread flour	
¹⁄₂ cup	granulated sugar	125 mL
1 tbsp	all-purpose flour	15 mL
¹⁄₂ tsp	fine kosher or sea salt	2 mL
2	eggs, beaten	2
1¹⁄₂ cups	small-curd cottage cheese (about 12 oz/375 g)	375 mL
¹⁄₄ cup	heavy or whipping (35%) cream	50 mL
1 tsp	vanilla extract	5 mL

1. *Form.* Divide the dough in half. Transfer one half to a floured surface and dust very lightly with flour. Flour your hands and the rolling pin. Working the dough as little as possible and adding flour as necessary, roll out into a 10-inch (25 cm) square. Drape the dough over the rolling pin and transfer to one of the baking pans, fitting the dough into the bottom and up the sides. Repeat with the remaining dough.

2. *Rest.* Cover with tea towels and let rest at room temperature for 40 minutes.

3. *Prepare oven for artisan baking.* About 30 minutes before baking, place the broiler pan on the lower shelf and the baking stone on the middle shelf of the oven. Preheat to 400°F (200°C).

4. *Prepare filling.* Five minutes before baking, in a food processor, combine sugar, flour, salt, eggs, cottage cheese, cream and vanilla; process until smooth. Pour half the filling into each pan.

5. *Place baking pans on baking stone and add water to broiler pan.* Using an oven mitt, carefully pull the middle rack of the oven out several inches. Place the baking pans on the hot stone. Push the middle rack back in place. Pull the lower rack out, pour the hot water into the broiler pan and push the lower rack back in place. Close the oven door immediately so the steam will envelop the oven.

6. *Bake.* Bake for 17 to 20 minutes or until filling has browned and crust is a medium reddish-brown. Transfer to a wire rack to cool in pans.

Apple Custard Kuchen

Makes 2 coffee cakes, to serve 12 to 16

Equipment:
- Rolling pin
- Two 8-inch (20 cm) square baking pans, buttered
- Broiler pan
- Baking stone

The cinnamon-spiced apple custard, paired with a sweet yeast dough, will have everyone wanting second and third pieces. Good thing this recipe makes two coffee cakes!

You Can Also Use
Challah Dough (page 186).

½	recipe prepared Easy Artisan Sweet Dough (page 184), about the size of a volleyball	½
	Unbleached bread flour	
½ cup	granulated sugar	125 mL
1	egg, beaten	1
1 cup	heavy or whipping (35%) cream	250 mL
1 cup	Honey Spice Applesauce (page 296) or other chunky homemade applesauce	250 mL

1. *Form.* Divide the dough in half. Transfer one half to a floured surface and dust very lightly with flour. Flour your hands and the rolling pin. Working the dough as little as possible and adding flour as necessary, roll out into a 10-inch (25 cm) square. Drape the dough over the rolling pin and transfer to one of the baking pans, fitting the dough into the bottom and up the sides. Repeat with the remaining dough.

2. *Rest.* Cover with tea towels and let rest at room temperature for 40 minutes.

3. *Prepare oven for artisan baking.* About 30 minutes before baking, place the broiler pan on the lower shelf and the baking stone on the middle shelf of the oven. Preheat to 400°F (200°C).

4. *Prepare filling.* Five minutes before baking, in a bowl, combine sugar, egg, cream and applesauce. Pour half the filling into each pan.

5. *Place baking pans on baking stone and add water to broiler pan.* Using an oven mitt, carefully pull the middle rack of the oven out several inches. Place the baking pans on the hot stone. Push the middle rack back in place. Pull the lower rack out, pour the hot water into the broiler pan and push the lower rack back in place. Close the oven door immediately so the steam will envelop the oven.

6. *Bake.* Bake for 17 to 20 minutes or until filling has browned and crust is a medium reddish-brown. Transfer to a wire rack to cool in pans.

Braided Challah

Makes 1 braided loaf, to serve 12

Equipment:
- Rolling pin
- Large baking sheet, lined with parchment paper
- Broiler pan
- Baking stone

Light, tender challah, a bread served on the Jewish Shabbat and Rosh Hashanah, is made without dairy products, so it can be served with a meal containing meat to follow kosher dietary rules. Challah is usually made in one of three forms: a boule, a braided loaf or a ram's horn. The boule and ram's horn variations are opposite. Challah dough also makes excellent egg rolls for small buffet sandwiches (see page 204). To get that airy, feathery texture, use unbleached bread flour, roll and turn the dough several times and bake in a 350°F (180°C) oven.

½	recipe prepared Challah Dough (page 186), about the size of a volleyball	½
	Unbleached bread flour	
1	egg, lightly beaten with 1 tbsp (15 mL) water	1
	Sesame or poppy seeds (optional)	
2 cups	hot water	500 mL

1. **Form.** Place dough on a floured surface and dust very lightly with flour. Flour your hands and the rolling pin. Working the dough as little as possible and adding flour as necessary, roll out the dough into a large rectangle, dusting with flour as necessary. Fold the dough in half, turn a quarter turn and roll out again. Repeat three more times. Roll up the dough into a cylinder. With a dough scraper, divide the dough into three equal portions. Dust very lightly with flour. Working the dough as little as possible and adding flour as necessary, roll each portion into a 16-inch (40 cm) long rope. Lay the ropes out vertically, parallel to each other and close, but not touching. Starting from the top, braid the ropes together snugly. Tuck the ends under to form an oblong loaf about 14 inches (35 cm) long.

2. **Rest.** Carefully transfer the loaf to the prepared baking sheet. Cover with a tea towel and let rest at room temperature for 40 minutes.

3. **Prepare oven for artisan baking.** About 30 minutes before baking, place the broiler pan on the lower shelf and the baking stone on the middle shelf of the oven. Preheat to 350°F (180°C).

4. **Add topping.** Carefully brush the loaf with egg wash. Sprinkle with sesame seeds (if using).

Tips

Enjoy right away with Artisan Butter (page 295) or wrap and freeze for up to 3 months.

Leftover challah (as if!) makes excellent French toast or bread pudding.

5. *Place baking sheet on baking stone and add water to broiler pan.* Using an oven mitt, carefully pull the middle rack of the oven out several inches. Place the baking sheet on the hot stone. Push the middle rack back in place. Pull the lower rack out, pour the hot water into the broiler pan and push the lower rack back in place. Close the oven door immediately so the steam will envelop the oven.

6. *Bake.* Bake for 40 to 42 minutes or until the crust is a shiny, medium brown and an instant-read thermometer inserted in the center of the loaf registers at least 190°F (90°C). Remove from pan and transfer to a wire rack to cool.

Change It Up

Round Challah: Form the dough into a 12-inch (30 cm) boule and proceed with the recipe.

Ram's Horn Challah: Form the dough into a 24-inch (60 cm) long rope, curl into a spiral and proceed with the recipe.

Challah or Egg Rolls

These light, airy, miniature sandwich or dinner rolls usually accompany a platter of sliced ham or turkey for buffet-style entertaining for a bridal shower, family gathering or funeral. It takes only minutes a day to make these rolls, so why not go for true, homemade comfort food?

You Can Also Use

Master Doughs #1 through #5 and all their variations.

1	recipe prepared Challah Dough (page 186)	1
	Unbleached bread flour	
1	egg, lightly beaten with 1 tbsp (15 mL) water	1
2 cups	hot water	500 mL

1. **Form.** Divide the dough in half. Transfer one half to a floured surface and dust very lightly with flour. Flour your hands. Working the dough as little as possible and adding flour as necessary, form the dough into a 16-inch (40 cm) cylinder. With a dough scraper, slice the cylinder into 2-inch (5 cm) pieces. Cut each piece in half. Pinch the cut sides closed and coax each piece into a 2-inch (5 cm) round. Pinch any seams together. Repeat with the remaining dough.

2. **Rest.** Place the rolls about 1 inch (2.5 cm) apart on the prepared baking sheets. Cover with tea towels and let rest at room temperature for 40 minutes.

3. **Prepare oven for artisan baking.** About 30 minutes before baking, place the broiler pan on the lower shelf and the baking stone on the middle shelf of the oven. Preheat to 350°F (180°C).

4. **Brush with egg wash.** Brush the top of each roll with egg wash.

5. **Place a baking sheet on baking stone and add water to broiler pan.** Using an oven mitt, carefully pull the middle rack of the oven out several inches. Place one of the baking sheets on the hot stone. Push the middle rack back in place. Pull the lower rack out, pour the hot water into the broiler pan and push the lower rack back in place. Close the oven door immediately so the steam will envelop the oven.

6. **Bake.** Bake for 20 to 22 minutes or until the rolls are domed and lightly browned and an instant-read thermometer inserted in the center of a roll registers at least 190°F (90°C). Remove from pan and transfer to a wire rack to cool. Repeat the baking with the remaining buns.

Apricot Kolache

Equipment:
- 2 large baking sheets, lined with parchment paper
- Broiler pan
- Baking stone

From Old World Bohemia, kolache are small, sweet, yeast-risen cakes filled with preserves and drizzled with glaze. They're a classic offering for a morning coffee break with neighbors or at Czech heritage festivals.

You Can Also Use
Challah Dough (page 186).

Change It Up

Poppy Seed Kolache: Substitute ¹/₂ cup (125 mL) Poppy Seed Filling (page 301) or prepared poppy seed filling for the apricot preserves and Lemon Glaze (variation, page 302) for the Almond Glaze.

Plum Kolache: Substitute ¹/₂ cup (125 mL) good-quality plum preserves for the apricot preserves.

¹/₂	recipe prepared Easy Artisan Sweet Dough (page 184), about the size of a volleyball	¹/₂
	Unbleached bread flour	
¹/₂ cup	good-quality apricot preserves	125 mL
2 cups	hot water	500 mL
	Almond Glaze (variation, page 302)	
	Clear or white sanding sugar	

1. *Form.* Divide the dough in half. Transfer one half to a floured surface and dust very lightly with flour. Flour your hands. Working the dough as little as possible and adding flour as necessary, form the dough into a 12-inch (30 cm) cylinder. With a dough scraper, slice the cylinder into 1-inch (2.5 cm) pieces. Roll each piece into a ball. Lightly flour any sticky places on the dough. The dough should feel soft and smooth all over, like a baby's skin, but not at all sticky. Repeat with the remaining dough.

2. *Rest.* Place the rolls about 2 inches (5 cm) apart on the prepared baking sheets. Cover with a tea towel and let rest for 45 minutes.

3. *Prepare oven for artisan baking.* About 30 minutes before baking, place the broiler pan on the lower shelf and the baking stone on the middle shelf of the oven. Preheat to 400°F (200°C).

4. *Fill.* With your knuckle or the handle of a wooden spoon, make an indentation in the center of each roll. Spoon 1 tsp (5 mL) preserves into each indentation.

5. *Place a baking sheet on baking stone and add water to broiler pan.* Using an oven mitt, carefully pull the middle rack of the oven out several inches. Place one of the baking sheets on the hot stone. Push the middle rack back in place. Pull the lower rack out, pour the hot water into the broiler pan and push the lower rack back in place. Close the oven door immediately so the steam will envelop the oven.

6. *Bake.* Bake for 8 to 10 minutes or until the rolls are puffed and lightly browned. Remove from pan and transfer to a wire rack set over a baking sheet to cool. Repeat the baking process with the remaining rolls. Once cool, drizzle with glaze. Dust with sanding sugar.

Easter Babka

Makes 1 large loaf, to serve 12

Equipment:
- Rolling pin
- Large, clean metal coffee can, buttered; large metal brioche pan, buttered; or a large sheet of coated panettone baking paper
- Broiler pan
- Baking stone

Polish and Russian bakers love this sweet bread, which looks like a glistening, snow-capped hill, for festive occasions like Easter. Flavored with almonds and cherries, babka can be baked in a large, clean coffee can or a large brioche pan, or on coated panettone baking paper.

1 cup	dried sour cherries or cranberries	250 mL
1/2 cup	lukewarm amaretto or other almond liqueur (about 100°F/38°C)	125 mL
1/2 cup	slivered almonds	125 mL
1 cup	candied cherries, halved	250 mL
1/2	recipe prepared Easy Artisan Sweet Dough (page 184), about the size of a volleyball	1/2
	Unbleached bread flour	
2 cups	hot water	500 mL
	Almond Glaze (variation, page 302)	
	Clear or white sanding sugar	

1. **Combine.** In a bowl, combine dried cherries and amaretto; let stand for 30 minutes or until cherries are plump. Drain and pat dry. Return to bowl and stir in almonds and candied cherries. Set aside.

2. **Form.** Place dough on a floured surface and dust very lightly with flour. Flour your hands and the rolling pin. Working the dough as little as possible and adding flour as necessary, roll out the dough into a 12- by 6-inch (30 by 15 cm) oval. Lightly flour any sticky places on the dough. The dough should feel soft and smooth all over, like a baby's skin, but not at all sticky.

3. **Fill.** Arrange one-quarter of the fruit and nut filling on the upper half of the dough oval and press into the dough with your hands. Fold the other half over the filling. Turn the dough a quarter turn. Working the dough as little as possible and adding flour as necessary, roll out the dough into an oval. Arrange another quarter of the fruit and nuts on the upper half of the oval and press into the dough with your hands. Fold the other half over the filling. Turn the dough a quarter turn. Working the dough as little as possible and adding flour as necessary, roll out the dough roll into an oval. Repeat this process twice more, sprinkling with flour as necessary, until all of the filling has been incorporated into the dough. Form the dough into a ball and place in the prepared can or pan, or on the paper.

4. *Rest.* Cover with a tea towel and let rest at room temperature for 40 minutes.

5. *Prepare oven for artisan baking.* About 30 minutes before baking, place the broiler pan on the lower shelf and the baking stone on the middle shelf of the oven. Preheat to 400°F (200°C).

6. *Place can, pan or paper on baking stone and add water to broiler pan.* Using an oven mitt, carefully pull the middle rack of the oven out several inches. Place the can, pan or paper on the hot stone. Push the middle rack back in place. Pull the lower rack out, pour the hot water into the broiler pan and push the lower rack back in place. Close the oven door immediately so the steam will envelop the oven.

7. *Bake.* Bake for 45 to 50 minutes or until an instant-read thermometer inserted in the center of the loaf registers at least 190°F (90°C). Transfer to a wire rack set over a baking sheet to cool. When cool, remove from the can or pan (but leave on the paper) and place on the rack. Drizzle the top of the loaf with glaze so that it drips down the sides. Dust with sanding sugar.

Brioche

Master Recipe #8
Easy Artisan Brioche Dough

Brioche is a sweet dough enriched with even more butter and eggs than sweet dough. With a slight tang of buttermilk to counter the richness, this dough makes fabulous festive breads, feathery rolls and wonderful beignets. With this easy recipe, Marie Antoinette's infamous retort, "Let them eat brioche," becomes a much more democratic possibility. No longer an exclusive specialty of French bakeries, rich and golden brioche can be made in your own kitchen. With brioche, you'll work with half the dough at a time. Brush traditional brioche shapes with an egg wash before baking. You won't need the egg wash for breads, rolls, beignets or savarins that are to be glazed or dusted with sugar.

Makes enough dough for bread, rolls, savarins or beignets to serve 12 to 16

Equipment:
- Instant-read thermometer
- 16-cup (4 L) mixing bowl
- Wooden spoon or Danish dough whisk

Tip
Before storing the dough in the refrigerator, use a permanent marker to write the date on the plastic wrap, so you'll know when you made your dough — and when to use it up 3 days later.

6½ cups	unbleached bread flour or a mixture of bread and all-purpose flour	1.625 L
½ cup	granulated sugar	125 mL
2 tbsp	instant or bread machine yeast	25 mL
1½ tbsp	fine kosher salt	22 mL
1 cup	unsalted butter, melted	250 mL
½ cup	buttermilk	125 mL
8	eggs, beaten	8
¾ cup	lukewarm water (about 100°F/38°C)	175 mL

1. *Measure.* Spoon the flour into a measuring cup, level with a knife or your finger, then dump the flour into the mixing bowl.

2. *Mix.* Add the sugar, yeast and salt to the flour. Stir together with a wooden spoon or Danish dough whisk. In a bowl, combine the butter and buttermilk. Add to the flour mixture, then add the eggs. Add the water and stir together until just moistened. Beat 40 strokes, scraping the bottom and the sides of the bowl, until the dough forms a lumpy, sticky mass.

3. *Rise.* Cover with plastic wrap and let rise at room temperature (72°F/22°C) in a draft-free place for 2 hours or until the dough has risen nearly to the top of the bowl and has a sponge-like appearance.

4. *Use right away or refrigerate.* Use that day or place the dough, covered with plastic wrap, in the refrigerator for up to 3 days before baking.

Baking with Canadian Flour

Canadian flour has a higher protein content than some U.S. flours and therefore absorbs more water. If you are using Canadian bread flour, start by adding about 1/2 cup (125 mL) less than called for, and add just enough of the remaining 1/2 cup (125 mL) to make a thick, paste-like dough. To get the best texture from your bread, you want to avoid a dough that is too dry.

Change It Up

Lemon-Scented Brioche Dough: Add 1 tbsp (15 mL) freshly grated lemon zest to the butter mixture.

Lemon–Poppy Seed Brioche Dough: Add 1 tbsp (15 mL) freshly grated lemon zest to the butter mixture. Grind 1/2 cup (125 mL) poppy seeds in a clean coffee or spice grinder and add to the butter mixture.

Orange-Scented Brioche Dough: Add 1 tbsp (15 mL) freshly grated orange zest to the butter mixture.

Easy Artisan Brioche Breads in Minutes a Day

Day 1	Stir the dough together and let rise. Bake, or cover and chill.
Days 2–3	Remove part of the dough, form and bake.

Butternut Brioche Dough

Equipment:
- Instant-read thermometer
- 16-cup (4 L) mixing bowl
- Wooden spoon or Danish dough whisk

Traditional brioche turns even more golden — and a little less rich — when you add puréed cooked squash or pumpkin to the dough. Brush traditional brioche shapes with an egg wash before baking. You won't need the egg wash for breads, rolls, beignets or savarins that are to be glazed or dusted with sugar.

Tip

To prepare the purée, simply cover frozen cubed butternut squash with water and cook until tender, then drain and purée in a food processor. Or, of course, you can use fresh squash, peeled, seeded, chopped and cooked until tender. One pound (500 g) of chopped peeled squash will yield about 1 cup (250 mL) puréed squash.

You Can Also Use

Canned pumpkin purée (not pumpkin pie filling), canned puréed squash or puréed sweet potatoes (canned or fresh or frozen, cooked).

6½ cups	unbleached bread flour or a mixture of bread and all-purpose flour	1.625 L
½ cup	granulated sugar	125 mL
2 tbsp	instant or bread machine yeast	25 mL
1½ tbsp	fine kosher salt	22 mL
1 cup	unsalted butter, melted	250 mL
½ cup	buttermilk	125 mL
8	eggs, beaten	8
1 cup	puréed cooked butternut squash or pumpkin	250 mL
¾ cup	lukewarm water (about 100°F/38°C)	175 mL

1. **Measure.** Spoon the flour into a measuring cup, level with a knife or your finger, then dump the flour into the mixing bowl.

2. **Mix.** Add the sugar, yeast and salt to the flour. Stir together with a wooden spoon or Danish dough whisk. In a bowl, combine the butter and buttermilk. Add to the flour mixture, then add the eggs. In another bowl, combine the squash and water. Add to the flour mixture and stir together until just moistened. Beat 40 strokes, scraping the bottom and the sides of the bowl, until the dough forms a lumpy, sticky mass.

3. **Rise.** Cover with plastic wrap and let rise at room temperature (72°F/22°C) in a draft-free place for 2 hours or until the dough has risen nearly to the top of the bowl and has a sponge-like appearance.

4. *Use right away or refrigerate.* Use that day or place the dough, covered with plastic wrap, in the refrigerator for up to 3 days before baking.

Baking with Canadian Flour
Canadian flour has a higher protein content than some U.S. flours and therefore absorbs more water. If you are using Canadian bread flour, start by adding about ½ cup (125 mL) less than called for, and add just enough of the remaining ½ cup (125 mL) to make a thick, paste-like dough.

Cider-Glazed Savarin

Equipment:
- 4-cup (1 L) metal ring mold, buttered
- Broiler pan
- Baking stone

Classic French savarin is a rich dough baked in a ring mold, then glazed. With its soft, honeycombed crumb, it's delicious as a brunch dish or dessert. When you turn out the glazed, golden ring onto a serving plate, you can fill the center with sautéed apples, a bowl of flavored Artisan Butter (page 295), fresh fruit, a prepared fruit curd or whipped cream. For delicious variations, try serving Lemon-Scented Savarin with a bowl of lemon curd, Butternut Savarin with apple or pumpkin butter.

You Can Also Use
Butternut Brioche Dough (page 212).

½	recipe prepared Easy Artisan Brioche Dough (page 210), about the size of a volleyball	½
	Unbleached all-purpose or bread flour	
2 cups	hot water	500 mL
	Cider Glaze with Rum (variation, page 302)	

1. *Form.* Place dough on a floured surface and dust very lightly with flour. Working the dough as little as possible and adding flour as necessary, form the dough into a 14-inch (35 cm) cylinder. Lightly flour any sticky places on the dough. The dough should feel soft and smooth all over, like a baby's skin, but not at all sticky.

2. *Rest.* Place the dough in the prepared ring mold, pinching the ring of dough closed. Cover with a tea towel and let rest at room temperature for 40 minutes.

3. *Prepare oven for artisan baking.* About 30 minutes before baking, place the broiler pan on the lower shelf and the baking stone on the middle shelf of the oven. Preheat to 425°F (220°C).

4. *Place ring mold on baking stone and add water to broiler pan.* Using an oven mitt, carefully pull the middle rack of the oven out several inches. Place ring mold on the hot stone. Push the middle rack back in place. Pull the lower rack out, pour the hot water into the broiler pan and push the lower rack back in place. Close the oven door immediately so the steam will envelop the oven.

5. *Bake.* Bake for 8 minutes, then reduce the temperature to 350°F (180°C). Bake for 15 to 17 minutes or until the crust is a medium dark brown and an instant-read thermometer inserted in the center of the loaf registers at least 190°F (90°C). With a knife or spatula, loosen the savarin from the sides of the mold and turn out onto a wire rack set over a baking sheet. Poke holes all over the surface with a cake tester. Brush the savarin all over with glaze until it is all absorbed.

Change It Up
Lemon-Scented Savarin: Use Lemon-Scented Brioche Dough (page 211) with Lemon or Cherry Glaze (page 302).

Orange-Scented Savarin: Use Orange-Scented Brioche Dough (page 211) with Orange Glaze (page 302).

Brioche à Tête

This is the classic brioche shape, baked in a fluted metal mold and with a topknot of dough in the center of the loaf, but with a rustic exterior. The egg wash gives it a deliciously dark sheen to set off the mellow, honeycombed crumb. You'll get accolades when you proudly serve this with Artisan Butter (page 295) and your best jams and jellies. And more good news: leftover brioche is delicious as French toast or used in desserts as you would pound cake.

Tip

Enjoy right away or let cool completely, wrap and freeze for up to 3 months.

½	recipe prepared Easy Artisan Brioche Dough (page 210), about the size of a volleyball	½
	Unbleached all-purpose or bread flour	
1	egg, lightly beaten with 1 tbsp (15 mL) water	1
3 cups	hot water	750 mL

1. **Form.** Place dough on a floured surface and dust very lightly with flour. Flour your hands. Pinch off a piece of dough the size of a tennis ball and roll into a teardrop shape. Working the dough as little as possible and adding flour as necessary, form the remaining dough into a round. With the handle of a wooden spoon or a bent pointing finger, make a depression in the center of the loaf, almost to the bottom. Place the small teardrop of dough, pointed end down, in the depression. Smooth the dough with your hands to form a soft, non-sticky skin. Pinch any seams together. Lightly flour any sticky places on the dough. The dough should feel soft and smooth all over, like a baby's skin, but not at all sticky.

2. **Rest.** Place the loaf in the prepared pan and brush with egg wash. Cover with a tea towel and let rest at room temperature for 40 minutes.

3. **Prepare oven for artisan baking.** About 30 minutes before baking, place the broiler pan on the lower shelf and the baking stone on the middle shelf of the oven. Preheat to 400°F (200°C).

4. **Place brioche pan on baking stone and add water to broiler pan.** Using an oven mitt, carefully pull the middle rack of the oven out several inches. Place the brioche pan on the hot stone. Push the middle rack back in place. Pull the lower rack out, pour the hot water into the broiler pan and push the lower rack back in place. Close the oven door immediately so the steam will envelop the oven.

5. **Bake.** Bake for 55 to 60 minutes or until the crust is a medium dark brown and an instant-read thermometer inserted in the center of the loaf registers at least 190°F (90°C). Remove from pan and transfer to a rack to cool.

Individual Brioches

Makes 8 individual brioche

Equipment:
- 8 individual metal brioche pans or muffin cups, buttered
- Broiler pan
- Baking stone

A basket of individual brioches, with their distinctively shiny topknots, can welcome friends and family to breakfast. Serve with Artisan Butter (page 295) and your best fruit preserves.

Tip

Enjoy right away or let cool completely, wrap and freeze for up to 3 months.

½	recipe prepared Easy Artisan Brioche Dough (page 210), about the size of a volleyball	½
	Unbleached all-purpose or bread flour	
1	egg, lightly beaten with 1 tbsp (15 mL) water	1
3 cups	hot water	750 mL

1. *Form.* Place dough on a floured surface and dust very lightly with flour. Flour your hands. Working the dough as little as possible and adding flour as necessary, form the dough into an 8-inch (20 cm) cylinder. With a dough scraper, cut the dough into 1-inch (2.5 cm) slices. Roll each slice into a ball. Lightly flour any sticky places on the dough.

2. *Rest.* Place each ball in a prepared cup and brush with egg wash. Cover with a tea towel and let rest at room temperature for 40 minutes.

3. *Prepare oven for artisan baking.* About 30 minutes before baking, place the broiler pan on the lower shelf and the baking stone on the middle shelf of the oven. Preheat to 400°F (200°C).

4. *Place brioche pans on baking stone and add water to broiler pan.* Using an oven mitt, carefully pull the middle rack of the oven out several inches. Place the brioche pans on the hot stone. Push the middle rack back in place. Pull the lower rack out, pour the hot water into the broiler pan and push the lower rack back in place. Close the oven door immediately so the steam will envelop the oven.

5. *Bake.* Bake for 15 to 18 minutes or until the crust is a medium dark brown and an instant-read thermometer inserted in the center of a roll registers at least 190°F (90°C). Remove from pan and transfer to a rack to cool.

Brioche Pull-Aparts

Makes 8 rolls

Equipment:
- Rolling pin
- 8-inch (20 cm) round cake pan, buttered
- Broiler pan
- Baking stone

Whether simply brushed with softened butter or with a more flavorful filling (see variations, below), these feathery-crumbed pull-aparts will have you looking for an occasion to serve them.

You Can Also Use

Butternut Brioche Dough (page 212) or Lemon- or Orange-Scented Brioche Dough (variations, page 211).

Change It Up

Orange Brioche Pull-Aparts: Stir 1 tbsp (15 mL) granulated sugar and $1/2$ tsp (2 mL) freshly grated orange zest into the butter.

Cinnamon Brioche Pull-Aparts: Sprinkle Cinnamon Sugar (page 301) over the butter on the dough.

$1/2$	recipe prepared Easy Artisan Brioche Dough (page 210), about the size of a volleyball	$1/2$
	Unbleached all-purpose or bread flour	
$1/4$ cup	unsalted butter, softened	50 mL
2 cups	hot water for broiler pan	500 mL

1. *Form.* Place dough on a floured surface and dust very lightly with flour. Flour your hands and the rolling pin. Working the dough as little as possible and adding flour as necessary, roll out the dough into a 12- by 8-inch (30 by 20 cm) rectangle. Spread the butter over the dough, leaving a $1/2$-inch (1 cm) perimeter. Starting with a short end, roll up the dough into a cylinder. If the dough begins to stick to the surface, use a dough scraper to push flour under the dough and scrape it up. Gently press and squeeze as you're rolling, to form the dough into a solid cylinder. With a pastry brush, brush off any excess flour. With the dough scraper, slice the cylinder into 1-inch (2.5 cm) pieces.

2. *Rest.* Place the rolls, cut side up, in the prepared pan so that they are almost touching. Cover with a tea towel and let rest at room temperature for 40 minutes.

3. *Prepare oven for artisan baking.* About 30 minutes before baking, place the broiler pan on the lower shelf and the baking stone on the middle shelf of the oven. Preheat to 400°F (200°C).

4. *Place cake pan on baking stone and add water to broiler pan.* Using an oven mitt, carefully pull the middle rack of the oven out several inches. Place the cake pan on the hot stone. Push the middle rack back in place. Pull the lower rack out, pour the hot water into the broiler pan and push the lower rack back in place. Close the oven door immediately so the steam will envelop the oven.

5. *Bake.* Bake for 32 to 34 minutes or until the crust is a medium dark brown and an instant-read thermometer inserted in the center of the rolls registers at least 190°F (90°C). Transfer to a wire rack to cool in pan.

Harvest Brioche Pull-Aparts

Makes 8 rolls

Equipment:
- Rolling pin
- 8-inch (20 cm) round cake pan, buttered
- Broiler pan
- Baking stone

Spicy apple or pumpkin butters add just the right note to rich brioche.

½	recipe prepared Butternut Brioche Dough (page 212), about the size of a volleyball	½
	Unbleached all-purpose or bread flour	
¼ cup	apple or pumpkin butter	50 mL
2 cups	hot water for broiler pan	500 mL

1. *Form.* Place dough on a floured surface and dust very lightly with flour. Flour your hands and the rolling pin. Working the dough as little as possible and adding flour as necessary, roll out the dough into a 12- by 8-inch (30 by 20 cm) rectangle. Spread the apple butter over the dough, leaving a ½-inch (1 cm) perimeter. Starting with a short end, roll up the dough into a cylinder. If the dough begins to stick to the surface, use a dough scraper to push flour under the dough and scrape it up. Gently press and squeeze as you're rolling, to form the dough into a solid cylinder. With a pastry brush, brush off any excess flour. With the dough scraper, slice the cylinder into 1-inch (2.5 cm) pieces.

2. *Rest.* Place the rolls, cut side up, in the prepared pan so that they are almost touching. Cover with a tea towel and let rest at room temperature for 40 minutes.

3. *Prepare oven for artisan baking.* About 30 minutes before baking, place the broiler pan on the lower shelf and the baking stone on the middle shelf of the oven. Preheat to 400°F (200°C).

4. *Place cake pan on baking stone and add water to broiler pan.* Using an oven mitt, carefully pull the middle rack of the oven out several inches. Place the cake pan on the hot stone. Push the middle rack back in place. Pull the lower rack out, pour the hot water into the broiler pan and push the lower rack back in place. Close the oven door immediately so the steam will envelop the oven.

5. *Bake.* Bake for 32 to 34 minutes or until the crust is a medium dark brown and an instant-read thermometer inserted in the center of the rolls registers at least 190°F (90°C). Transfer to a wire rack to cool in pan.

Polish Poppy Seed Pull-Aparts

Makes 8 rolls

Equipment:
- Rolling pin
- 8-inch (20 cm) round cake pan, buttered
- Broiler pan
- Baking stone

The contrast of light and dark, buttery citrus against crunchy poppy seeds, is one of those appearance and taste marriages made in heaven. You'll need the bracing effects of hot coffee in the morning or tea in the afternoon to accompany this treat, because these pull-aparts will make you weak in the knees.

¹/₂	recipe prepared Lemon-Scented Brioche Dough (variation, page 211), about the size of a volleyball	¹/₂
	Unbleached all-purpose or bread flour	
1 cup	Poppy Seed Filling (page 301)	250 mL
2 cups	hot water	500 mL
	Lemon Glaze (variation, page 302)	

1. **Form.** Place dough on a floured surface and dust very lightly with flour. Flour your hands and the rolling pin. Working the dough as little as possible and adding flour as necessary, roll out the dough into a 12- by 8-inch (30 by 20 cm) rectangle. Spread the poppy seed filling over the dough, leaving a ¹/₂-inch (1 cm) perimeter. Starting with a short end, roll up the dough into a cylinder. If the dough begins to stick to the surface, use the dough scraper to push flour under the dough and scrape it up. Gently press and squeeze as you're rolling, to form the dough into a solid cylinder. With a pastry brush, brush off any excess flour. With the dough scraper, slice the cylinder into 1-inch (2.5 cm) pieces.

2. **Rest.** Place the rolls, cut side up, in the prepared pan so that they are almost touching. Cover with a tea towel and let rest at room temperature for 40 minutes.

3. **Prepare oven for artisan baking.** About 30 minutes before baking, place the broiler pan on the lower shelf and the baking stone on the middle shelf of the oven. Preheat to 425°F (220°C).

4. **Place cake pan on baking stone and add water to broiler pan.** Using an oven mitt, carefully pull the middle rack of the oven out several inches. Place the cake pan on the hot stone. Push the middle rack back in place. Pull the lower rack out, pour the hot water into the broiler pan, and push the lower rack back in place. Close the oven door immediately so the steam will envelop the oven.

5. **Bake.** Bake for 8 minutes, then reduce the temperature to 350°F (180°C). Bake for 24 to 26 minutes more or until the crust is a medium dark brown and an instant-read thermometer inserted in the center of the rolls registers at least 190°F (90°C). Transfer to a wire rack to cool in pan. Once cool, brush with glaze.

Tip

You can use prepared poppy seed filling instead of making your own.

You Can Also Use

Sweet Cream Cheese Filling (page 300), Orange Cream Cheese Filling (variation, page 300) or Coconut Cream Cheese Filling (variation, page 300).

Change It Up

Polish Lemon and Poppy Seed Savarin: Roll out the dough into a 14- by 8-inch (35 by 20 cm) rectangle and spread with filling. Starting with a long side, roll up the dough into a cylinder. Lightly flour any sticky places on the dough. Place the dough in a buttered 4-cup (1 L) metal ring mold, pinching the ring of dough closed. Bake at 425°F (220°C) for 8 minutes, then reduce the temperature to 350°F (180°C). Bake for 17 to 20 minutes or until the crust is a medium dark brown and an instant-read thermometer inserted in the center of the loaf registers at least 190°F (90°C). With a knife or spatula, loosen the savarin from the sides of the mold and turn out onto a wire rack set over a baking sheet. Poke holes all over the surface with a cake tester. Brush the savarin all over with glaze until it is all absorbed.

Pan Dolce

Equipment:
- Rolling pin
- Large, clean metal coffee can, buttered; large metal brioche pan, buttered; or a large sheet of coated panettone baking paper
- Broiler pan
- Baking stone

If you like Italian panettone, that domed bread in the red package usually available at Christmastime, you'll love homemade pan dolce, or "sweet bread," from Liguria. Bejeweled with dried fruits soaked in heady spirits, this festive bread with a feathery crumb can be baked in a large, clean coffee can or a large brioche pan, or on coated panettone baking paper.

2 cups	mixed dried fruit (see tip, at right), snipped into ½-inch (1 cm) pieces	500 mL
½ cup	lukewarm brandy, cognac, sherry or other fortified wine (about 100°F/38°C)	125 mL
½	recipe prepared Easy Artisan Brioche Dough (page 210), about the size of a volleyball	½
	Unbleached all-purpose or bread flour	
2 cups	hot water	500 mL
	Almond Glaze (variation, page 302)	
	Colored sprinkles	

1. *Combine.* In a bowl, combine dried fruit and brandy; let stand for 30 minutes or until fruit is plump. Drain and pat dry.

2. *Form.* Place dough on a floured surface and dust very lightly with flour. Flour your hands and the rolling pin. Working the dough as little as possible and adding flour as necessary, roll out the dough into a 12- by 6-inch (30 by 15 cm) oval. Lightly flour any sticky places on the dough. The dough should feel soft and smooth all over, like a baby's skin, but not at all sticky.

3. *Fill.* Arrange one-quarter of the fruit filling on the upper half of the dough oval and press into the dough with your hands. Fold the other half over the filling. Turn the dough a quarter turn. Working the dough as little as possible and adding flour as necessary, roll out the dough into an oval. Arrange another quarter of the fruit on the upper half of the oval and press into the dough with your hands. Fold the other half over the filling. Turn the dough a quarter turn. Working the dough as little as possible and adding flour as necessary, roll out the dough roll into an oval. Repeat this process twice more, sprinkling with flour as necessary, until all of the fruit has been incorporated into the dough. Form the dough into a ball and place in the prepared can or pan, or on the paper.

4. *Rest.* Cover with a tea towel and let rest at room temperature for 40 minutes.

For the mixed fruit, you can use apricots, apples, cherries, cranberries, dates, figs and/or raisins. Use kitchen shears to snip larger fruit into small pieces.

5. *Prepare oven for artisan baking.* About 30 minutes before baking, place the broiler pan on the lower shelf and the baking stone on the middle shelf of the oven. Preheat to 425°F (220°C).

6. **Place can, pan or paper on baking stone and add water to broiler pan.** Using an oven mitt, carefully pull the middle rack of the oven out several inches. Place the can, pan or paper on the hot stone. Push the middle rack back in place. Pull the lower rack out, pour the hot water into the broiler pan and push the lower rack back in place. Close the oven door immediately so the steam will envelop the oven.

7. *Bake.* Bake for 10 minutes, then reduce the temperature to 350°F (180°C). Bake for 35 to 40 minutes or until an instant-read thermometer inserted in the center of the loaf registers at least 190°F (90°C). Transfer to a wire rack set over a baking sheet to cool. When cool, remove from the can or pan (but leave on the paper) and place on the rack. Drizzle the top of the loaf with glaze so that it drips down the sides. Sprinkle with colored sprinkles.

Brioche Beignets

Makes 36 beignets

Equipment:
- Rolling pin
- Deep skillet or electric skillet
- Candy/deep-fry thermometer

There are beignets and there are beignets. The square fritters now served at a famous café in New Orleans taste like cardboard compared to these. So put on a pot of chicory coffee and laissez les bon temps roulez.

½	recipe prepared Easy Artisan Brioche Dough (page 210), about the size of a volleyball	½
	Vegetable oil	
	Confectioner's (icing) sugar	

1. **Form.** Place dough on a floured surface and dust very lightly with flour. Flour your hands and the rolling pin. Working the dough as little as possible and adding flour as necessary, roll out the dough into a 12-inch (30 cm) square. With a pizza wheel or a sharp knife, cut the dough into 2-inch (5 cm) squares. Lightly dust each square with flour, if necessary, to keep it from being sticky.

2. **Rest.** Cover with a tea towel and let rest at room temperature for 40 minutes.

3. **Fry.** In the skillet, heat 3 inches (7.5 cm) of oil over medium-high heat until it registers 350°F (180°C) on thermometer. Fry the beignets, about six at a time, for about 1 minute per side or until golden brown. Using a slotted spoon, remove to a plate lined with paper towels to drain. Sprinkle with confectioners' sugar while still hot.

Pocketbook Beignets

Makes 36 beignets

Equipment:
- Rolling pin
- Deep skillet or electric skillet
- Candy/deep-fry thermometer

When you are adept at frying delectable and habit-forming beignets, take it a step further and make these filled "pocketbook" fritters. To counteract the richness of fried brioche, use a very tart filling, such as apricot preserves, as at right, or orange marmalade, quince preserves, red currant jelly or apple butter. Mix and match the finishing glaze with the filling.

You Can Also Use

Lemon- or Orange-Scented Brioche Dough (variations, page 211) or Butternut Brioche Dough (page 212).

½	recipe prepared Easy Artisan Brioche Dough (page 210), about the size of a volleyball	½
	Unbleached all-purpose or bread flour	
¾ cup	apricot preserves	175 mL
	Vegetable oil	
	Almond Glaze (variation, page 302)	

1. *Form.* Place dough on a floured surface and dust very lightly with flour. Flour your hands and the rolling pin. Working the dough as little as possible and adding flour as necessary, roll out the dough into a 12-inch (30 cm) square. With a pizza wheel or a sharp knife, cut the dough into 2-inch (5 cm) squares. Lightly dust each square with flour, if necessary, to keep it from being sticky. Place ½ tsp (2 mL) preserves in the center of each square. Draw up the sides of the dough and pinch closed. Loosely form into an egg or ball shape. Lightly dust with flour again, if necessary, to keep it from being sticky.

2. *Rest.* Cover with a tea towel and let rest at room temperature for 40 minutes.

3. *Fry.* In the skillet, heat 3 inches (7.5 cm) of oil over medium-high heat until it registers 350°F (180°C) on thermometer. Fry the pocketbook beignets, about six at a time, for about 1 minute per side or until golden brown. Using a slotted spoon, remove to a plate lined with paper towels to drain. While still warm, transfer to a wire rack placed over a baking sheet and drizzle with glaze.

Change It Up

Orange Pocketbook Beignets: Use Orange-Scented Brioche Dough (variation, page 211), orange marmalade for the filling and Orange Glaze (variation, page 302).

Cranberry Orange Pocketbook Beignets: Use Orange-Scented Brioche Dough (variation, page 211), cranberry sauce for the filling and Orange Glaze (variation, page 302).

Cinnamon Apple Pocketbook Beignets: Use tart apple jelly for the filling and dust with Cinnamon Sugar (page 301).

Pumpkin Spice Pocketbook Beignets: Use Butternut Brioche Dough (page 212) and pumpkin butter for the filling, and dust with Cinnamon Sugar (page 301).

Part 3
Master Baking

We've gone from beginner through intermediate artisan baking, and now we're ready for recipes that use the skills you've learned: mixing and flavoring doughs, rolling and cutting, adding toppings and fillings, forming all the different shapes and artisan baking. The recipes and techniques in this chapter are for the dedicated amateur artisan baker — the person who wants an authentic bagel, flaky and buttery croissants that taste the way you get them in Paris, real Danish pastry and sourdough bread made with a natural starter.

Hungry? Intrigued? Then, let's take out the bowl and dough whisk again.

Naturally Leavened Breads

Easy Artisan Naturally Leavened Starter

"Naturally leavened" means just that — the rising or leavening power comes from nature. Wild yeasts in the air, rather than manufactured ones, allow fermentation to take place, creating those bubbles that rise to the surface and help your artisan bread rise.

There are many different recipes for homemade sourdough starters. For example, traditional artisan baker's levain starts with a simple mixture of unbleached flour, spring water and organic purple grapes; it takes 2 weeks to ferment, then another week or so to feed before it can be used in baking. The Easy Artisan way to acquire sourdough starter is to buy ready-made starter online from a source such as King Arthur Flour Company (www.kingarthurflour.com) or Sourdoughs International (www.sourdo.com), or to get some from a friend — like Carl Griffith, who was famous for his 1847 Oregon Trail starter (http://home.att.net/~carlsfriends). I used the King Arthur sourdough starter, a descendant of a 250-year-old starter.

Follow the specific instructions from your source for feeding your starter until it is bubbling, active and looks ready to use for baking. Once your starter is going, you can keep feeding it, wrap and chill it in the refrigerator for up to a week between feedings, or put it in hibernation in the freezer until you're ready to thaw, feed and bake with it again.

Makes about 2 cups (500 mL)

Equipment:
- Instant-read thermometer
- 4-cup (1 L) bowl or glass measuring cup
- Wooden spoon or metal whisk

1	portion prepared sourdough starter	1
2 cups	lukewarm filtered or bottled spring water (110°F/43°C)	500 mL
2 cups	unbleached all-purpose or bread flour (preferably organic)	500 mL

1. *Revive the starter.* Let the starter come to room temperature. Pour the starter into the bowl and follow the directions from your online source or friend for reviving it. Wrap loosely with plastic wrap and keep at a constant room temperature (72°F/22°C). Starter is less active when cold, but develops a very sour flavor if it gets above 80°F (27°C).

2. *Feed.* Feed the starter mixture according to instructions. Stir it occasionally, cover loosely and let it sit until it bubbles, forms a thick, spongy mass and rises almost to the top of the bowl, usually 1 to 3 days after it is revived.

3. *Use starter for baking.* Remove 2 cups (500 mL) of the starter to use for baking.

4. *Keep feeding remaining starter, or wrap and chill, or wrap and freeze.* Stir water and flour into the remaining starter. Cover and let stand for 24 hours or until bubbly. Use right away for baking, or cover and refrigerate for up to 1 week before use. If the starter does not produce bubbles, has an "off" aroma (not clean, sour or tangy) or turns pink, discard it and start over. You can also freeze the starter in 1-cup (250 mL) or 2-cup (500 mL) airtight containers.

Tips

To revive frozen or refrigerated starter, let it thaw at room temperature. Remove 1 cup (250 mL) of the starter and discard. Stir 2 cups (500 mL) lukewarm (110°F/43°C) filtered or bottled spring water and 2 cups (500 mL) unbleached all-purpose or bread flour (preferably organic) into the remaining starter. Cover and let stand in a warm spot for 24 hours or until it is bubbly and a clear liquid has formed on the top. Stir the liquid back into the starter. When it bubbles and rises to the top of the bowl, it's ready to use for baking.

You'll know when a sourdough starter is ready for action because it will look active — bubbles will rise to the surface and slowly burst, and the starter will rise nearly to the top of the bowl. If your starter is new, you may need to give it a little more time to do its thing. But be assured that it will signal you when it's ready for baking.

When in doubt, give your starter another day to ferment, bubble and rise.

Naturally Leavened Starter in Minutes a Day

Day 1	Revive the starter. Cover loosely and let ferment at room temperature.
Day 2	Feed the starter. Cover loosely and let ferment at room temperature.
Day 3	Use in baking, or wrap and chill for up to 1 week, or freeze indefinitely in 1-cup (250 mL) or 2-cup (500 mL) portions.

Maintaining Naturally Leavened Starter in Minutes a Day

Day 1	Thaw 1 cup (250 mL) frozen starter or let refrigerated starter come to room temperature. Stir in 2 cups (500 mL) lukewarm filtered or bottled spring water and 2 cups (500 mL) unbleached all-purpose or bread flour (preferably organic). Let ferment for 24 hours. When starter bubbles and rises to the top of the bowl, it's ready to use in baking.
Day 2	Use starter in baking, or cover and chill for up to 1 week before feeding again, or freeze indefinitely.
Day 9	Let refrigerated starter come to room temperature. Stir in 2 cups (500 mL) lukewarm filtered or bottled spring water and 2 cups (500 mL) unbleached all-purpose or bread flour (preferably organic). Let ferment for 24 hours. When starter bubbles and rises to the top of the bowl, it's ready to use in baking.
Day 10	Use starter in baking, or cover and chill for 1 week before feeding again, or freeze indefinitely.

Master Recipe #9
Easy Artisan Naturally Leavened Dough

Easy Artisan Naturally Leavened Dough, much like Easy Artisan Slow-Rise Dough, is looser than a kneaded dough, so it's good that you've had some practice before you tackle this one. The looseness comes from extra moisture, which is needed to replace kneading and help create the honeycombed crumb that is the hallmark of this bread. You'll use a "fed" starter, or one that is ready for baking — bubbles are rising and forming on the top, and it has increased in bulk to almost double its size.

When the dough made with the starter rises three-quarters of the way to the top of the bowl, it is ready to form into loaves. Naturally leavened breads need a lot of time to get the starter working and develop flavor and texture. Use the best ingredients — organic flour, filtered or bottled spring water, kosher or sea salt — for true artisan bread. Just like love, as the old song says, you can't hurry this dough.

Makes enough dough for artisan loaves, rolls and flatbreads to serve 16 to 32

Equipment:
- Instant-read thermometer
- 16-cup (4 L) mixing bowl
- Wooden spoon or Danish dough whisk

4½ cups	unbleached bread flour (preferably organic)	1.125 L
1 cup	whole-grain flour, such as white whole wheat (preferably organic)	250 mL
1½ tbsp	fine kosher salt	22 mL
2½ cups	filtered or bottled spring water, at room temperature	625 mL
2 cups	prepared and "fed" starter (page 000)	500 mL

1. **Measure.** One at a time, spoon the bread flour and whole-grain flour into a measuring cup, level with a knife or your finger, then dump into the mixing bowl. Combine well.

2. **Mix.** Add the salt to the flours. Stir together with a wooden spoon or Danish dough whisk. Pour in the water and starter and stir together until just moistened. Beat 40 strokes, scraping the bottom and the sides of the bowl, until the dough forms a thick, spongy mass.

3. **Ferment.** Cover the bowl with plastic wrap and let ferment at room temperature (72°F/22°C) in a draft-free place for 12 to 24 hours or until the dough is bubbly on the surface, has a spongy appearance and has risen three-quarters of the way to the top of the bowl.

4. **Use right away or refrigerate.** Use right away or place the bowl, covered with plastic wrap, in the refrigerator for up to 3 days before baking.

Tip

Use a floured flexible cutting board and a dough scraper in tandem to scoop under naturally leavened baguettes, boules and batards after forming, and let them take their longer rest on the cutting board. When ready to bake, use the dough scraper to loosen the dough, flouring as needed, and transfer it to the prepared baker's peel.

Baking with Canadian Flour

Canadian flour has a higher protein content than some U.S. flours and therefore absorbs more water. If you are using Canadian bread flour, start by adding about $1/2$ cup (125 mL) less than called for, and add just enough of the remaining $1/2$ cup (125 mL) to make a thick, paste-like dough. To get the best texture from your bread, you want to avoid a dough that is too dry. You don't need to adjust the amount of whole-grain flour.

Troubleshooting

If breads made with Easy Artisan Naturally Leavened Dough don't rise in the oven and have a gummy texture, it means your starter wasn't strong enough. Give your starter more time to ferment, then try again, making a half batch of dough.

If breads made with Easy Artisan Naturally Leavened Dough don't rise as high in the oven but still have a good flavor and honeycombed crumb, it means the formed loaf needed more rising time. Give your dough more time to rest and rise next time.

Naturally Leavened Breads in Minutes a Day

Day 1	Make dough with starter. Let dough rest and rise.
Days 2–3	Form and rest dough, bake bread.

Naturally Leavened Herbed Polenta Dough

Equipment:
- Instant-read thermometer
- 16-cup (4 L) mixing bowl
- Wooden spoon or Danish dough whisk

A slightly sour flavor takes this dough to the next level.

Baking with Canadian Flour

Canadian flour has a higher protein content than some U.S. flours and therefore absorbs more water. If you are using Canadian bread flour, start by adding about ½ cup (125 mL) less than called for, and add just enough of the remaining ½ cup (125 mL) to make a thick, paste-like dough. To get the best texture from your bread, you want to avoid a dough that is too dry. You don't need to adjust the amount of whole-grain flour.

4½ cups	unbleached bread flour (preferably organic)	1.125 L
½ cup	whole-grain flour, such as white whole wheat (preferably organic)	125 mL
½ cup	cornmeal	125 mL
1½ tbsp	fine kosher salt	22 mL
1 tbsp	dried rosemary	15 mL
1 tbsp	dried basil	15 mL
2½ cups	filtered or bottled spring water, at room temperature	625 mL
2 cups	prepared and "fed" starter (page 228)	500 mL

1. **Measure.** One at a time, spoon the bread flour, whole-grain flour and cornmeal into a measuring cup, level with a knife or your finger, then dump into the mixing bowl. Combine well.

2. **Mix.** Add the salt, rosemary and basil to the flour mixture. Stir together with a wooden spoon or Danish dough whisk. Pour in the water and starter and stir together until just moistened. Beat 40 strokes, scraping the bottom and the sides of the bowl, until the dough forms a thick, spongy mass.

3. **Ferment.** Cover the bowl with plastic wrap and let ferment at room temperature (72°F/22°C) in a draft-free place for 12 to 24 hours or until the dough is bubbly on the surface, has a spongy appearance and has risen three-quarters of the way to the top of the bowl.

4. **Use right away or refrigerate.** Use right away or place the bowl, covered with plastic wrap, in the refrigerator for up to 3 days before baking.

Naturally Leavened Graham Dough

Equipment:
- Instant-read thermometer
- 16-cup (4 L) mixing bowl
- Wooden spoon or Danish dough whisk

Just a bit of graham or "shaggy" whole wheat flour adds interesting texture to this bread.

Baking with Canadian Flour

Canadian flour has a higher protein content than some U.S. flours and therefore absorbs more water. If you are using Canadian bread flour, start by adding about ½ cup (125 mL) less than called for, and add just enough of the remaining ½ cup (125 mL) to make a thick, paste-like dough. You don't need to adjust the amount of stone-ground wheat flour.

4½ cups	unbleached bread flour (preferably organic)	1.125 L
½ cup	stone-ground wheat or graham flour	125 mL
1½ tbsp	fine kosher salt	22 mL
2½ cups	filtered or bottled spring water, at room temperature	625 mL
2 cups	prepared and "fed" starter (page 228)	500 mL

1. *Measure.* One at a time, spoon the bread flour and wheat flour into a measuring cup, level with a knife or your finger, then dump into the mixing bowl. Combine well.

2. *Mix.* Add the salt to the flours. Stir together with a wooden spoon or Danish dough whisk. Pour in the water and starter and stir together until just moistened. Beat 40 strokes, scraping the bottom and the sides of the bowl, until the dough forms a thick, spongy mass.

3. *Ferment.* Cover the bowl with plastic wrap and let ferment at room temperature (72°F/22°C) in a draft-free place for 12 to 24 hours or until the dough is bubbly on the surface, has a spongy appearance and has risen three-quarters of the way to the top of the bowl.

4. *Use right away or refrigerate.* Use right away or place the bowl, covered with plastic wrap, in the refrigerator for up to 3 days before baking.

Naturally Leavened Sour Rye Dough

Makes enough dough for artisan loaves, rolls and flatbreads to serve 16 to 32

Equipment:
- Instant-read thermometer
- 16-cup (4 L) mixing bowl
- Wooden spoon or Danish dough whisk

I love this dough formed into crescents for dinner rolls.

Baking with Canadian Flour

Canadian flour has a higher protein content than some U.S. flours and therefore absorbs more water. If you are using Canadian bread flour, start by adding about 1/2 cup (125 mL) less than called for, and add just enough of the remaining 1/2 cup (125 mL) to make a thick, paste-like dough. To get the best texture from your bread, you want to avoid a dough that is too dry. You don't need to adjust the amount of rye flour.

4 1/2 cups	unbleached bread flour (preferably organic)	1.125 L
1/2 cup	rye flour	125 mL
1 1/2 tbsp	fine kosher salt	22 mL
2 1/2 cups	filtered or bottled spring water, at room temperature	625 mL
2 cups	prepared and "fed" starter (page 228)	500 mL

1. *Measure.* One at a time, spoon the bread flour and rye flour into a measuring cup, level with a knife or your finger, then dump into the mixing bowl. Combine well.

2. *Mix.* Add the salt to the flours. Stir together with a wooden spoon or Danish dough whisk. Pour in the water and starter and stir together until just moistened. Beat 40 strokes, scraping the bottom and the sides of the bowl, until the dough forms a thick, spongy mass.

3. *Ferment.* Cover the bowl with plastic wrap and let ferment at room temperature (72°F/22°C) in a draft-free place for 12 to 24 hours or until the dough is bubbly on the surface, has a spongy appearance and has risen three-quarters of the way to the top of the bowl.

4. *Use right away or refrigerate.* Use right away or place the bowl, covered with plastic wrap, in the refrigerator for up to 3 days before baking.

Naturally Leavened Wild Rice Dough

Makes enough dough for artisan loaves, rolls and flatbreads to serve 16 to 32

Equipment:
- Instant-read thermometer
- 16-cup (4 L) mixing bowl
- Wooden spoon or Danish dough whisk

This dough makes handsome rolls that go well with a dinner of game meat.

Baking with Canadian Flour

Canadian flour has a higher protein content than some U.S. flours and therefore absorbs more water. If you are using Canadian bread flour, start by adding about ½ cup (125 mL) less than called for, and add just enough of the remaining ½ cup (125 mL) to make a thick, paste-like dough. You don't need to adjust the amount of rye flour.

4½ cups	unbleached bread flour (preferably organic)	1.125 L
½ cup	stone-ground rye flour	125 mL
2 cups	cooked wild rice or short-grain black rice, cooled and patted dry	500 mL
1½ tbsp	fine kosher salt	22 mL
1 tbsp	freshly ground white pepper	15 mL
2½ cups	filtered or bottled spring water, at room temperature	625 mL
2 cups	prepared and "fed" starter (page 228)	500 mL

1. *Measure.* One at a time, spoon the bread flour, rye flour and wild rice into a measuring cup, level with a knife or your finger, then dump into the mixing bowl. Combine well.

2. *Mix.* Add the salt and pepper to the flour mixture. Stir together with a wooden spoon or Danish dough whisk. Pour in the water and starter and stir together until just moistened. Beat 40 strokes, scraping the bottom and the sides of the bowl, until the dough forms a thick, spongy mass.

3. *Ferment.* Cover the bowl with plastic wrap and let ferment at room temperature (72°F/22°C) in a draft-free place for 12 to 24 hours or until the dough is bubbly on the surface, has a spongy appearance and has risen three-quarters of the way to the top of the bowl.

4. *Use right away or refrigerate.* Use right away or place the bowl, covered with plastic wrap, in the refrigerator for up to 3 days before baking.

Classic French Baguettes

Equipment:
- Flexible cutting board, floured
- Baker's peel
- Broiler pan
- Baking stone
- Plastic spray bottle of water

All the practicing you did with previous doughs will come in handy as you wrangle this one into shape with a dough scraper and flour. The longer resting time means the dough will get sticky again, but it's easier to flour under and around the dough on the flexible cutting board than it is on the cornmeal-dusted baker's peel. After the dough has rested, you can simply scrape, flour and slide it off the cutting board and onto the baker's peel. Spraying the loaves with water before and during baking helps promote that blistered crust effect.

½	recipe prepared Easy Artisan Naturally Leavened Dough (page 230)	½
	Unbleached bread flour	
	Olive oil spray	
½ cup	cornmeal	125 mL
2 cups	hot water	500 mL

1. *Turn.* Place dough on a generously floured surface and dust generously with flour. Flour your hands. Using a dough scraper, scrape the dough up and over itself, flouring and turning it as you go, for 12 to 15 turns or until the dough is soft and not sticky. Cut the dough in half and dust very lightly with flour.

2. *Form.* Flour your hands. Working the dough as little as possible and adding flour as necessary, form each half into a 12- to 14-inch (30 to 35 cm) cylinder. Smooth the dough with your hands to form a soft, non-sticky skin. Pinch any seams together. Pinch each end into a point. Lightly flour any sticky places on the dough. The dough should feel soft and smooth all over, like a baby's skin, but not at all sticky.

3. *Rest.* Scoop under each baguette with the dough scraper and cutting board so that they're parallel to each other and 4 inches (10 cm) apart on the cutting board. Spray plastic wrap with olive oil spray and cover the dough with the oiled side touching the dough. Cover the cutting board with a tea towel. Let rest at room temperature for 4 hours or until slightly risen and expanded.

4. *Prepare oven for artisan baking.* About 30 minutes before baking, place the broiler pan on the lower shelf and the baking stone on the middle shelf of the oven. Preheat to 450°F (230°C).

5. *Slash baguettes with serrated knife.* Remove the plastic wrap from the baguettes. Using a serrated knife, make three evenly spaced diagonal slashes, about 1 inch (2.5 cm) deep, across each baguette, exposing the moist dough under the surface.

You Can Also Use

Easy Artisan Slow-Rise Dough (page 148).

6. *Transfer baguettes to baker's peel.* Sprinkle the cornmeal on the baker's peel. Using the dough scraper and flouring the dough if it sticks to the board, loosen and nudge the baguettes from the cutting board onto the peel so that they're parallel to each other and 4 inches (10 cm) apart.

7. *Slide baguettes onto baking stone and add water to broiler pan.* Using an oven mitt, carefully pull the middle rack of the oven out several inches. Hold the baker's peel level with the rack so that the first baguette will slide sideways onto the hot stone. With a quick forward jerk of your arms, slide the first baguette from the peel to the back of the stone. With another jerk, slide the second baguette onto the front of the stone. Push the middle rack back in place. Pull the lower rack out, pour the hot water into the broiler pan and push the lower rack back in place. Spray the baguettes with water. Close the oven door immediately so the steam will envelop the oven.

8. *Bake.* Bake for 18 to 22 minutes, spraying the baguettes with water three times during baking, until the crust is a blistered medium golden brown and an instant-read thermometer inserted in the center of the baguettes registers at least 190°F (90°C). Wearing oven mitts, remove baguettes by hand to cool on a wire rack.

Change It Up

Whole-Grain Baguettes: Make Easy Artisan Naturally Leavened Dough with coarser, stone-ground whole-grain flour (wheat or rye).

Wood-Burning Oven Technique: Place $1/4$ cup (50 mL) fine dry wood chips (such as mesquite or apple) in a small metal pan, moisten with 2 tbsp (25 mL) water and place next to the broiler pan on the lower shelf of the oven. They will start to smolder and release wisps of smoke. Remove the pan of smoldering wood chips after baking. Let the wood chips cool completely, then discard. Be sure your kitchen is well ventilated.

Rustic Italian Batard

Makes 1 large loaf, to serve 8

Equipment:
- Flexible cutting board, floured
- Baker's peel
- Broiler pan
- Baking stone
- Plastic spray bottle of water

Traditionally, Italian bread is made in the batard shape, perfect for slicing and then mopping up a delicious pasta sauce. Brush slices of batard with olive oil, rub with a garlic clove and grill for the best-ever bruschetta.

This larger loaf takes longer to rest and develop flavor, 5 to 8 hours or more. Naturally leavened and slow-rise doughs have more of a "fudge factor" — you're not bound by exact timing on resting and rising. So you could form the loaf in the evening and let it rest and slightly rise overnight. The longer rest and rise will mean more developed sourdough flavor in the loaf.

½	recipe prepared Easy Artisan Naturally Leavened Dough (page 230)	½
	Unbleached bread flour	
	Olive oil spray	
½ cup	cornmeal	125 mL
2 cups	hot water	500 mL

1. *Turn.* Place dough on a generously floured surface and dust generously with flour. Flour your hands. Using a dough scraper, scrape the dough up and over itself, flouring and turning it as you go, for 12 to 15 turns or until the dough is soft and not sticky. Dust very lightly with flour.

2. *Form.* Flour your hands. Working the dough as little as possible and adding flour as necessary, form the dough into a wide 10- to 12-inch (25 to 30 cm) cylinder. Pinch the ends and any seams closed. Lightly flour any sticky places on the dough. The dough should feel soft and smooth all over, like a baby's skin, but not at all sticky.

3. *Rest.* Scoop under the batard with the dough scraper and cutting board so that the batard rests on the cutting board. Spray plastic wrap with olive oil spray and cover the dough with the oiled side touching the dough. Cover the cutting board with a tea towel. Let rest at room temperature for 5 to 8 hours (or more) or until the batard has slightly risen and expanded.

4. *Prepare oven for artisan baking.* About 30 minutes before baking, place the broiler pan on the lower shelf and the baking stone on the middle shelf of the oven. Preheat to 450°F (230°C).

5. *Slash batard with serrated knife.* Remove the plastic wrap from the batard. Using a serrated knife, make five crosshatch slashes, about ½ inch (1 cm deep), diagonally across the top of the batard, exposing the moist dough under the surface.

6. *Transfer batard to baker's peel.* Sprinkle the cornmeal on the baker's peel. Using the dough scraper and flouring the dough if it sticks to the board, loosen and nudge the batard from the cutting board onto the peel.

Tip

Cut leftover bread into cubes, then toast on a baking sheet in the oven to make croutons. They're delicious on vegetable soups and in salads. Store the croutons in a sealable plastic bag for up to 1 week.

7. *Slide batard onto baking stone and add water to broiler pan.* Using an oven mitt, carefully pull the middle rack of the oven out several inches. Hold the baker's peel level with the rack so that the loaf will slide onto the center of the hot stone. With a quick jerk of your arms, slide the loaf from the peel to the stone. Push the middle rack back in place. Pull the lower rack out, pour the hot water into the broiler pan and push the lower rack back in place. Spray the batard with water. Close the oven door immediately so the steam will envelop the oven.

8. *Bake.* Bake for 27 to 30 minutes, spraying the loaf with water three times during baking, until the crust is a blistered medium golden brown and an instant-read thermometer inserted in the center of the loaf registers at least 190°F (90°C). Wearing oven mitts, remove the loaf by hand to cool on a wire rack.

Change It Up

Wood-Burning Oven Technique: Place $\frac{1}{4}$ cup (50 mL) fine dry wood chips (such as mesquite or apple) in a small metal pan, moisten with 2 tbsp (25 mL) water and place next to the broiler pan on the lower shelf of the oven. They will start to smolder and release wisps of smoke. Remove the pan of smoldering wood chips after baking. Let the wood chips cool completely, then discard. Be sure your kitchen is well ventilated.

Thyme and Olive Boule

Equipment:
- Rolling pin
- Flexible cutting board, floured
- Baker's peel
- Broiler pan
- Baking stone
- Plastic spray bottle of water

This is a version of my favorite loaf at WheatFields, an artisan bakery in Lawrence, Kansas, where I spent some time learning how to form and bake artisan bread. You already know how to make a boule from Master Dough #1 and how to fold filling ingredients into the dough from Master Dough #4; now you make the slashes deeper. Try the fabulous Thyme and Olive Artisan Rolls too (variation, page 243).

You Can Also Use

Any of the variations of Easy Artisan Slow-Rise Dough (pages 148–153) or Easy Artisan Naturally Leavened Dough (pages 232–235).

1½ cups	oil-cured olives, pitted and sliced	375 mL
1 tsp	dried thyme	5 mL
½	recipe prepared Easy Artisan Naturally Leavened Dough (page 230)	½
	Unbleached bread flour	
	Olive oil spray	
½ cup	cornmeal	125 mL
2 cups	hot water	500 mL

1. *Combine.* In a small bowl, combine olives and thyme. Set aside.

2. *Turn.* Place dough on a generously floured surface and dust generously with flour. Flour your hands. Using a dough scraper, scrape the dough up and over itself, flouring and turning it as you go, for 12 to 15 turns or until the dough is soft and not sticky. Dust very lightly with flour.

3. *Fill.* Flour your hands and the rolling pin. Working the dough as little as possible and adding flour as necessary, roll out the dough into a large rectangle. Arrange one-quarter of the olive filling on the upper half of the dough and press into the dough with your hands. Fold the other half over the filling. Turn the dough a quarter turn. Working the dough as little as possible and adding flour as necessary, roll out the dough into a rectangle. Arrange another quarter of the filling on the upper half of the dough and press into the dough with your hands. Fold the other half over the filling. Turn the dough a quarter turn. Working the dough as little as possible and adding flour as necessary, roll out the dough into a rectangle. Repeat the process twice more, until all of the filling has been incorporated into the dough. Let rest for 5 minutes.

4. *Form.* Working the dough as little as possible and adding flour as necessary, form the dough into an 8- to 10-inch (20 to 25 cm) round. Smooth the dough with your hands to form a soft, non-sticky skin. Pinch any seams together. Lightly flour any sticky places on the dough. The dough should feel soft and smooth all over, like a baby's skin, but not at all sticky.

5. *Rest.* Scoop under the boule with the dough scraper and cutting board so that the boule rests on the cutting board. Spray plastic wrap with olive oil spray and cover the dough with the oiled side touching the dough. Cover the cutting board with a tea towel. Let rest at room temperature for 4 hours or until slightly risen and expanded.

6. *Prepare oven for artisan baking.* About 30 minutes before baking, place the broiler pan on the lower shelf and the baking stone on the middle shelf of the oven. Preheat to 450°F (230°C).

7. *Slash boule with serrated knife.* Remove the plastic wrap from the boule. Using a serrated knife, make three evenly spaced slashes, about 1½ inches (4 cm) deep, across the boule, exposing the moist dough under the surface.

8. *Transfer boule to baker's peel.* Sprinkle the cornmeal on the baker's peel. Using the dough scraper and flouring the dough if it sticks to the board, loosen and nudge the boule from the cutting board onto the peel.

9. *Slide boule onto baking stone and add water to broiler pan.* Using an oven mitt, carefully pull the middle rack of the oven out several inches. Hold the baker's peel level with the rack so that the dough round will slide onto the center of the hot stone. With a quick forward jerk of your arms, slide the dough round from the peel to the stone. Push the middle rack back in place. Pull the lower rack out, pour the hot water into the broiler pan and push the lower rack back in place. Spray the boule with water. Close the oven door immediately so the steam will envelop the oven.

10. *Bake.* Bake for 27 to 30 minutes, spraying the loaf with water three times during baking, until the crust is a blistered medium golden brown and an instant-read thermometer inserted in the center of the loaf registers at least 190°F (90°C). Wearing oven mitts, remove the loaf by hand to cool on a wire rack.

Rosemary Walnut Artisan Rolls

Equipment:
- Rolling pin
- Flexible cutting board, floured
- Baking sheet, lined with parchment paper
- Broiler pan
- Baking stone
- Plastic spray bottle of water

Serve these savory rolls with a holiday or celebration dinner.

½	recipe prepared Easy Artisan Naturally Leavened Dough (page 230)	½
	Unbleached bread flour	
1 cup	Rosemary Walnuts (page 297)	250 mL
	Olive oil spray	
½ cup	cornmeal	125 mL
2 cups	hot water	500 mL

1. *Turn.* Place dough on a generously floured surface and dust generously with flour. Flour your hands. Using a dough scraper, scrape the dough up and over itself, flouring and turning it as you go, for 12 to 15 turns or until the dough is soft and not sticky. Dust very lightly with flour.

2. *Fill.* Flour your hands and the rolling pin. Working the dough as little as possible and adding flour as necessary, roll out the dough into a large rectangle. Arrange one-quarter of the walnuts on the upper half of the dough and press into the dough with your hands. Fold the other half over the walnuts. Turn the dough a quarter turn. Working the dough as little as possible and adding flour as necessary, roll out the dough into a rectangle. Arrange another quarter of the walnuts on the upper half of the dough and press into the dough with your hands. Fold the other half over the walnuts. Turn the dough a quarter turn. Working the dough as little as possible and adding flour as necessary, roll out the dough into a rectangle. Repeat the process twice more, until all of the walnuts have been incorporated into the dough. Let rest for 5 minutes.

3. *Form.* Working the dough as little as possible and adding flour as necessary, form the dough into a 16-inch (40 cm) cylinder. Smooth the dough with your hands to form a soft, non-sticky skin. With the dough scraper, cut the dough into 2-inch (5 cm) pieces. Form each piece into a roll.

Any of the variations of Easy Artisan Slow-Rise Dough (pages 148–153) or Easy Artisan Naturally Leavened Dough (pages 232–235).

4. *Rest.* Place the rolls about 2 inches (5 cm) apart on the prepared baking sheet. Spray plastic wrap with olive oil spray and cover the rolls with the oiled side touching the dough. Cover the baking sheet with a tea towel. Let rest at room temperature for 4 hours or until slightly risen and expanded.

5. *Prepare oven for artisan baking.* About 30 minutes before baking, place the broiler pan on the lower shelf and the baking stone on the middle shelf of the oven. Preheat to 450°F (230°C).

6. *Place baking sheet on baking stone and add water to broiler pan.* Using an oven mitt, carefully pull the middle rack of the oven out several inches. Place the baking sheet on the hot stone. Push the middle rack back in place. Pull the lower rack out, pour the hot water into the broiler pan and push the lower rack back in place. Spray the rolls with water. Close the oven door immediately so the steam will envelop the oven.

7. *Bake.* Bake for 15 to 17 minutes, spraying the rolls with water three times during baking, until risen and brown. Transfer to a wire rack to cool on pan.

Change It Up

Thyme and Olive Artisan Rolls: Use the filling from Thyme and Olive Boule (page 240) instead of the walnuts.

Golden Onion Sourdough Rye

**Makes 1 boule,
to serve 8 to 12**

Equipment:
- Rolling pin
- Flexible cutting board, floured
- Baker's peel
- Broiler pan
- Baking stone
- Plastic spray bottle of water

Sour rye meets golden onion with savory ground white pepper. Make these into rolls, following the instructions for Thyme and Olive Artisan Rolls (variation, page 243) for wonderful sandwiches.

Filling

3 tbsp	olive oil	45 mL
1	large onion, chopped	1
1/2 tsp	freshly ground white pepper	2 mL
1/2 tsp	garlic salt	2 mL
1/2	recipe prepared Naturally Leavened Sour Rye Dough (page 234)	1/2
	Unbleached bread flour	
	Olive oil spray	
1/2 cup	cornmeal	125 mL
2 cups	hot water	500 mL

1. *Prepare filling.* In a medium skillet, heat oil over medium-high heat. Sauté onion for 7 to 10 minutes or until transparent. Season with pepper and garlic salt. Remove from heat and let cool.

2. *Turn.* Place dough on a generously floured surface and dust generously with flour. Flour your hands. Using a dough scraper, scrape the dough up and over itself, flouring and turning it as you go, for 12 to 15 turns or until the dough is soft and not sticky. Dust very lightly with flour.

3. *Fill.* Flour your hands and the rolling pin. Working the dough as little as possible and adding flour as necessary, roll out the dough into a large rectangle. Arrange one-quarter of the filling on the upper half of the dough and press into the dough with your hands. Fold the other half over the filling. Turn the dough a quarter turn. Working the dough as little as possible and adding flour as necessary, roll out the dough into a rectangle. Arrange another quarter of the filling on the upper half of the dough and press into the dough with your hands. Fold the other half over the filling. Turn the dough a quarter turn. Working the dough as little as possible and adding flour as necessary, roll out the dough into a rectangle. Repeat the process twice more, until all of the filling has been incorporated into the dough. Let rest for 5 minutes.

4. *Form.* Working the dough as little as possible and adding flour as necessary, form the dough into an 8- to 10-inch (20 to 25 cm) round. Smooth the dough with your hands to form a soft, non-sticky skin. Pinch any seams together. Lightly flour any sticky places on the dough. The dough should feel soft and smooth all over, like a baby's skin, but not at all sticky.

5. *Rest.* Scoop under the boule with the dough scraper and cutting board so that the boule rests on the cutting board. Spray plastic wrap with olive oil spray and cover the dough with the oiled side touching the dough. Cover the cutting board with a tea towel. Let rest at room temperature for 4 hours or until slightly risen and expanded.

6. *Prepare oven for artisan baking.* About 30 minutes before baking, place the broiler pan on the lower shelf and the baking stone on the middle shelf of the oven. Preheat to 450°F (230°C).

7. *Slash boule with serrated knife.* Remove the plastic wrap from the boule. Using a serrated knife, make three evenly spaced slashes, about $1\frac{1}{2}$ inches (4 cm) deep, across the boule, exposing the moist dough under the surface.

8. *Transfer boule to baker's peel.* Sprinkle the cornmeal on the baker's peel. Using the dough scraper and flouring the dough if it sticks to the board, loosen and nudge the boule from the cutting board onto the peel.

9. *Slide boule onto baking stone and add water to broiler pan.* Using an oven mitt, carefully pull the middle rack of the oven out several inches. Hold the baker's peel level with the rack so that the dough round will slide onto the center of the hot stone. With a quick forward jerk of your arms, slide the dough round from the peel to the stone. Push the middle rack back in place. Pull the lower rack out, pour the hot water into the broiler pan and push the lower rack back in place. Spray the boule with water. Close the oven door immediately so the steam will envelop the oven.

10. *Bake.* Bake for 27 to 30 minutes, spraying the loaf with water three times during baking, until the crust is a blistered medium golden brown and an instant-read thermometer inserted in the center of the loaf registers at least 190°F (90°C). Wearing oven mitts, remove the loaf by hand to cool on a wire rack.

Naturally Leavened Wild Rice Stalks

Makes 2 bread stalks, to serve 12 to 16

Equipment:
- Flexible cutting board, floured
- Baking sheet, lined with parchment paper
- Broiler pan
- Baking stone
- Plastic spray bottle of water

Naturally Leavened Wild Rice Dough is handsome — there's no other word for it. A pale, creamy yellow with black flecks of cooked wild or short-grain black rice, this dough makes a fine boule, batard or baguette. You can go a step further, as here, and cut it into the classic pain d'épi, *or wheat sheaf shape, for a standout on the buffet or dinner table. You already have experience with forming a baguette and, if you've made the Swedish Tea Ring (page 192), with snipping the dough at intervals and fanning it out. That's exactly the two-step forming process for this recipe.*

½	recipe prepared Naturally Leavened Wild Rice Dough (page 235)	½
	Unbleached bread flour	
	Olive oil spray	
2 cups	hot water	500 mL

1. *Turn.* Place dough on a generously floured surface and dust generously with flour. Flour your hands. Using a dough scraper, scrape the dough up and over itself, flouring and turning it as you go, for 12 to 15 turns or until the dough is soft and not sticky. Cut the dough in half and dust very lightly with flour.

2. *Form.* Flour your hands. Working the dough as little as possible and adding flour as necessary, form each half into a 12- to 14-inch (30 to 35 cm) cylinder. Lightly flour any sticky places on the dough. The dough should feel soft and smooth all over, like a baby's skin, but not at all sticky.

3. *Cut.* Scoop under each loaf with the dough scraper and cutting board and transfer the loaves to the prepared baking sheet, placing them 4 inches (10 cm) apart. Using kitchen shears, with the blades almost flat against the dough, and starting from the bottom end of each cylinder, make seven V-shaped cuts almost all the way through the dough, at even intervals, up the length of the dough. Raise and turn each V-shaped notch up and out to alternating sides, right then left, to form the wild rice stalk.

4. *Rest.* Spray plastic wrap with olive oil spray and cover the dough with the oiled side touching the dough. Cover the baking sheet with a tea towel. Let rest at room temperature for 4 hours or until slightly risen and expanded.

5. *Prepare oven for artisan baking.* About 30 minutes before baking, place the broiler pan on the lower shelf and the baking stone on the middle shelf of the oven. Preheat to 450°F (230°C).

You Can Also Use
Any of the variations of Easy Artisan Slow-Rise Dough (pages 148–153) or Easy Artisan Naturally Leavened Dough (pages 232–235).

6. *Place baking sheet on baking stone and add water to broiler pan.* Using an oven mitt, carefully pull the middle rack of the oven out several inches. Place the baking sheet on the hot stone. Push the middle rack back in place. Pull the lower rack out, pour the hot water into the broiler pan and push the lower rack back in place. Spray the loaves with water. Close the oven door immediately so the steam will envelop the oven.

7. *Bake.* Bake for 18 to 22 minutes, spraying the loaves with water three times during baking, until lightly browned and an instant-read thermometer inserted in the center of the loaf registers at least 190°F (90°C). Transfer to a rack to cool on pan.

Change It Up

Naturally Leavened Wheat Sheaves: Use Easy Artisan Naturally Leavened Dough (page 230), made with stone-ground wheat, in place of the Naturally Leavened Wild Rice Dough.

Country French Couronne

**Makes 1 crown loaf,
to serve 8 to 12**

Equipment:
- Rolling pin
- Flexible cutting board, floured
- Baking sheet, lined with parchment paper
- Broiler pan
- Baking stone
- Plastic spray bottle of water

A couronne is the classic crown or circlet shape often seen in artisan breads. This is another variation on the Swedish Tea Ring (page 192), so if you've already made that, this recipe is a snap. You'll roll the dough out to a rectangle, sprinkle on the seeds, then roll the dough into a cylinder. To keep the circle from becoming something else when you try to slide it onto the baking stone, we'll use a baking sheet. The interior sprinkling of seeds forms a pleasing pattern when the slices are turned out, much like a quilted design on a vintage Provençal boutis, or quilt.

½	recipe prepared Easy Artisan Naturally Leavened Dough (page 230)	½
	Unbleached bread flour	
2 tbsp	fennel seeds	25 mL
2 tbsp	poppy seeds	25 mL
2 tbsp	millet or golden sesame seeds	25 mL
	Olive oil spray	
2 cups	hot water	500 mL

1. *Turn.* Place dough on a generously floured surface and dust generously with flour. Flour your hands. Using a dough scraper, scrape the dough up and over itself, flouring and turning it as you go, for 12 to 15 turns or until the dough is soft and not sticky. Dust very lightly with flour.

2. *Form and fill.* Flour your hands and the rolling pin. Working the dough as little as possible and adding flour as necessary, roll out the dough into an 18- by 12-inch (45 by 30 cm) rectangle. Sprinkle the dough with the fennel, poppy and millet seeds and press into the dough with your hands. Starting with a long end, roll up the dough into a cylinder. If the dough begins to stick to the surface, use a dough scraper to push flour under the dough and scrape it up. Gently press and squeeze as you're rolling, to form the dough into a solid cylinder. Pinch the long seam closed. Bring the ends together to form a circle and pinch closed. Lightly flour any sticky places on the dough. The dough should feel soft and smooth all over, like a baby's skin, but not at all sticky.

3. *Cut.* Scoop under the ring with the dough scraper and cutting board and transfer the ring to the prepared baking sheet, seam side down. With kitchen shears, starting from the outer rim, cut diagonal slashes in the ring, three-quarters of the way through the dough, at 2-inch (5 cm) intervals all around the ring. Gently fan the slices, going in the same direction, so the filling shows.

4. *Rest.* Spray plastic wrap with olive oil spray and cover the dough with the oiled side touching the dough. Cover the baking sheet with a tea towel. Let rest at room temperature for 4 hours or until slightly risen and expanded.

You Can Also Use

Easy Artisan Dough (page 34), Easy Artisan Slow-Rise Dough (page 148) or Easy Artisan Whole-Grain Dough (page 56), made with white whole wheat flour. Follow the original recipe's instructions for resting and rising, but form, fill, cut and bake according to this recipe.

5. *Prepare oven for artisan baking.* About 30 minutes before baking, place the broiler pan on the lower shelf and the baking stone on the middle shelf of the oven. Preheat to 450°F (230°C).

6. *Place baking sheet on baking stone and add water to broiler pan.* Using an oven mitt, carefully pull the middle rack of the oven out several inches. Place the baking sheet on the hot stone. Push the middle rack back in place. Pull the lower rack out, pour the hot water into the broiler pan and push the lower rack back in place. Spray the couronne with water. Close the oven door immediately so the steam will envelop the oven.

7. *Bake.* Bake for 20 to 22 minutes, spraying the ring with water three times during baking, until risen and browned and an instant-read thermometer inserted in the center of the loaf registers at least 190°F (90°C). Remove from pan and transfer to a wire rack to cool.

Change It Up

Rosemary Walnut Couronne: Sprinkle the dough rectangle with 1 cup (250 mL) chopped Rosemary Walnuts (page 297) instead of the seeds.

Toasted Hazelnut Flatbread with Roasted Asparagus and Goat Cheese

Makes 1 large flatbread, to serve 12 to 16 as an appetizer, or 6 to 8 as a main course

Equipment:
- Rolling pin
- Flexible cutting board, floured
- Large baking sheet, lined with parchment paper
- Broiler pan
- Baking stone

Serve this delicious flatbread as an appetizer, with a Cabernet or Pinot Noir, or as the main course of a casual meal, as you would a quiche.

You Can Also Use

Master Doughs #1 through #5 or Slow-Rise Ciabatta dough (page 164). Follow the original recipe's instructions for resting and rising, then top and bake according to this recipe.

½	recipe prepared Easy Artisan Naturally Leavened Dough (page 230)	½
	Unbleached bread flour	
	Olive oil spray	
1 cup	toasted hazelnuts, coarsely chopped	250 mL
8 oz	thin-stalked asparagus, trimmed	250 g
1 tbsp	olive oil	15 mL
8 oz	fresh goat cheese, crumbled	250 g
	Additional olive oil	
2 cups	hot water	500 mL

1. *Turn.* Place dough on a generously floured surface and dust generously with flour. Flour your hands. Using a dough scraper, scrape the dough up and over itself, flouring and turning it as you go, for 12 to 15 turns or until the dough is soft and not sticky. Dust very lightly with flour.

2. *Fill.* Flour your hands and the rolling pin. Working the dough as little as possible and adding flour as necessary, roll out the dough into a large rectangle. Arrange one-quarter of the hazelnuts on the upper half of the dough and press into the dough with your hands. Fold the other half over the nuts. Turn the dough a quarter turn. Working the dough as little as possible and adding flour as necessary, roll out the dough into a rectangle. Arrange another quarter of the nuts on the upper half of the dough and press into the dough with your hands. Fold the other half over the nuts. Turn the dough a quarter turn. Working the dough as little as possible and adding flour as necessary, roll out the dough into a rectangle. Repeat the process twice more, until all of the nuts have been incorporated into the dough. Let rest for 5 minutes.

3. *Form.* Working the dough as little as possible and adding flour as necessary, roll out the dough into a 16- by 10-inch (40 by 25 cm) oval. Lightly flour any sticky places on the dough. The dough should feel soft and smooth all over, like a baby's skin, but not at all sticky.

4. *Rest.* Scoop under the dough oval with the dough scraper and cutting board and transfer the oval to the prepared baking sheet. Spray plastic wrap with olive oil spray and cover the dough with the oiled side touching the dough. Cover the baking sheet with a tea towel. Let rest at room temperature for 4 hours or until slightly risen and expanded.

5. *Prepare topping.* Cut the asparagus on the diagonal into 2-inch (5 cm) pieces, place in a bowl and toss with 1 tbsp (15 mL) olive oil.

6. *Prepare oven for artisan baking.* About 30 minutes before baking, place the broiler pan on the lower shelf and the baking stone on the middle shelf of the oven. Preheat to 450°F (230°C).

7. *Top.* Using a spoon, dollop the goat cheese on the flatbread. Scatter the asparagus over the cheese and drizzle with olive oil.

8. *Place baking sheet on baking stone and add water to broiler pan.* Using an oven mitt, carefully pull the middle rack of the oven out several inches. Place the baking sheet on the hot stone. Push the middle rack back in place. Pull the lower rack out, pour the hot water into the broiler pan and push the lower rack back in place. Close the oven door immediately so the steam will envelop the oven.

9. *Bake.* Bake for 20 to 22 minutes or until the crust is lightly browned. Remove from pan and transfer to a wire rack to cool.

Apricot and Pistachio Flatbread with Feta and Honey

Makes 1 large flatbread, to serve 12 to 16 as an appetizer, or 6 to 8 as a main course

Equipment:
- Rolling pin
- Flexible cutting board, floured
- Large baking sheet, lined with parchment paper
- Broiler pan
- Baking stone

½ cup	snipped dried apricots	125 mL
½ cup	roasted pistachios	125 mL
½	recipe prepared Easy Artisan Naturally Leavened Dough (page 230)	½
	Unbleached bread flour	
	Olive oil spray	
8 oz	feta cheese, crumbled	250 g
	Olive oil	
2 tbsp	liquid honey	25 mL
2 cups	hot water	500 mL

1. *Combine.* In a small bowl, combine apricots and pistachios.

2. *Turn.* Place dough on a generously floured surface and dust generously with flour. Flour your hands. Using a dough scraper, scrape the dough up and over itself, flouring and turning it as you go, for 12 to 15 turns or until the dough is soft and not sticky. Dust very lightly with flour.

3. *Fill.* Flour your hands and the rolling pin. Working the dough as little as possible and adding flour as necessary, roll out the dough into a large rectangle. Arrange one-quarter of the apricot mixture on the upper half of the dough and press into the dough with your hands. Fold the other half over the filling. Turn the dough a quarter turn. Working the dough as little as possible and adding flour as necessary, roll out the dough into a rectangle. Arrange another quarter of the filling on the upper half of the dough and press into the dough with your hands. Fold the other half over the filling. Turn the dough a quarter turn. Working the dough as little as possible and adding flour as necessary, roll out the dough into a rectangle. Repeat the process twice more, until all of the filling has been incorporated into the dough. Let rest for 5 minutes.

You Can Also Use

Master Doughs #1 through #5 or Slow-Rise Ciabatta dough (page 164). Follow the original recipe's instructions for resting and rising, then top and bake according to this recipe.

4. *Form.* Working the dough as little as possible and adding flour as necessary, roll out the dough into a 16- by 10-inch (40 by 25 cm) oval. Lightly flour any sticky places on the dough. The dough should feel soft and smooth all over, like a baby's skin, but not at all sticky.

5. *Rest.* Scoop under the dough oval with the dough scraper and cutting board and transfer the oval to the prepared baking sheet. Spray plastic wrap with olive oil spray and cover the dough with the oiled side touching the dough. Cover the baking sheet with a tea towel. Let rest at room temperature for 4 hours or until slightly risen and expanded.

6. *Prepare oven for artisan baking.* About 30 minutes before baking, place the broiler pan on the lower shelf and the baking stone on the middle shelf of the oven. Preheat to 450°F (230°C).

7. *Top.* Using a spoon, dollop the feta cheese on the flatbread. Drizzle with olive oil, then with honey.

8. *Place baking sheet on baking stone and add water to broiler pan.* Using an oven mitt, carefully pull the middle rack of the oven out several inches. Place the baking sheet on the hot stone. Push the middle rack back in place. Pull the lower rack out, pour the hot water into the broiler pan and push the lower rack back in place. Close the oven door immediately so the steam will envelop the oven.

9. *Bake.* Bake for 20 to 22 minutes or until the crust is lightly browned. Remove from pan and transfer to a wire rack to cool.

Bagels and Bialys

Master Recipe #10
Easy Artisan Bagel Dough

Bagels (and bialys) came to North America from Eastern Europe with Polish and German émigrés. The hallmarks of a good bagel are a shiny texture (from boiling them first) and a chewy crumb (from unbleached bread flour). The secret ingredient is barley malt, or malt syrup, a thick, dark brown sweetener made from sprouted barley. Bagel dough is easy to make, but the technique involved in forming the bagels takes a little practice. But even an imperfect homemade bagel is something to cheer!

Makes enough dough for bagels or bialys to serve 12 to 16

Equipment:
- Instant-read thermometer
- 16-cup (4 L) mixing bowl
- 4-cup (1 L) glass measuring cup
- Wooden spoon or Danish dough whisk

Tips

Look for barley malt in the syrup section at better grocery stores or health food shops, or online.

Before storing the dough in the refrigerator, use a permanent marker to write the date on the plastic wrap, so you'll know when you made your dough — and when to use it up 3 days later.

6$\frac{1}{2}$ cups	unbleached bread flour	1.625 L
2$\frac{1}{2}$ tbsp	instant or bread machine yeast	32 mL
1$\frac{1}{2}$ tbsp	kosher salt	22 mL
2	eggs, beaten	2
$\frac{1}{2}$ cup	barley malt (malt syrup)	125 mL
$\frac{1}{4}$ cup	vegetable oil	50 mL
	Hot water	

1. *Measure.* Spoon the flour into a measuring cup, level with a knife or your finger, then dump the flour into the mixing bowl.

2. *Mix.* Add the yeast and salt to the flour. Stir together with a wooden spoon or Danish dough whisk. In the glass measuring cup, combine eggs, barley malt and oil. Pour in enough hot water to reach the 4-cup (1 L) mark and carefully whisk to blend. Pour into the flour mixture and stir together until just moistened. Beat 40 strokes, scraping the bottom and the sides of the bowl, until the dough forms a lumpy, sticky mass.

3. *Rise.* Cover the bowl with plastic wrap and let rise at room temperature (72°F/22°C) in a draft-free place for 2 hours or until the dough has risen nearly to the top of the bowl and has a sponge-like appearance.

4. *Use right away or refrigerate.* Use that day or place the dough, covered with plastic wrap, in the refrigerator for up to 3 days before baking.

continued…

Polish Poppy Seed Pull-Aparts (page 218)

Brioche Beignets
(page 222)

Thyme and Olive Boule (page 240)

Rustic Italian Batard (page 238)

New York Bagels (variations, page 260–261)
top to bottom: Salt Bagels, Poppy Seed Bagels, Asiago Bagels

Flaky, Buttery Croissants (page 276)

Apricot and Almond Galettes (page 286)

clockwise from top: Artisan Butter (page 295), Honey Spice Applesauce (page 296) and Rosemary Walnuts (page 297)

Baking with Canadian Flour

Canadian flour has a higher protein content than some U.S. flours and therefore absorbs more water. If you are using Canadian bread flour, start by adding about $\frac{1}{2}$ cup (125 mL) less than called for, and add just enough of the remaining $\frac{1}{2}$ cup (125 mL) to make a thick, paste-like dough.

Change It Up

Montreal Bagel Dough: Omit the salt. (You will also boil them in sweetened water and shape them smaller; see recipe, page 264.)

Bialy Dough: Substitute 2 tbsp (25 mL) granulated sugar for the barley malt.

Bagels and Bialys in Minutes a Day

Day 1	Stir the dough together and let rise. Bake, or cover and chill.
Days 2–3	Remove part of the dough, form and bake bagels and bialys.

Bagel and Bialy Flavorings

Flavoring	How Used	Flavor
Caraway seeds	Mixed into dough	Caraway
Dehydrated onion flakes	Sprinkled on boiled bagels before baking	Toasted onion
Dill seeds	Sprinkled on boiled bagels before baking	Dill
Fennel seeds	Sprinkled on boiled bagels before baking	Licorice
Ground cinnamon	Mixed with sugar and sprinkled on dough before baking	Cinnamon
Nigella seeds	Sprinkled on boiled bagels before baking	Onion
Poppy seeds	Sprinkled on boiled bagels before baking	Sweet
Sesame seeds	Sprinkled on boiled bagels before baking	Sesame

Whole-Grain Bagel Dough

Makes enough dough for bagels or bialys to serve 12 to 16

Equipment:
- Instant-read thermometer
- 16-cup (4 L) mixing bowl
- 4-cup (1 L) glass measuring cup
- Wooden spoon or Danish dough whisk

4½ cups	unbleached bread flour	1.125 L
2 cups	whole-grain flour, such as white whole wheat	500 mL
2½ tbsp	instant or bread machine yeast	32 mL
1½ tbsp	kosher salt	22 mL
1 tbsp	Artisan Bread Dough Enhancer (page 294)	15 mL
2	eggs, beaten	2
½ cup	barley malt (malt syrup)	125 mL
¼ cup	vegetable oil	50 mL
	Hot water	

Tips

Look for barley malt in the syrup section at better grocery stores or health food shops, or online.

Before storing the dough in the refrigerator, use a permanent marker to write the date on the plastic wrap, so you'll know when you made your dough — and when to use it up 3 days later.

1. *Measure.* One at a time, spoon the bread flour and whole-grain flour into a measuring cup, level with a knife or your finger, then dump into the mixing bowl. Combine well.

2. *Mix.* Add the yeast, salt and dough enhancer to the flours. Stir together with a wooden spoon or Danish dough whisk. In the glass measuring cup, combine eggs, barley malt and oil. Pour in enough hot water to reach the 4-cup (1 L) mark and carefully whisk to blend. Pour into the flour mixture and stir together until just moistened. Beat 40 strokes, scraping the bottom and the sides of the bowl, until the dough forms a lumpy, sticky mass.

3. *Rise.* Cover the bowl with plastic wrap and let rise at room temperature (72°F/22°C) in a draft-free place for 2 hours or until the dough has risen nearly to the top of the bowl and has a sponge-like appearance.

4. *Use right away or refrigerate.* Use that day or place the dough, covered with plastic wrap, in the refrigerator for up to 3 days before baking.

Baking with Canadian Flour

If you are using Canadian bread flour, start by adding about ½ cup (125 mL) less than called for, and add just enough of the remaining ½ cup (125 mL) to make a thick, paste-like dough. You don't need to adjust the amount of whole-grain flour.

Caraway Rye Bagel Dough

Makes enough dough for bagels or bialys to serve 12 to 16

Equipment:
- Instant-read thermometer
- 16-cup (4 L) mixing bowl
- 4-cup (1 L) glass measuring cup
- Wooden spoon or Danish dough whisk

4½ cups	unbleached bread flour	1.125 L
2 cups	rye flour	500 mL
2½ tbsp	instant or bread machine yeast	32 mL
2 tbsp	caraway seeds	25 mL
1½ tbsp	kosher salt	22 mL
1 tbsp	Artisan Bread Dough Enhancer (page 294)	15 mL
2	eggs, beaten	2
½ cup	barley malt (malt syrup)	125 mL
¼ cup	vegetable oil	50 mL
	Hot water	

Tips

Look for barley malt in the syrup section at better grocery stores or health food shops, or online.

Before storing the dough in the refrigerator, use a permanent marker to write the date on the plastic wrap, so you'll know when you made your dough — and when to use it up 3 days later.

1. *Measure.* One at a time, spoon the bread flour and rye flour into a measuring cup, level with a knife or your finger, then dump into the mixing bowl. Combine well.

2. *Mix.* Add the yeast, caraway seeds, salt and dough enhancer to the flours. Stir together with a wooden spoon or Danish dough whisk. In the glass measuring cup, combine eggs, barley malt and oil. Pour in enough hot water to reach the 4-cup (1 L) mark and carefully whisk to blend. Pour into the flour mixture and stir together until just moistened. Beat 40 strokes, scraping the bottom and the sides of the bowl, until the dough forms a lumpy, sticky mass.

3. *Rise.* Cover the bowl with plastic wrap and let rise at room temperature (72°F/22°C) in a draft-free place for 2 hours or until the dough has risen nearly to the top of the bowl and has a sponge-like appearance.

4. *Use right away or refrigerate.* Use that day or place the dough, covered with plastic wrap, in the refrigerator for up to 3 days before baking.

Baking with Canadian Flour
If you are using Canadian bread flour, start by adding about ½ cup (125 mL) less than called for, and add just enough of the remaining ½ cup (125 mL) to make a thick, paste-like dough. You don't need to adjust the amount of rye flour.

New York Bagels

Makes 8 large bagels

Equipment:
- Rolling pin
- Large baking sheet, lined with parchment paper
- Broiler pan
- Baking stone

Artisan bagels look like they were freshly made by an artisan's hand — yours! They are imperfectly shaped, crinkly and wrinkly; in short, quite unlike their smooth mass-produced cousins. But the flavor and texture are truly authentic — and addictive. They're crisp-crusted, with the right amount of "bite" and chewier crumb that authentic bagels have. You boil them first, then bake. Note that bagels need 2 hours to rest before they are boiled and baked.

½	recipe prepared Easy Artisan Bagel Dough (page 256), about the size of a volleyball	½
	Unbleached bread flour	
2 cups	hot water	500 mL

1. **Form.** Place dough on a floured surface and dust very lightly with flour. Flour your hands and the rolling pin. Working the dough as little as possible and adding flour as necessary, roll out the dough into a large rectangle. Fold the dough in half, turn a quarter turn and roll out again. Repeat three more times. Form the dough into an 8-inch (20 cm) cylinder. Smooth the dough with your hands to form a soft, non-sticky skin. Pinch any seams together. Cut the cylinder into 1-inch (2.5 cm) pieces. Lightly flour any sticky places on the dough. The dough should feel soft and smooth all over, like a baby's skin, but not at all sticky. With your hands, pull, stretch, squeeze and roll each portion into an 8- to 9-inch (20 to 23 cm) rope. Hold one end of each rope between your thumb and forefinger in the palm of your hand. Drape the rest of the rope around the back of your hand until the other end touches the end you're holding. Pinch and squeeze the ends together.

2. **Rest.** Place the bagels on the prepared baking sheet. With your fingers, neaten them up into a bagel shape, making sure they're 2 inches (5 cm) apart. Cover with a slightly moistened tea towel and let rest at room temperature for 2 hours.

3. **Prepare oven for artisan baking and boil water.** About 30 minutes before baking, place the broiler pan on the lower shelf and the baking stone on the middle shelf of the oven. Preheat to 450°F (230°C). Bring a large pot of water to a boil over medium-high heat.

4. **Boil.** Using a slotted spoon or a metal pancake turner, place four bagels in the boiling water. Boil for 1 minute. Gently turn them over and boil for 1 minute. Drain well and return to the baking sheet, placing them 2 inches (5 cm) apart. Repeat with the remaining bagels.

Artisan bagels taste best the same day they're made.

5. *Place baking sheet on baking stone and add water to broiler pan.* Using an oven mitt, carefully pull the middle rack of the oven out several inches. Place the baking sheet on the hot stone. Push the middle rack back in place. Pull the lower rack out, pour the hot water into the broiler pan and push the lower rack back in place. Close the oven door immediately so the steam will envelop the oven.

6. *Bake.* Bake for 25 to 27 minutes or until the crust is a medium dark brown and an instant-read thermometer inserted in the center of the bagels registers at least 190°F (90°C). Transfer to a wire rack to cool on pan.

Change It Up

Poppy Seed Bagels: Sprinkle boiled bagels with poppy seeds before baking.

Salt Bagels: Sprinkle boiled bagels with coarse kosher or sea salt before baking.

Onion Bagels: Sprinkle boiled bagels with dehydrated onion flakes before baking.

Asiago Bagels: Sprinkle boiled bagels with shredded Asiago cheese before baking.

Sesame Bagels: Sprinkle boiled bagels with sesame seeds before baking.

Cinnamon Raisin Bagels: In a bowl, combine $1/2$ cup (125 mL) packed light or dark brown sugar and 1 tbsp (15 mL) ground cinnamon. Sprinkle this mixture onto the dough rectangle, leaving a 1-inch (2.5 cm) perimeter, then sprinkle with $1/2$ cup (125 mL) raisins before rolling the dough up into a cylinder.

Marbled Bagels

Makes 8 large bagels

Equipment:
- Rolling pin
- Large baking sheet, lined with parchment paper
- Broiler pan
- Baking stone

Caraway Rye Bagel Dough, which has caraway seeds added, is my favorite whole-grain dough to use in Marbled Bagels, but feel free to use other whole-grain doughs. Note that bagels need 2 hours to rest before they are boiled and baked.

¼	recipe prepared Easy Artisan Bagel Dough (page 256), about the size of a softball	¼
¼	recipe prepared Caraway Rye Bagel Dough (page 259), about the size of a softball	¼
	Unbleached bread flour	
2 cups	hot water	500 mL

1. *Form.* Place the dough portions on a floured surface and dust very lightly with flour. Flour your hands and the rolling pin. Working the dough as little as possible and adding flour as necessary, roll out each dough portion into a 10- by 9-inch (25 by 23 cm) rectangle. Stack one rectangle on top of the other. Starting with a long end, roll up the dough into a cylinder. Roll out the dough into a large rectangle. Fold the dough in half, turn a quarter turn and roll out again. Repeat two more times. Form the dough into an 8-inch (20 cm) cylinder. Smooth the dough with your hands to form a soft, non-sticky skin. Pinch any seams together. Cut the cylinder into 1-inch (2.5 cm) pieces. Lightly flour any sticky places on the dough. The dough should feel soft and smooth all over, like a baby's skin, but not at all sticky. With your hands, pull, stretch, squeeze and roll each portion into an 8- to 9-inch (20 to 23 cm) rope. Hold one end of each rope between your thumb and forefinger in the palm of your hand. Drape the rest of the rope around the back of your hand until the other end touches the end you're holding. Pinch and squeeze the ends together.

2. *Rest.* Place the bagels on the prepared baking sheet. With your fingers, neaten them up into a bagel shape, making sure they're 2 inches (5 cm) apart. Cover with a slightly moistened tea towel and let rest at room temperature for 2 hours.

3. *Prepare oven for artisan baking and boil water.* About 30 minutes before baking, place the broiler pan on the lower shelf and the baking stone on the middle shelf of the oven. Preheat to 450°F (230°C). Bring a large pot of water to a boil over medium-high heat.

4. *Boil.* Using a slotted spoon or a metal pancake turner, place four bagels in the boiling water. Boil for 1 minute. Gently turn them over and boil for 1 minute. Drain well and return to the baking sheet, placing them 2 inches (5 cm) apart. Repeat with the remaining bagels.

5. *Place baking sheet on baking stone and add water to broiler pan.* Using an oven mitt, carefully pull the middle rack of the oven out several inches. Place the baking sheet on the hot stone. Push the middle rack back in place. Pull the lower rack out, pour the hot water into the broiler pan and push the lower rack back in place. Close the oven door immediately so the steam will envelop the oven.

6. *Bake.* Bake for 25 to 27 minutes or until the crust is a medium dark brown and an instant-read thermometer inserted in the center of the bagels registers at least 190°F (90°C). Transfer to a wire rack to cool on pan.

Montreal Bagels

Montreal bagels are made with a salt-free dough. They're smaller than New York bagels and are boiled in water sweetened with barley malt. Then they're usually baked in a wood-burning oven. To simulate that, I put on my BBQ Queen tiara to offer a way to get a slightly smoky flavor in your oven, using hardwood chips meant for the grill or smoker. Note that bagels need 2 hours to rest before they are boiled and baked.

1/2	recipe prepared Montreal Bagel Dough (variation, page 257), about the size of a volleyball	1/2
	Unbleached bread flour	
1/2 cup	barley malt (malt syrup)	125 mL
2 cups	hot water	500 mL

1. **Form.** Place dough on a floured surface and dust very lightly with flour. Flour your hands and the rolling pin. Working the dough as little as possible and adding flour as necessary, roll out the dough into a large rectangle. Fold the dough in half, turn a quarter turn and roll out again. Repeat three more times. Form the dough into a 12-inch (30 cm) cylinder. Smooth the dough with your hands to form a soft, non-sticky skin. Pinch any seams together. Cut the cylinder into 1-inch (2.5 cm) pieces. Lightly flour any sticky places on the dough. The dough should feel soft and smooth all over, like a baby's skin, but not at all sticky. With your hands, pull, stretch, squeeze and roll each portion into a 6-inch (15 cm) rope. Hold one end of each rope between your thumb and forefinger in the palm of your hand. Drape the rest of the rope around the back of your hand until the other end touches the end you're holding. Pinch and squeeze the ends together.

2. **Rest.** Place the bagels on the prepared baking sheet. With your fingers, neaten them up into a bagel shape, making sure they're 2 inches (5 cm) apart. Cover with a slightly moistened tea towel and let rest at room temperature for 2 hours.

3. **Prepare oven for artisan baking and boil water.** About 30 minutes before baking, place the broiler pan on the lower shelf and the baking stone on the middle shelf of the oven. Preheat to 450°F (230°C). For the wood-burning oven technique, place the moistened wood chips in a small metal pan next to the broiler pan on the lower shelf. They will start to smolder and release wisps of smoke. Bring a large pot of water, sweetened with the barley malt, to a boil over medium-high heat.

Tips

Artisan bagels taste best the same day they're made.

If using the wood chips, be sure your kitchen is well ventilated.

4. *Boil.* Using a slotted spoon or a metal pancake turner, place four bagels in the boiling water. Boil for 1 minute. Gently turn them over and boil for 1 minute. Drain well and return to the baking sheet, placing them 2 inches (5 cm) apart. Repeat with the remaining bagels.

5. *Place baking sheet on baking stone and add water to broiler pan.* Using an oven mitt, carefully pull the middle rack of the oven out several inches. Place the baking sheet on the hot stone. Push the middle rack back in place. Pull the lower rack out, pour the hot water into the broiler pan and push the lower rack back in place. Close the oven door immediately so the steam will envelop the oven.

6. *Bake.* Bake for 22 to 25 minutes or until the crust is a medium dark brown and an instant-read thermometer inserted in the center of the bagels registers at least 190°F (90°C). Transfer to a wire rack to cool on pan. Remove the smoldering wood chips from the oven, let cool completely, then discard.

Change It Up

Poppy Seed Bagels: Sprinkle boiled bagels with poppy seeds before baking.

Salt Bagels: Sprinkle boiled bagels with coarse kosher or sea salt before baking.

Onion Bagels: Sprinkle boiled bagels with dehydrated onion flakes before baking.

Asiago Bagels: Sprinkle boiled bagels with shredded Asiago cheese before baking.

Sesame Bagels: Sprinkle boiled bagels with sesame seeds before baking.

Cinnamon Raisin Montreal Bagels

Add a "schmear" of cream cheese and you've got a great snack.

½ cup	packed light or dark brown sugar	125 mL
1 tbsp	ground cinnamon	15 mL
½	recipe prepared Montreal Bagel Dough (variation, page 257), about the size of a volleyball	½
	Unbleached bread flour	
½ cup	raisins	125 mL
½ cup	barley malt (malt syrup)	125 mL
2 cups	hot water	500 mL

1. **Combine.** In a small bowl, combine brown sugar and cinnamon.

2. **Form and fill.** Place dough on a floured surface and dust very lightly with flour. Flour your hands and the rolling pin. Working the dough as little as possible and adding flour as necessary, roll out the dough into a large rectangle. Fold the dough in half, turn a quarter turn and roll out again. Repeat three more times. Sprinkle the dough with the brown sugar mixture, leaving a 1-inch (2.5 cm) perimeter. Sprinkle raisins over the brown sugar. Form the dough into a 12-inch (30 cm) cylinder. Smooth the dough with your hands to form a soft, non-sticky skin. Pinch any seams together. Cut the cylinder into 1-inch (2.5 cm) pieces. Lightly flour any sticky places on the dough. The dough should feel soft and smooth all over, like a baby's skin, but not at all sticky. With your hands, pull, stretch, squeeze and roll each portion into a 6-inch (15 cm) rope. Hold one end of each rope between your thumb and forefinger in the palm of your hand. Drape the rest of the rope around the back of your hand until the other end touches the end you're holding. Pinch and squeeze the ends together.

3. **Rest.** Place the bagels on the prepared baking sheet. With your fingers, neaten them up into a bagel shape, making sure they're 2 inches (5 cm) apart. Cover with a slightly moistened tea towel and let rest at room temperature for 2 hours.

Tips

Artisan bagels taste best the same day they're made.

If using the wood chips, be sure your kitchen is well ventilated.

4. *Prepare oven for artisan baking and boil water.* About 30 minutes before baking, place the broiler pan on the lower shelf and the baking stone on the middle shelf of the oven. Preheat to 450°F (230°C). For the wood-burning oven technique, place the moistened wood chips in a small metal pan next to the broiler pan on the lower shelf. They will start to smolder and release wisps of smoke. Bring a large pot of water, sweetened with the barley malt, to a boil over medium-high heat.

5. *Boil.* Using a slotted spoon or a metal pancake turner, place four bagels in the boiling water. Boil for 1 minute. Gently turn them over and boil for 1 minute. Drain well and return to the baking sheet, placing them 2 inches (5 cm) apart. Repeat with the remaining bagels.

6. *Place baking sheet on baking stone and add water to broiler pan.* Using an oven mitt, carefully pull the middle rack of the oven out several inches. Place the baking sheet on the hot stone. Push the middle rack back in place. Pull the lower rack out, pour the hot water into the broiler pan and push the lower rack back in place. Close the oven door immediately so the steam will envelop the oven.

7. *Bake.* Bake for 22 to 25 minutes or until the crust is a medium dark brown and an instant-read thermometer inserted in the center of the bagels registers at least 190°F (90°C). Transfer to a wire rack to cool on pan. Remove the smoldering wood chips from the oven, let cool completely, then discard.

Bialys

Makes 8 large bialys

Equipment:
- Rolling pin
- Large baking sheet, lined with parchment paper
- Baking stone

Brought to New York in the 1900s from Bialystock, Poland, bialys (or Bialystock kuchen) are similar to bagels, but are rolled into rimmed circles and topped with a signature mixture of finely minced onion, poppy seeds, vegetable oil and salt. Unlike bagels, they're not boiled before they're baked.

Topping

3 tbsp	finely minced onion	45 mL
2 tsp	poppy seeds	10 mL
1 tsp	vegetable oil	5 mL
¼ tsp	kosher or sea salt	1 mL
½	recipe prepared Bialy Dough (variation, page 257), about the size of a volleyball	½
	Unbleached bread flour	

1. **Combine.** In a small bowl, combine onion, poppy seeds, oil and salt. Set aside, giving the flavors time to combine.

2. **Form.** Place dough on a floured surface and dust very lightly with flour. Flour your hands and the rolling pin. Working the dough as little as possible and adding flour as necessary, roll out the dough into a large rectangle. Fold the dough in half, turn a quarter turn and roll out again. Repeat three more times. Form the dough into an 8-inch (20 cm) cylinder. Smooth the dough with your hands to form a soft, non-sticky skin. Pinch any seams together. Cut the cylinder into 1-inch (2.5 cm) pieces. Lightly flour any sticky places on the dough. The dough should feel soft and smooth all over, like a baby's skin, but not at all sticky. Roll out each piece into a 3-inch (7.5 cm) circle.

3. **Rest.** Place the circles 2 inches (5 cm) apart on the prepared baking sheet. Cover with a slightly moistened tea towel and let rest at room temperature for 2 hours.

4. **Fill.** Using the bottom of a shot glass or small drinking glass, make a well in the center of each circle, using a circular motion to create a donut-like shape with a 1-inch (2.5 cm) perimeter of raised dough. Spoon some of the topping into each depression and swirl it around with the back of the spoon. Let rest again, covered with a tea towel, while the oven preheats.

Tip

Artisan bialys taste best the same day they're made.

5. *Prepare oven for artisan baking.* Place the baking stone on the middle shelf of the oven. Preheat to 450°F (230°C).

6. *Place baking sheet on baking stone.* Using an oven mitt, carefully pull the middle rack of the oven out several inches. Place the baking sheet on the hot stone. Push the middle rack back in place.

7. *Bake.* Bake for 20 to 25 minutes or until the crust is a medium dark brown and the bialys have risen. Transfer to a wire rack to cool on pan.

Pletzel

Makes 1 large pletzel, to serve 16

Equipment:
- Rolling pin
- Large baking sheet, lined with parchment paper
- Broiler pan
- Baking stone

A pletzel is a flatbread made with bialy or bagel dough, sort of a Jewish deep-dish pizza topped with sautéed onions and sprinkled with poppy seeds. True comfort food, pletzel is delicious with slow-simmered soups and stews, salads or beer.

Topping

1/4 cup	vegetable oil (preferably olive oil)	50 mL
2	onions, chopped	2
1/2	recipe prepared Bialy Dough (variation, page 257), about the size of a volleyball	1/2
	Unbleached bread flour	
1	egg, beaten	1
	Poppy seeds	
2 cups	hot water	500 mL

1. **Prepare topping.** In a large skillet, heat oil over medium-high heat. Sauté onions for 7 to 10 minutes or until transparent. Remove from heat and let cool.

2. **Form.** Place dough on a floured surface and dust very lightly with flour. Flour your hands and the rolling pin. Working the dough as little as possible and adding flour as necessary, roll out the dough into a 12- by 10-inch (30 by 25 cm) rectangle. Lightly flour any sticky places on the dough. The dough should feel soft and smooth all over, like a baby's skin, but not at all sticky.

3. **Rest.** Transfer the dough to the prepared baking sheet. Brush the dough with beaten egg, then spread with the topping, leaving a 1-inch (2.5 cm) perimeter. Sprinkle with poppy seeds. Cover with a tea towel and let rest at room temperature for 1 hour.

4. **Prepare oven for artisan baking.** About 30 minutes before baking, place the broiler pan on the lower shelf and the baking stone on the middle shelf of the oven. Preheat to 450°F (230°C).

You Can Also Use

Easy Artisan Bagel Dough (page 256), Easy Artisan Dough (page 34), Easy Artisan Whole-Grain Dough (page 56), made with white whole wheat flour, Easy Artisan Slow-Rise Dough (page 148) or Easy Artisan Naturally Leavened Dough (page 230).

5. *Place baking sheet on baking stone and add water to broiler pan.* Using an oven mitt, carefully pull the middle rack of the oven out several inches. Place the baking sheet on the hot stone. Push the middle rack back in place. Pull the lower rack out, pour the hot water into the broiler pan and push the lower rack back in place. Close the oven door immediately so the steam will envelop the oven.

6. *Bake.* Bake for 20 to 22 minutes or until the crust is puffed and golden brown. Transfer to a rack to cool on pan. Cut into slices to serve.

Change It Up

Wood-Burning Oven Technique: Place $1/4$ cup (50 mL) fine dry wood chips (such as mesquite or apple) in a small metal pan, moisten with 2 tbsp (25 mL) water and place next to the broiler pan on the lower shelf of the oven. They will start to smolder and release wisps of smoke. Remove the pan of smoldering wood chips after baking. Let the wood chips cool completely, then discard. Be sure your kitchen is well ventilated.

Buttery Yeast Breads

Master Dough #11
Easy Artisan Buttery Yeast Dough

Buttery Yeast Dough takes us a step or two beyond Easy Artisan Sweet Dough and Easy Artisan Brioche Dough, with filling and folding techniques picked up in previous chapters. This dough starts with what's known as the detrempe *(a sweet yeast dough), to which you add a butter layer, or* buerrage, *to create a laminated dough, or one in which layers of butter create rich flakiness during baking. Traditional recipes have you pound cold butter into rectangles, a tricky proposition. This streamlined method cuts the butter in with some of the flour, as you would do for a pie crust. The buerrage is then rolled into the dough. A little orange juice in the detrempe adds a nuanced flavor note and helps cut some of the richness. Because the structure of this dough does best rolled into linear shapes, we'll stick to rectangles and avoid circles.*

Makes enough dough for pastries, braids and galettes to serve 16 to 24

Equipment:
- Instant-read thermometer
- 16-cup (4 L) mixing bowl
- Wooden spoon or Danish dough whisk
- Pastry blender or food processor
- Rolling pin

Tip
It's very important to keep laminated doughs cold, so the butter layers stay intact. Use a marble pastry work surface, if possible, and work in a cool room.

Detrempe

2¹⁄₂ cups	unbleached all-purpose flour	625 mL
¹⁄₃ cup	granulated sugar	75 mL
1 tbsp	instant or bread machine yeast	15 mL
1 tsp	kosher salt	5 mL
¹⁄₂ cup	milk (whole or 2%)	125 mL
2	eggs, beaten	2
¹⁄₄ cup	freshly squeezed orange juice	50 mL

Buerrage

1 cup	unbleached all-purpose flour	250 mL
1 cup	cold unsalted butter, cut into 16 pieces	250 mL

1. **Measure.** Spoon the flour into a measuring cup, level with a knife or your finger, then dump the flour into the mixing bowl.

2. **Mix.** Add the sugar, yeast and salt to the flour. Stir together with a wooden spoon or Danish dough whisk. Pour in the milk. Whisk the eggs with the juice, then stir into the flour mixture just until moistened. Beat 40 strokes, scraping the bottom and the sides of the bowl, until the dough forms a lumpy, sticky mass.

3. **Rise.** Cover the bowl with plastic wrap and let rise at room temperature (72°F/22°C) in a draft-free place for 2 hours or until the dough has risen nearly to the top of the bowl and has a sponge-like appearance.

4. **Refrigerate.** Place the dough, covered with plastic wrap, in the refrigerator for up to 3 days before baking. (For the best flavor, refrigerate for at least 8 hours or overnight.)

Croissants and Danish Pastry in Minutes a Day

Day 1	Make the detrempe and the buerrage. Cover and refrigerate.
Day 2	Roll the detrempe and buerrage together for laminated dough. Cover and refrigerate.
Day 3	Roll out the dough, cut and form into shapes. Cover and refrigerate, or let rise and bake.
Day 4 (optional)	Let rise and bake.

5. *Prepare the buerrage.* Place the flour in a bowl. Using the pastry blender, cut in butter until the butter is the size of small peas or smaller. (Or place the flour and butter in the food processor and pulse until the butter is the size of small peas or smaller.) Do not overwork; you want the butter to stay cold and solid. Cover and refrigerate for at least 1 hour or for up to 1 day.

6. *Laminate the dough.* Place the dough on a floured surface and dust very lightly with flour. Flour your hands and the rolling pin. Working the dough as little as possible and adding flour as necessary, roll out the dough into an 18- by 12-inch (45 by 30 cm) rectangle, using a dough scraper and your hands to lift and help form the dough into an even rectangle with the long sides on your right and left. Sprinkle half the buerrage on the top two-thirds of the dough, leaving a 1½-inch (4 cm) border on the right and left sides. With your hands, lightly press the buerrage into the dough so it will stick. Fold the bottom third of the dough up and over some of the filling, like you're folding a business letter. Fold the top third of the dough down so the filling is completely covered and you have a 12- by 6-inch (30 by 15 cm) rectangle. Use your hands to scoop up stray buerrage and tuck it back under the dough, and to help form the dough into an even rectangle. Turn the dough a quarter turn, lightly flouring under and on top of the dough as necessary, and roll out into an 18- by 12-inch (45 by 30 cm) rectangle with the long sides on your right and left. Repeat the process with the remaining buerrage. Wrap with plastic wrap and refrigerate for 30 minutes. Roll out the dough into a rectangle and fold like a business letter two more times. Use your hands to help form the dough into an even 12- by 6-inch (30 by 15 cm) rectangle of laminated dough. Lightly flour any sticky places on the dough. The dough should feel firm all over, with flattened pieces of butter visible within the dough, but not at all sticky.

7. *Rest and chill.* Wrap the dough with plastic wrap and refrigerate for at least 30 minutes or for up to 24 hours before using.

Flaky, Buttery Croissants

Makes 20 croissants

Equipment:
- Rolling pin
- 2 large baking sheets, lined with parchment paper
- Broiler pan
- Baking stone

If you've ever watched an artisan baker make croissants, you know it looks easy. Cut the dough into triangles, stretch them at the top and down the length and roll into a crescent — there you go. Once you practice doing this, it will be easy and you can go on to filled croissants, either sweet or savory.

1	recipe prepared Buttery Yeast Dough (page 274)	1
	Unbleached all-purpose flour	
1	egg, lightly beaten with 1 tbsp (15 mL) water	1
2 cups	hot water	500 mL

1. *Form.* Remove the dough rectangle from the refrigerator and cut in half. Rewrap one half and return to the refrigerator. Transfer the other half to a generously floured surface and dust very lightly with flour. Flour your hands and the rolling pin. Roll out the dough to a 15- by 6-inch (38 by 15 cm) rectangle with the long sides horizontal. The dough should feel cold, firm and smooth all over, but not at all sticky. With a paring knife or pizza wheel, starting at a short side, mark the top and bottom of the dough at 3-inch (7.5 cm) intervals. From the left-hand edge of the bottom, make a diagonal cut up to the first 3-inch (7.5 cm) mark to form a long triangle with a 3-inch (7.5 cm) base at the top. Make another diagonal cut down to reach the next 3-inch (7.5 cm) mark at the bottom, creating another triangle. Repeat the process until you have 10 triangles. Lift each triangle and gently press and pull the top and down along the length of the triangle to stretch the base to 4 to 5 inches (10 to 12.5 cm) wide. Starting at the base, tightly roll each triangle into a crescent, stretching and pulling it as you go. Repeat the process with the remaining dough.

2. *Chill or rise.* Place croissants 2 inches (5 cm) apart on the prepared baking sheets, arranging them so that the pointed tip is visible. Cover the baking sheets with plastic wrap and refrigerate for up to 24 hours, or let rise in a warm (72°F/22°C) place for 2 hours or until about doubled in size. (If chilling first, let the croissants come to room temperature, then let rise.)

3. *Prepare oven for artisan baking.* About 30 minutes before baking, place the broiler pan on the lower shelf and the baking stone on the middle shelf of the oven. Preheat to 400°F (200°C).

Tips

It's very important to keep laminated doughs cold, so the butter layers stay intact. Use a marble pastry work surface, if possible, and work in a cool room. The dough should be at a warm room temperature only during the final rise.

You can wrap and freeze formed but unbaked croissants for up to 3 months. Simply thaw and let rise before baking.

4. *Brush with egg wash.* Brush the croissants with egg wash.

5. *Place a baking sheet on baking stone and add water to broiler pan.* Using an oven mitt, carefully pull the middle rack of the oven out several inches. Place one of the baking sheets on the hot stone. Push the middle rack back in place. Pull the lower rack out, pour the hot water into the broiler pan and push the lower rack back in place. Close the oven door immediately so the steam will envelop the oven.

6. *Bake.* Bake for 8 to 10 minutes or until the pastry is golden brown. Transfer to a wire rack to cool on pan. Repeat the baking process with the remaining croissants. Enjoy right away or let cool, wrap and freeze for up to 3 months.

Change It Up

Almond Croissants: Place a generous teaspoon (5 mL) of Danish Almond Filling (page 299) in the center of each triangle and roll up, then proceed with the recipe.

Chocolate Croissants: Place 2 tsp (10 mL) chopped bittersweet or dark chocolate in the center of each triangle and roll up, then proceed with the recipe.

Ham and Cheese Croissants: Place a generous teaspoon (5 mL) each chopped ham and shredded Gruyère or Cheddar cheese in the center of each triangle and roll up, then proceed with the recipe.

Danish Orange Pinwheels

Makes 32 pinwheels

Equipment:
- Rolling pin
- 2 large baking sheets, lined with parchment paper
- Broiler pan
- Baking stone

It's great to wake up to the fresh taste of orange in the morning — especially if it's in a tender, flaky, buttery Danish pastry like this one. Make a big batch of pinwheels to give as holiday gifts from your kitchen.

1	recipe prepared Danish Pastry Dough (variation, page 275)	1
	Unbleached all-purpose flour	
1 cup	Orange Cream Cheese Filling (variation, page 300), softened	250 mL
1	egg, lightly beaten with 1 tbsp (15 mL) water	1
2 cups	hot water	500 mL
	Orange Glaze (variation, page 302)	

1. **Form.** Remove the dough rectangle from the refrigerator and cut in half. Rewrap one half and return to the refrigerator. Transfer the other half to a generously floured surface and dust very lightly with flour. Flour your hands and the rolling pin. Roll out the dough to a 12-inch (30 cm) square. The dough should feel cold, firm and smooth all over, but not at all sticky. With a sharp knife or pizza wheel, cut the dough into sixteen 3-inch (7.5 cm) squares. Place a generous teaspoon (7 mL) filling in the center of each square. Bring each corner of the square up and over the filling to meet in the middle and pinch them closed with your fingers. Repeat the process with the remaining dough.

2. **Chill or rise.** Place the pinwheels 2 inches (5 cm) apart on the prepared baking sheets. Cover the baking sheets with plastic wrap and refrigerate for up to 24 hours, or let rise in a warm (72°F/22°C) place for 2 hours or until about doubled in size. (If chilling first, let the pinwheels come to room temperature, then let rise.)

3. **Prepare oven for artisan baking.** About 30 minutes before baking, place the broiler pan on the lower shelf and the baking stone on the middle shelf of the oven. Preheat to 400°F (200°C).

4. **Brush with egg wash.** Brush the pinwheels with egg wash.

Tips

It's very important to keep laminated doughs cold, so the butter layers stay intact. Use a marble pastry work surface, if possible, and work in a cool room. Only keep the dough at warm room temperature during the final rise.

You can freeze baked pinwheels in plastic freezer bags for up to 3 months. To thaw, place frozen pastries on a baking sheet, cover lightly with foil and warm in a 350°F (180°C) oven for 15 minutes.

You Can Also Use

Buttery Yeast Dough (page 274).

5. *Place a baking sheet on baking stone and add water to broiler pan.* Using an oven mitt, carefully pull the middle rack of the oven out several inches. Place one of the baking sheets on the hot stone. Push the middle rack back in place. Pull the lower rack out, pour the hot water into the broiler pan and push the lower rack back in place. Close the oven door immediately so the steam will envelop the oven.

6. *Bake.* Bake for 10 to 12 minutes or until the pastry is golden brown. Transfer to a wire rack set over a baking sheet and let cool on pan for 5 minutes, then drizzle with glaze. Repeat the baking process with the remaining pinwheels. Enjoy right away or let cool, wrap and freeze for up to 3 months.

Danish Almond Plait

Equipment:
- Rolling pin
- Flexible cutting board
- Large baking sheet, lined with parchment paper
- Broiler pan
- Baking stone

Not only does this long, braided pastry look terribly impressive on a breakfast or brunch table, but it's also easy to make. All you do, really, is crisscross fingers of dough over the central filling, and it looks like you slaved all day. That's the Easy Artisan way.

1	recipe prepared Buttery Yeast Dough (page 274)	1
	Unbleached all-purpose flour	
	Danish Almond Filling (page 299)	
1	egg, lightly beaten with 1 tbsp (15 mL) water	1
	Pearl sugar, white sanding sugar or coarse sugar	
2 cups	hot water	500 mL

1. **Form.** Remove the dough rectangle from the refrigerator and cut in half. Rewrap one half and return to the refrigerator. Transfer the other half to a generously floured surface and dust very lightly with flour. Flour your hands and the rolling pin. Roll out the dough to an 18- by 14-inch (45 by 35 cm) rectangle with the long sides to the left and right. The dough should feel cold, firm and smooth all over, but not at all sticky. Spoon half the filling down the center of the rectangle, leaving a 2-inch (5 cm) perimeter. With a paring knife or a pizza wheel, cut a diagonal line from the right side of the bottom of the filling through the dough to the end. Cut a diagonal line from the left side of the bottom of the filling through the dough to the end. Fold the resulting trapezoid of dough up and over the filling. Repeat with the top of the dough. Cut the pastry on either side of the filling into diagonal strips about $1/2$ inch (1 cm) wide. Fold the strips over the filling, alternating strips from each side, to create a braid effect, brushing away excess flour with a pastry brush. Trim any ends and gently press the braided dough together. Repeat the process with the remaining dough.

2. **Chill or rise.** Using a flexible cutting board, scoop under each pastry and carefully transfer to the prepared baking sheet. Cover the baking sheet with plastic wrap and refrigerate for up to 24 hours, or let rise in a warm (72°F/22°C) place for 2 hours or until about doubled in size. (If chilling first, let the pastry come to room temperature, then let rise.)

Tips

It's very important to keep laminated doughs cold, so the butter layers stay intact. Use a marble pastry work surface, if possible, and work in a cool room. The dough should be at a warm room temperature only during the final rise.

Both pearl sugar and white sanding sugar are available at baking supply shops or online.

You Can Also Use

Danish Pastry Dough (variation, page 275).

3. *Prepare oven for artisan baking.* About 30 minutes before baking, place the broiler pan on the lower shelf and the baking stone on the middle shelf of the oven. Preheat to 400°F (200°C).

4. *Add topping.* Gently brush the pastry with egg wash and sprinkle with sugar.

5. *Place baking sheet on baking stone and add water to broiler pan.* Using an oven mitt, carefully pull the middle rack of the oven out several inches. Place the baking sheet on the hot stone. Push the middle rack back in place. Pull the lower rack out, pour the hot water into the broiler pan and push the lower rack back in place. Close the oven door immediately so the steam will envelop the oven.

6. *Bake.* Bake for 15 to 17 minutes or until the top of the pastry is deep brown and the rest is puffed and golden. Transfer to a wire rack to cool on pan. Enjoy right away or let cool, wrap and freeze for up to 3 months.

Change It Up

Caramel Apple Plait: Use Caramel Apple Filling (page 298) in place of the Danish Almond Filling.

Sweet Cream Cheese Plait: Use Sweet Cream Cheese Filling (page 300) in place of the Danish Almond Filling. Serve each slice with fruit compote.

Danish Crescents

Similar to croissants, these crescents have a sweet or nutty filling and a drizzle of glaze at the end.

1	recipe prepared Danish Pastry Dough (variation, page 275)	1
	Unbleached all-purpose flour	
½ cup	apricot, cherry or plum preserves or Danish Almond Filling (page 299)	125 mL
1	egg, lightly beaten with 1 tbsp (15 mL) water	1
2 cups	hot water	500 mL
	Easy Artisan Glaze (page 302)	

1. **Form.** Remove the dough rectangle from the refrigerator and cut in half. Rewrap one half and return to the refrigerator. Transfer the other half to a generously floured surface and dust very lightly with flour. Flour your hands and the rolling pin. Roll out the dough to a 15- by 6-inch (38 by 15 cm) rectangle with the long sides horizontal. The dough should feel cold, firm and smooth all over, but not at all sticky. With a paring knife or pizza wheel, starting at a short side, mark the top and bottom of the dough at 3-inch (7.5 cm) intervals. From the left-hand edge of the bottom, make a diagonal cut up to the first 3-inch (7.5 cm) mark to form a long triangle with a 3-inch (7.5 cm) base at the top. Make another diagonal cut down to reach the next 3-inch (7.5 cm) mark at the bottom, creating another triangle. Repeat the process until you have 10 triangles. Lift each triangle and gently press and pull the top and down along the length of the triangle to stretch the base to 4 to 5 inches (10 to 12.5 cm) wide. Mound 2 tsp (10 mL) preserves about 1 inch (2.5 cm) from the edge of the base. Starting at the base, tightly roll each triangle into a crescent, stretching and pulling it as you go. Repeat the process with the remaining dough.

2. **Chill or rise.** Place crescents 2 inches (5 cm) apart on the prepared baking sheets, arranging them so that the pointed tip is visible. Cover the baking sheets with plastic wrap and refrigerate for up to 24 hours, or let rise in a warm (72°F/22°C) place for 2 hours or until about doubled in size. (If chilling first, let the crescents come to room temperature, then let rise.)

Tip

It's very important to keep laminated doughs cold, so the butter layers stay intact. Use a marble pastry work surface, if possible, and work in a cool room. Only keep the dough at warm room temperature during the final rise.

You Can Also Use

Buttery Yeast Dough (page 274).

3. *Prepare oven for artisan baking.* About 30 minutes before baking, place the broiler pan on the lower shelf and the baking stone on the middle shelf of the oven. Preheat to 400°F (200°C).

4. *Brush with egg wash.* Brush the crescents with egg wash.

5. *Place a baking sheet on baking stone and add water to broiler pan.* Using an oven mitt, carefully pull the middle rack of the oven out several inches. Place one of the baking sheets on the hot stone. Push the middle rack back in place. Pull the lower rack out, pour the hot water into the broiler pan and push the lower rack back in place. Close the oven door immediately so the steam will envelop the oven.

6. *Bake.* Bake for 8 to 10 minutes or until the pastry is golden brown. Transfer to a wire rack set over a baking sheet and let cool on pan for 5 minutes, then drizzle with glaze. Repeat the baking process with the remaining crescents. Enjoy right away or let cool, wrap and freeze for up to 3 months.

Danish Bear Claws

Makes 16 bear claws

Equipment:
- Rolling pin
- 2 large baking sheets, lined with parchment paper
- Broiler pan
- Baking stone

Bear claws start out as squares. Then they're filled, folded and cut so that the edge of the pastry resembles stubby toes, which separate and spread out during baking. These pastries also get a drizzle of glaze at the end.

1	recipe prepared Danish Pastry Dough (variation, page 275)	1
	Unbleached all-purpose flour	
1/2 cup	apricot, cherry or plum preserves or Danish Almond Filling (page 299)	125 mL
1	egg, lightly beaten with 1 tbsp (15 mL) water	1
2 cups	hot water	500 mL
	Easy Artisan Glaze (page 302)	

1. *Form.* Remove the dough rectangle from the refrigerator and cut in half. Rewrap one half and return to the refrigerator. Transfer the other half to a generously floured surface and dust very lightly with flour. Flour your hands and the rolling pin. Roll out the dough to a 16- by 8-inch (40 by 20 cm) rectangle. The dough should feel cold, firm and smooth all over, but not at all sticky. With a paring knife or pizza wheel, cut the dough into eight 4-inch (10 cm) squares. Mound 2 tsp (10 mL) preserves in the center of each square. Brush one side of each square with egg wash, then fold the opposite side over the filling, pressing the edges together to seal. Make three cuts on the folded side, almost but not quite to the seam side. Repeat the process with the remaining dough.

2. *Chill or rise.* Place the bear claws 2 inches (5 cm) apart on the prepared baking sheets. Gently fan the "toes" slightly. Cover the baking sheets with plastic wrap and refrigerate for up to 24 hours, or let rise in a warm (72°F/22°C) place for 2 hours or until about doubled in size. (If chilling first, let the bear claws come to room temperature, then let rise.)

3. *Prepare oven for artisan baking.* About 30 minutes before baking, place the broiler pan on the lower shelf and the baking stone on the middle shelf of the oven. Preheat to 400°F (200°C).

4. *Brush with egg wash.* Brush the bear claws with egg wash.

Tip

It's very important to keep laminated doughs cold, so the butter layers stay intact. Use a marble pastry work surface, if possible, and work in a cool room. Only keep the dough at warm room temperature during the final rise.

You Can Also Use

Buttery Yeast Dough (page 274).

5. *Place a baking sheet on baking stone and add water to broiler pan.* Using an oven mitt, carefully pull the middle rack of the oven out several inches. Place one of the baking sheets on the hot stone. Push the middle rack back in place. Pull the lower rack out, pour the hot water into the broiler pan and push the lower rack back in place. Close the oven door immediately so the steam will envelop the oven.

6. *Bake.* Bake for 10 to 12 minutes or until the pastry is golden brown. Transfer to a wire rack set over a baking sheet and let cool on pan for 5 minutes, then drizzle with glaze. Repeat the baking process with the remaining bear claws. Enjoy right away or let cool, wrap, and freeze for up to 3 months.

Apricot and Almond Galettes

Equipment:
- Rolling pin
- Large baking sheet, lined with parchment paper
- Broiler pan
- Baking stone

These pastries are like sweet, buttery, yeasty freeform tarts, and they're favorites at French pâtisseries and boulangeries. Once you've got your dough, they're easy to make.

12	fresh apricots, halved (or 24 canned apricot halves, drained)	12
1/2 cup	white, dark or spiced rum	125 mL
1/2	recipe prepared Buttery Yeast Dough (page 274)	1/2
	Unbleached all-purpose flour	
1	egg, lightly beaten with 1 tbsp (15 mL) water	1
1/4 cup	heavy or whipping (35%) cream	50 mL
1/4 cup	raw or turbinado sugar crystals or pearl sugar	50 mL
1/4 cup	sliced almonds	50 mL
2 cups	hot water	500 mL

1. *Combine.* In a bowl, combine apricots and rum; let stand for 30 minutes, then drain and pat apricots dry. Reserve the rum for another use.

2. *Form.* Place dough on a generously floured surface and dust very lightly with flour. Flour your hands and the rolling pin. Roll out the dough to a 16- by 8-inch (40 by 20 cm) rectangle. The dough should feel cold, firm and smooth all over, but not at all sticky. With a sharp knife or a pizza wheel, cut the dough into 4-inch (10 cm) squares.

3. *Chill or rise.* Place the squares 2 inches (5 cm) apart on the prepared baking sheet. Cover the baking sheet with plastic wrap and refrigerate for up to 24 hours, or let rise in a warm (72°F/22°C) place for 2 hours or until about doubled in size. (If chilling first, let the galettes come to room temperature, then let rise.)

4. *Prepare oven for artisan baking.* About 30 minutes before baking, place the broiler pan on the lower shelf and the baking stone on the middle shelf of the oven. Preheat to 425°F (220°C).

Tip

It's very important to keep laminated doughs cold, so the butter layers stay intact. Use a marble pastry work surface, if possible, and work in a cool room. Only keep the dough at warm room temperature during the final rise.

You Can Also Use

Danish Pastry Dough (variation, page 275).

5. *Add topping.* Brush the pastry squares with egg wash. Place 3 apricot halves, cut side down, in the center of each square. Brush the apricots with cream and sprinkle with raw sugar and almonds.

6. *Place baking sheet on baking stone and add water to broiler pan.* Using an oven mitt, carefully pull the middle rack of the oven out several inches. Place the baking sheet on the hot stone. Push the middle rack back in place. Pull the lower rack out, pour the hot water into the broiler pan and push the lower rack back in place. Close the oven door immediately so the steam will envelop the oven.

7. *Bake.* Bake for 8 minutes, then reduce the temperature to 350°F (180°C). Bake for 10 to 12 minutes or until the pastry is golden brown. Transfer to a wire rack to cool on pan. Enjoy right away or let cool, wrap and freeze for up to 3 months.

Caramel Apple Galettes

Equipment:
- Rolling pin
- Large baking sheet, lined with parchment paper
- Broiler pan
- Baking stone

Tip

It's very important to keep laminated doughs cold, so the butter layers stay intact. Use a marble pastry work surface, if possible, and work in a cool room. Only keep the dough at warm room temperature during the final rise.

¹⁄₂	recipe prepared Buttery Yeast Dough (page 274)	¹⁄₂
	Unbleached all-purpose flour	
1	egg, lightly beaten with 1 tbsp (15 mL) water	1
1 cup	Caramel Apple Filling (page 298)	250 mL
¹⁄₄ cup	chopped pecans or sliced almonds	50 mL
2 cups	hot water	500 mL

1. *Form.* Place dough on a generously floured surface and dust very lightly with flour. Flour your hands and the rolling pin. Roll out the dough to a 16- by 8-inch (40 by 20 cm) rectangle. The dough should feel cold, firm and smooth all over, but not at all sticky. With a sharp knife or a pizza wheel, cut the dough into 4-inch (10 cm) squares.

2. *Chill or rise.* Place the squares 2 inches (5 cm) apart on the prepared baking sheet. Cover the baking sheet with plastic wrap and refrigerate for up to 24 hours, or let rise in a warm (72°F/22°C) place for 2 hours or until about doubled in size. (If chilling first, let the galettes come to room temperature, then let rise.)

3. *Prepare oven for artisan baking.* About 30 minutes before baking, place the broiler pan on the lower shelf and the baking stone on the middle shelf of the oven. Preheat to 425°F (220°C).

4. *Add topping.* Brush the pastry squares with egg wash. Spoon 2 tbsp (25 mL) Caramel Apple Filling in the center of each square. Sprinkle with pecans.

You Can Also Use

Danish Pastry Dough
(variation, page 275).

5. *Place baking sheet on baking stone and add water to broiler pan.* Using an oven mitt, carefully pull the middle rack of the oven out several inches. Place the baking sheet on the hot stone. Push the middle rack back in place. Pull the lower rack out, pour the hot water into the broiler pan and push the lower rack back in place. Close the oven door immediately so the steam will envelop the oven.

6. *Bake.* Bake for 8 minutes, then reduce the temperature to 350°F (180°C). Bake for 10 to 12 minutes or until the pastry is golden brown. Transfer to a wire rack to cool on pan. Enjoy right away or let cool, wrap and freeze for up to 3 months.

Berries 'n' Cream Galettes

Tip

It's very important to keep laminated doughs cold, so the butter layers stay intact. Use a marble pastry work surface, if possible, and work in a cool room. Only keep the dough at warm room temperature during the final rise.

½	recipe prepared Buttery Yeast Dough (page 274)	½
	Unbleached all-purpose flour	
1	egg, lightly beaten with 1 tbsp (15 mL) water	1
1 cup	Sweet Cream Cheese Filling (page 300)	250 mL
¼ cup	fresh berries	50 mL
¼ cup	sliced almonds	50 mL
2 cups	hot water	500 mL

1. *Form.* Place dough on a generously floured surface and dust very lightly with flour. Flour your hands and the rolling pin. Roll out the dough to a 16- by 8-inch (40 by 20 cm) rectangle. The dough should feel cold, firm and smooth all over, but not at all sticky. With a sharp knife or a pizza wheel, cut the dough into 4-inch (10 cm) squares.

2. *Chill or rise.* Place the squares 2 inches (5 cm) apart on the prepared baking sheet. Cover the baking sheet with plastic wrap and refrigerate for up to 24 hours, or let rise in a warm (72°F/22°C) place for 2 hours or until about doubled in size. (If chilling first, let the galettes come to room temperature, then let rise.)

3. *Prepare oven for artisan baking.* About 30 minutes before baking, place the broiler pan on the lower shelf and the baking stone on the middle shelf of the oven. Preheat to 425°F (220°C).

4. *Add topping.* Brush the pastry squares with egg wash. Spoon 2 tbsp (25 mL) Sweet Cream Cheese Filling in the center of each square. Sprinkle with berries and almonds.

You Can Also Use

Danish Pastry Dough (variation, page 275).

5. *Place baking sheet on baking stone and add water to broiler pan.* Using an oven mitt, carefully pull the middle rack of the oven out several inches. Place the baking sheet on the hot stone. Push the middle rack back in place. Pull the lower rack out, pour the hot water into the broiler pan and push the lower rack back in place. Close the oven door immediately so the steam will envelop the oven.

6. *Bake.* Bake for 8 minutes, then reduce the temperature to 350°F (180°C). Bake for 10 to 12 minutes or until the pastry is golden brown. Transfer to a wire rack to cool on pan. Enjoy right away or let cool, wrap and freeze for up to 3 months.

The Artisan Pantry

Artisan Bread Dough Enhancer

Dough enhancer contains ingredients that help heavy doughs rise better and unbleached all-purpose flour do the heavy lifting of bread flour. So if bread flour is not always available in your area, make a batch of dough enhancer and keep it in a tightly closed jar in your refrigerator. To increase the level of protein in unbleached all-purpose flour so you can use it in place of bread flour, add 1 tsp (5 mL) Easy Artisan Dough Enhancer to each cup (250 mL) of all-purpose flour. However, you'll need to search for dough enhancer ingredients. Boxes of vital wheat gluten, nonfat dry milk and ground ginger are available in the baking aisle. Unflavored gelatin is with puddings and gelatin mixes. Boxes of pectin and ascorbic acid are available where canning and preserving items are shelved; ascorbic acid is sometimes also shelved with Jewish foods. Soy-lecithin granules (Bob's Red Mill brand is one) can be found in the baking or health foods aisle. You can also buy ready-made powdered dough enhancer in the baking aisle of better grocery stores.

Makes about 1¾ cups (425 mL)

1 cup	vital wheat gluten	250 mL
½ cup	instant nonfat dry milk powder	125 mL
2 tbsp	soy-lecithin granules	25 mL
2 tbsp	powdered pectin	25 mL
2 tbsp	unflavored gelatin powder	25 mL
1 tsp	ground ginger	5 mL
1 tsp	ascorbic acid crystals	5 mL

1. In a glass jar, combine gluten, dry milk, soy-lecithin granules, pectin, gelatin, ginger and ascorbic acid crystals. Close the lid and shake to blend. Keeps, refrigerated, indefinitely.

Artisan Butter

Farm wives used to make their spending money by churning butter by hand to sell at the market. We can count ourselves fortunate that the food processor now takes the place of the old wooden churn in the home kitchen. If you're making Easy Artisan bread, you should also serve delicious but equally artisan butter, and this is it. This recipe produces unsalted butter; if you like, add sea salt to taste. Ultra-pasteurized cream will take a little longer to process, but still makes delicious butter.

2 cups	heavy or whipping (35%) cream	500 mL

1. Line a sieve with a single layer of cheesecloth or a clean terrycloth tea towel and place the sieve over a bowl. Pour the cream into the food processor and process for about 5 minutes. The cream will go, in stages, from liquid to whipped cream to thick whipped cream to a solid mass of butter that separates from the milky liquid, or whey.

2. Transfer the butter to the lined sieve and press the butter with a wooden spoon or spatula to release more of the whey. When the butter does not release any more whey, scoop it from the sieve and cover with plastic wrap.

3. Use right away, keep covered in the refrigerator for up to 1 month or freeze indefinitely.

Change It Up

Garlic Herb Butter: In a bowl, combine 1 cup (250 mL) softened butter with 1 large clove garlic, minced, and 2 tbsp (25 mL) mixed chopped fresh herbs, such as flat-leaf (Italian) parsley, dill, tarragon, chives, oregano and/or rosemary, or to taste.

Savory Whipped Onion Butter: In a food processor, combine 1 cup (250 mL) softened butter, $1/4$ cup (50 mL) minced onion, $1/4$ cup (50 mL) minced flat-leaf (Italian) parsley, 2 tsp (10 mL) Worcestershire sauce, $1/2$ tsp (2 mL) dry mustard and $1/2$ tsp (2 mL) cracked black pepper; process until light and fluffy.

Honey Butter: In a bowl, combine 1 cup (250 mL) softened butter with 1 tbsp (15 mL) medium-colored liquid clover or wildflower honey, or to taste.

Raspberry Butter: In a bowl, combine 1 cup (250 mL) softened butter with 1 cup (250 mL) mashed fresh or thawed frozen raspberries. (Or use strawberries for Strawberry Butter.)

Spiced Pumpkin Butter: In a bowl, combine 1 cup (250 mL) softened butter with $1/3$ cup (75 mL) canned pumpkin purée (not pie filling), 1 tsp (5 mL) grated orange zest and 1 tsp (5 mL) pumpkin pie spice.

Pomegranate Orange Butter: In a bowl, combine 1 cup (250 mL) softened butter with $1/4$ cup (50 mL) pomegranate molasses and 1 tbsp (15 mL) grated orange zest.

Honey Spice Applesauce

Makes about 4 cups (1 L)

Dark with spices, this applesauce is wonderful served warm with artisan bread, as a topping for Apple Custard Kuchen (page 201) or as a flavorful ingredient in artisan loaves such as Honey Spice Applesauce Bread (variation, page 129).

4 cups	unsweetened applesauce	1 L
1 cup	clover or other mild honey	250 mL
2 tsp	ground cinnamon	10 mL
1/4 tsp	freshly grated nutmeg	1 mL
1/4 tsp	kosher salt, or to taste	1 mL
1 tsp	freshly squeezed lemon juice, or to taste	5 mL

1. In a large saucepan, heat applesauce, honey, cinnamon and nutmeg over medium-high heat until bubbling. Reduce heat and simmer for 5 minutes or until thickened. Taste, then add salt and lemon juice as needed.

2. Use right away or let cool, transfer to airtight containers and freeze for up to 6 months.

Rosemary Walnuts

Makes about 2 cups (500 mL)

- Preheat oven to 400°F (200°C)

Equipment:
- Baking sheet, lined with parchment paper

For years, my BBQ Queen co-author, Karen Adler (300 Big & Bold Barbecue & Grilling Recipes), has been making roasted rosemary walnuts for the holidays. As I was experimenting with the Easy Artisan techniques, I put two and two together: wouldn't those walnuts taste great in bread? Fold this mixture into bread dough, as instructed in Easy Artisan Seeded and Filled Dough (page 90), and into slow-rise and naturally leavened doughs as well.

2 tsp	crushed dried rosemary	10 mL
½ tsp	kosher salt	2 mL
½ tsp	cayenne pepper	2 mL
2 tbsp	unsalted butter	25 mL
2 cups	walnut halves	500 mL

1. In a small bowl, stir together rosemary, salt and cayenne until well blended, with no lumps or clumps.

2. In a large saucepan, melt butter over medium-high heat. Stir in the rosemary mixture. Add walnuts and stir for 2 to 3 minutes or until evenly coated.

3. Using a spatula, spread walnuts on prepared baking sheet. Bake in preheated oven for 10 to 15 minutes or until walnuts are lightly toasted but not burned.

4. Let cool, use right away or store in an airtight container at room temperature for up to 2 months.

Caramel Apple Filling

**Makes about 2 cups
(500 mL)**

*As a filling for pull-aparts,
coffee cakes, swirled loaves,
tea rings, Danish pastries
or croissants, this has no
peer. After you make it, the
problem will be disciplining
yourself to try only a little
taste and save the rest for
the recipe.*

¼ cup	unsalted butter	50 mL
½ cup	packed light or dark brown sugar	125 mL
4	large tart apples (such as Granny Smith or Fuji), peeled and cut into small dice	4
	Freshly squeezed lemon juice	

1. In a large skillet, melt butter over medium-high heat. Stir in brown sugar until well blended. Stir in apples and cook, stirring, for about 12 minutes or until softened. Remove from heat and stir in lemon juice to taste. Let cool completely.

2. Use right away once cool, or transfer to an airtight container and refrigerate for up to 3 days.

Cinnamon Filling

**Makes about ¾ cup
(175 mL)**

*This is the classic filling for
cinnamon rolls, Swedish tea
rings and other pastries. This
mild version uses granulated
sugar and regular grocery-
store cinnamon (usually from
Indonesia).*

6 tbsp	granulated sugar	90 mL
2 tbsp	ground cinnamon	25 mL
¾ cup	unsalted butter, softened	175 mL

1. In a bowl, combine sugar and cinnamon. Using a fork, beat in butter until smooth and well blended.

Change It Up

For a stronger-flavored cinnamon filling, use packed light or dark brown sugar in place of granulated and Vietnamese or Chinese cassia cinnamon.

Danish Almond Filling

Makes about 2¹/₂ cups (625 mL)

- Preheat oven to 300°F (150°C)

8 oz	sliced almonds (about 1¹/₂ cups/375 mL)	250 g
1 cup	granulated sugar	250 mL
1 tsp	almond or vanilla extract	5 mL
2	egg whites	2

Midwesterners of Scandinavian descent love a vanilla-scented almond filling. If you prefer a stronger almond flavoring, use the almond extract. This filling tastes best if it has several days to mature.

Tips

Toasting the nuts first gives this filling a better flavor.

For wonderful ready-made fillings, check out American Almond Products Company (1-800-825-6663 or www.lovenbake.com).

1. Spread almonds in a single layer on a baking sheet. Toast in preheated oven for 10 to 15 minutes or until nuts are golden and have a toasty aroma. (Check after 10 minutes, and do not let brown.) Let cool, then discard any nuts that have turned dark brown.

2. In a food processor or blender, grind cooled almonds to a fine paste. Add sugar and process until the mixture resembles coarse flour. Add almond extract and egg whites; process for 2 to 3 minutes or until a stiff paste forms.

3. Transfer to an airtight container and refrigerate until ready to use, up to 3 days.

Change It Up

Toasted Hazelnut Filling: Substitute hazelnuts for the almonds and rub off the skins after toasting. Omit the extract.

Pistachio Filling: Substitute unsalted roasted pistachios for the almonds and skip Step 1. Use almond extract.

Sweet Cream Cheese Filling

Makes about 1⅓ cups (325 mL)

Delicious as a filling for pull-aparts, crescent rolls, Danish pastries, coffee cake or swirled loafs, this cream cheese mixture can be flavored in many different ways (see variations, at right).

1	package (8 oz/250 g) cream cheese, softened	1
1	egg yolk	1
¼ cup	granulated sugar	50 mL
2 tbsp	all-purpose flour	25 mL
1 tsp	vanilla extract	5 mL

1. In a food processor, combine cream cheese, egg yolk, sugar, flour and vanilla; process until smooth.

2. Use right away or transfer to an airtight container and refrigerate for up to 3 days.

Change It Up

Almond Cream Cheese Filling: Use 1 tsp (5 mL) almond extract in place of the vanilla.

Lemon Cream Cheese Filling: Use 1 tsp (5 mL) lemon extract or grated lemon zest in place of the vanilla.

Orange Cream Cheese Filling: Use 1 tsp (5 mL) orange extract or grated orange zest in place of the vanilla.

Sweet Spice Cream Cheese Filling: Add 1 tsp (5 mL) apple pie spice.

Coconut Cream Cheese Filling: Add ½ cup (125 mL) sweetened flaked coconut.

Poppy Seed Filling

Makes about 1 cup (250 mL)

Artisan bakers of Polish and Slavic descent love the combination of sweet, crunchy poppy seeds and tart lemon in festive breads and pastries. Polish bakeries often sell bags of poppy seeds already ground, but it's easy to do at home.

1 cup	poppy seeds	250 mL
1/2 cup	milk	125 mL
2 tbsp	granulated sugar	25 mL
1 tbsp	honey	15 mL
1 tsp	ground allspice	5 mL

1. Grind the poppy seeds, in batches if necessary, in a clean coffee grinder, spice grinder or small food processor, or by hand using a mortar and pestle.

2. In a saucepan, combine ground poppy seeds, milk, sugar, honey and allspice; bring to a boil over medium-high heat. Reduce heat and simmer for 10 minutes, stirring frequently, until sugar and honey are well dissolved and the mixture has thickened slightly. Remove from the heat and let cool.

3. Use right away or transfer to an airtight container and refrigerate for up to 1 week.

Cinnamon Sugar

Makes about 1/4 cup (50 mL)

Like everything else, there is a difference between ready-made and homemade cinnamon sugar — and it's the degree of cinnamon-iness. I prefer to use the strongest type of cinnamon, that which is grown in Vietnam and labeled either Vietnamese or Saigon cinnamon. Use this mixture to make cinnamon rolls, to sprinkle on hot beignets or to make great cinnamon toast.

| 1/4 cup | granulated sugar | 50 mL |
| 1 1/2 tsp | ground cinnamon | 7 mL |

1. In a small bowl, combine sugar and cinnamon until well blended.

Easy Artisan Glaze

Makes about 1¼ cups (300 mL)

Add a final sweet touch to your baked goods with a homemade glaze, thinner than either a frosting or an icing. A glaze is meant to give baked goods a sweet sheen and an initial flavor. Make glaze right before you're ready to use it; otherwise, it can harden and get lumpy.

1 cup	confectioner's (icing) sugar	250 mL
¼ cup	whole milk, half-and-half (10%) cream or heavy or whipping (35%) cream	50 mL
1 tsp	vanilla extract	5 mL

1. In a small bowl, whisk together confectioner's sugar and milk until smooth. Whisk in vanilla. Use right away.

Change It Up

Almond Glaze: Use 1 tsp (5 mL) almond extract in place of the vanilla.

Coffee Glaze: Use 1 tsp (5 mL) coffee extract in place of the vanilla, or substitute 2 tbsp (25 mL) freshly brewed strong coffee for half the milk.

Lemon Glaze: Use 1 tsp (5 mL) lemon extract or grated lemon zest in place of the vanilla.

Orange Glaze: Use ¼ cup (50 mL) freshly squeezed orange juice in place of the milk and 1 tsp (5 mL) orange extract or grated orange zest in place of the vanilla.

Cider Glaze: Use ¼ cup (50 mL) unsweetened apple cider in place of the milk.

Cider Glaze with Rum: Use ¼ cup (50 mL) unsweetened apple cider and 1 to 2 tbsp (15 to 25 mL) light or dark rum in place of the milk.

Cherry Glaze: Use ¼ cup (50 mL) cherry juice in place of the milk and 1 tsp (5 mL) almond extract in place of the vanilla.

Cranberry Orange Glaze: Use ¼ cup (50 mL) cranberry juice in place of the milk and 1 tsp (5 mL) orange extract or grated orange zest in place of the vanilla.

Chocolate Glaze

Makes about ¹/₂ cup (125 mL)

Sometimes a pastry just calls out for a drizzle of chocolate. This easy method also results in easy cleanup.

Tip

If you use larger, button-size chocolate chips, it might be necessary to microwave on High for 15 to 30 seconds longer, until the chocolate has melted enough to knead smooth.

| ¹/₂ cup | small semisweet chocolate chips | 125 mL |
| 2 tbsp | heavy or whipping (35%) cream | 25 mL |

1. In a small microwave-safe sealable plastic bag, combine chocolate chips and cream. Seal and microwave on High for 30 seconds. Remove the bag and knead the mixture until smooth and well blended.

2. Cut a tiny corner from the bottom of the bag and squeeze glaze over a cooled loaf in a decorative pattern.

Easy Caramelized Onions

Makes about 2 cups (500 mL)

Who doesn't like caramelized onions? They're so adaptable as pizza and flatbread toppings, and savory roll and sandwich fillings, that you just have to have a batch on hand in the refrigerator or freezer. This recipe is adapted from one by Kathryn Moore and Roxanne Wyss (www. pluggedintocooking.com), and it's fabulous.

Tip

For caramelized onions on the stovetop, heat the oil and butter in a large saucepan over medium-low heat. Stir in the onions and cook, stirring occasionally, for 20 to 30 minutes or until the onions have caramelized. Season to taste with salt and pepper.

4	large onions, thinly sliced	4
2 tbsp	olive oil	25 mL
2 tbsp	unsalted butter	25 mL
	Salt and freshly ground black pepper	

1. In a small (2- to 4-quart) slow cooker, combine onions, oil and butter. Cover and cook on High for 6 to 8 hours or until onions are medium brown and wilted. Season to taste with salt and pepper. Let cool.

2. Use right away or transfer to an airtight container and refrigerate for up to 1 week or freeze for up to 3 months.

Caramelized Shallots and Garlic with Red Wine

Makes about 3 cups (750 mL)

As a topping for artisan flatbreads, this heady mixture shines. Serve with a good red wine and artisan cheese as an appetizer or a snack.

2 tbsp	olive oil	25 mL
25	small shallots	25
20	cloves garlic	20
2 tbsp	granulated sugar	25 mL
3 cups	dry red wine, divided	750 mL
	Coarse salt and freshly ground black pepper	

1. In a large skillet, heat oil over medium-high heat. Add shallots and garlic; cook, stirring occasionally, for about 10 minutes or until shallots are golden brown. Add sugar, stir well and cook for about 4 minutes or until sugar caramelizes. Add 2 cups (500 mL) of the wine, reduce heat to low, cover and simmer for 20 to 25 minutes or until shallots are soft. Add the remaining wine and simmer, uncovered, for 10 to 15 minutes or until wine has evaporated. Season to taste with salt and pepper. Let cool.

2. Use right away or transfer to an airtight container and refrigerate for up to 5 days.

Library and Archives Canada Cataloguing in Publication

Fertig, Judith M.
    200 fast & easy artisan breads : no knead, one bowl / Judith Fertig.

Includes index.
ISBN 978-0-7788-0211-2

    1. Cookery (Bread). 2. Bread. I. Title. II. Title: Two hundred fast & easy artisan breads.
III. Title: 200 fast and easy artisan breads.

TX769.F47 2009   641.8'15   C2009-902261-3

Index

Gluten-Free Grilled Chicken and Vegetable Pizza, 181
Squash or Pumpkin Dough, 127
Strawberry Butter, 295
Sun-Dried Tomato Dough, 125
   Sun-Dried Tomato and Feta Flatbread, 144
   Sun-Dried Tomato and Pesto Batard, 142
Swedish Tea Ring Dough, 187
   Cardamom and Cinnamon–Scented Swedish Tea Ring, 192
Sweet Cream Cheese Filling, 300
   Berries 'n' Cream Galettes, 290
   Chocolate Swirl Bread, 140
   Danish Almond Plait (variation), 280
   Danish Orange Pinwheels, 278
Swiss Rye Boule, 96

T

tapioca flour
   Easy Artisan Gluten-Free Dough (Master Recipe #6), 170
   Gluten-Free Caraway "Rye" Dough, 173
   Gluten-Free Cornmeal Pepper Dough, 172
   Gluten-Free Sandwich Buns, 178
Three-Seed Batard, 100
Three-Seed Breadsticks, 40
Thyme and Olive Artisan Rolls, 243
Thyme and Olive Boule, 240
Toasted Hazelnut Filling, 299
   Chocolate Hazelnut Swirl Loaf, 188
Toasted Hazelnut Flatbread with Roasted Asparagus and Goat Cheese, 250
tomatoes, 121. *See also* Sun-Dried Tomato Dough
   Caprese Swirl Rolls, 50
   Coca Mallorquina, 162
   Flatbread with Caramelized Onions and Brie (variation), 44
   Greek-Style Pizza, 52
   White Whole Wheat Pizza with Grilled Vegetables, 86

Traditional Naan Dough, 67
   Afghan Flatbread with Cilantro and Green Onions, 112
   Nigella Naan, 116
   Peshawari Naan, 114
   Traditional Naan, 72

V

vegetables. *See also specific vegetables*
   Fig and Gorgonzola Swirl Loaf (variation), 48
   Greek-Style Pizza, 52
   Leaf-Wrapped Slow-Rise Breadsticks, 166
   Toasted Hazelnut Flatbread with Roasted Asparagus and Goat Cheese, 250
   White Whole Wheat Pizza with Grilled Vegetables, 86

W

walnuts, 185. *See also* Rosemary Walnuts
   Roquefort and Walnut Fougasse, 104
White Whole Wheat Pizza with Grilled Vegetables, 86
Whole-Grain Bagel Dough, 258
Whole-Grain Baguettes, 237
Whole Wheat Cheddar Boule, 94
Whole Wheat Soy Dough, 63
wild rice
   Naturally Leavened Wild Rice Dough, 235
   Northern Lakes Wild Rice Dough, 61

Y

yeast, 15
yogurt
   Slow-Rise Sour Rye Dough, 153
   Traditional Naan Dough, 67

Z

zucchini
   Coca Mallorquina, 162
   Gluten-Free Grilled Chicken and Vegetable Pizza, 181

More Great Books
from Robert Rose

Appliance Cooking

- The Mixer Bible Second Edition
  by Meredith Deeds and Carla Snyder
- The Dehydrator Bible
  by Jennifer MacKenzie, Jay Nutt & Don Mercer
- The Juicing Bible Second Edition
  by Pat Crocker

- 200 Best Panini Recipes
  by Tiffany Collins
- 200 Best Pressure Cooker Recipes
  by Cinda Chavich
- 300 Slow Cooker Favorites
  by Donna-Marie Pye
- The 150 Best Slow Cooker Recipes
  by Judith Finlayson

- Delicious & Dependable Slow Cooker Recipes
  by Judith Finlayson
- 125 Best Vegetarian Slow Cooker Recipes
  by Judith Finlayson
- The Healthy Slow Cooker
  by Judith Finlayson
- The Best Convection Oven Cookbook
  by Linda Stephen

- 250 Best American Bread Machine Baking Recipes
  by Donna Washburn and Heather Butt
- 250 Best Canadian Bread Machine Baking Recipes
  by Donna Washburn and Heather Butt

Baking

- The Cheesecake Bible
  by George Geary
- 1500 Best Bars, Cookies, Muffins, Cakes & More
  by Esther Brody
- The Complete Book of Baking
  by George Geary
- The Complete Book of Bars & Squares
  by Jill Snider
- The Complete Book of Pies
  by Julie Hasson
- 125 Best Chocolate Recipes
  by Julie Hasson
- 125 Best Cupcake Recipes
  by Julie Hasson
- Complete Cake Mix Magic
  by Jill Snider

Healthy Cooking

- The Vegetarian Cook's Bible
  by Pat Crocker
- The Vegan Cook's Bible
  by Pat Crocker
- 125 Best Vegetarian Recipes
  by Byron Ayanoglu with contributions from Algis Kemezys
- The Smoothies Bible
  by Pat Crocker
- 125 Best Vegan Recipes
  by Maxine Effenson Chuck and Beth Gurney

- 200 Best Lactose-Free Recipes
  by Jan Main
- 500 Best Healthy Recipes
  Edited by Lynn Roblin, RD
- Complete Gluten-Free Cookbook
  by Donna Washburn and Heather Butt
- 125 Best Gluten-Free Recipes
  by Donna Washburn and Heather Butt
- The Best Gluten-Free Family Cookbook
  by Donna Washburn and Heather Butt

- Diabetes Meals for Good Health
  by Karen Graham, RD
- Canada's Diabetes Meals for Good Health
  by Karen Graham, RD
- America's Complete Diabetes Cookbook
  Edited by Katherine E. Younker, MBA, RD
- Canada's Complete Diabetes Cookbook
  Edited by Katherine E. Younker, MBA, RD

Recent Bestsellers

- The Complete Book of Pickling
  by Jennifer MacKenzie
- Baby Blender Food
  by Nicole Young
- 125 Best Ice Cream Recipes
  by Marilyn Linton and Tanya Linton

- The Convenience Cook
  by Judith Finlayson
- Easy Indian Cooking
  by Suneeta Vaswani
- Simply Thai Cooking
  by Wandee Young and Byron Ayanoglu

Health

- 55 Most Common Medicinal Herbs Second Edition
  by Dr. Heather Boon, B.Sc.Phm., Ph.D. and Michael Smith, B.Pharm, M.R.Pharm.S., ND
- Canada's Baby Care Book
  by Dr. Jeremy Friedman MBChB, FRCP(C), FAAP, and Dr. Norman Saunders MD, FRCP(C)
- The Baby Care Book
  by Dr. Jeremy Friedman MBChB, FRCP(C), FAAP, and Dr. Norman Saunders MD, FRCP(C)

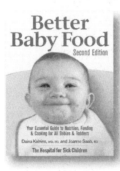

- Better Baby Food Second Edition
  by Daina Kalnins, MSc, RD, and Joanne Saab, RD
- Better Food for Pregnancy
  by Daina Kalnins, MSc, RD, and Joanne Saab, RD
- Crohn's & Colitis
  by Dr. A. Hillary Steinhart, MD, MSc, FRCP(C)
- Crohn's & Colitis Diet Guide
  by Dr. A. Hillary Steinhart, MD, MSc, FRCP(C), and Julie Cepo, BSc, BASc, RD

Also Available
from Robert Rose

300 Big & Bold
Barbecue
& Grilling
recipes

Karen Adler and Judith Fertig

ISBN 978-0-7788-0212-9 $27.95 Canada / $24.95 U.S.

For more great books, see previous pages

Robert
ROSE